Mastering Algorithms with Python

A Practical Approach to Problem Solving and Python Implementation

Chenyang Shi

Apress®

Mastering Algorithms with Python: A Practical Approach to Problem Solving and Python Implementation

Chenyang Shi
Austin, TX, USA

ISBN-13 (pbk): 979-8-8688-1798-4　　　　　　ISBN-13 (electronic): 979-8-8688-1799-1
https://doi.org/10.1007/979-8-8688-1799-1

Copyright © 2025 by Chenyang Shi

This work is subject to copyright. All rights are reserved by the Publisher, whether the whole or part of the material is concerned, specifically the rights of translation, reprinting, reuse of illustrations, recitation, broadcasting, reproduction on microfilms or in any other physical way, and transmission or information storage and retrieval, electronic adaptation, computer software, or by similar or dissimilar methodology now known or hereafter developed.

Trademarked names, logos, and images may appear in this book. Rather than use a trademark symbol with every occurrence of a trademarked name, logo, or image we use the names, logos, and images only in an editorial fashion and to the benefit of the trademark owner, with no intention of infringement of the trademark.

The use in this publication of trade names, trademarks, service marks, and similar terms, even if they are not identified as such, is not to be taken as an expression of opinion as to whether or not they are subject to proprietary rights.

While the advice and information in this book are believed to be true and accurate at the date of publication, neither the authors nor the editors nor the publisher can accept any legal responsibility for any errors or omissions that may be made. The publisher makes no warranty, express or implied, with respect to the material contained herein.

　　Managing Director, Apress Media LLC: Welmoed Spahr
　　Acquisitions Editor: Celestin Suresh John
　　Development Editor: Jim Markham
　　Coordinating Editor: Gryffin Winkler

Cover image designed by Freepik (www.freepik.com)

Distributed to the book trade worldwide by Springer Science+Business Media New York, 1 New York Plaza, New York, NY 10004. Phone 1-800-SPRINGER, fax (201) 348-4505, e-mail orders-ny@springer-sbm.com, or visit www.springeronline.com. Apress Media, LLC is a Delaware LLC and the sole member (owner) is Springer Science + Business Media Finance Inc (SSBM Finance Inc). SSBM Finance Inc is a **Delaware** corporation.

For information on translations, please e-mail booktranslations@springernature.com; for reprint, paperback, or audio rights, please e-mail bookpermissions@springernature.com.

Apress titles may be purchased in bulk for academic, corporate, or promotional use. eBook versions and licenses are also available for most titles. For more information, reference our Print and eBook Bulk Sales web page at http://www.apress.com/bulk-sales.

Any source code or other supplementary material referenced by the author in this book is available to readers on GitHub. For more detailed information, please visit https://www.apress.com/gp/services/source-code.

If disposing of this product, please recycle the paper

To Shuoshuo, Gilbert, Herbert, and
in loving memory of my grandparents, Youyu and Yanlan.

Table of Contents

About the Author ix

About the Technical Reviewer xi

Acknowledgments xiii

Introduction xv

Chapter 1: Recursion 1

    Basics of Recursion 1

    Simple Recursion Examples.. 3

    Number of Paths in a Grid 4

    H-Tree 6

    Tower of Hanoi 9

    Application 12

    Summary 16

Chapter 2: Divide and Conquer 19

    Guess a Number 19

    Merge Sort 22

    Quick Sort 28

    Multiplication of Two Positive Integers 32

    Fast Fourier Transform 38

    Application 50

    Summary 54

Chapter 3: Greedy Algorithm 53

    Coin Change 53

    Class Scheduling 55

    Jumping Frog 57

Build TV Towers 61
Minimum Spanning Tree: Kruskal's Algorithm 64
Minimum Spanning Tree: Prim's Algorithm 76
Application 82
Summary 88

Chapter 4: Dynamic Programming 89

Fibonacci Number 89
The Generic Way of Designing a Dynamic Programming Solution 93
Longest Common Subsequence and Substring 97
Knapsack 102
Application 108
Summary 115

Chapter 5: RSA Cryptosystem 117

Caesar Cipher 117
RSA Initial Encounter 120
Greatest Common Divisor 121
Find Prime Numbers 123
An Improved Version of RSA 125
Application 134
Summary 134

Chapter 6: Monte Carlo 135

Generate a Random Number 135
Test Uniformity and Independence of Random Numbers 138
Examples of Simple Monte Carlo Simulations 144
Monte Carlo Integration 149
How Likely Will It Rain Tomorrow? 154
Metropolis–Hastings 160
Application 165
Summary 171

Chapter 7: A Tale of Ten Cities 173

A Traveling Consultant: Part 1 173

A Traveling Consultant: Part 2 180

A Traveling Consultant: Part 3 186

Build a Warehouse 194

Group the Cities 199

Application 204

Summary 208

Chapter 8: Chess 211

Binary Tree and Its Traversals 211

N-ary Tree and Its Traversals 215

Knight's Tour 218

Minimum Jumps for a Knight 225

Eight Queens 228

Monte Carlo Tree Search 235

Application 243

    Binary Trees and N-ary Trees 243

    DFS, BFS, and Backtracking 244

    Monte Carlo Tree Search 248

Summary 250

Appendix A: A Quick Review of Python 251

Appendix B: Environment Setup and Package Installation 267

Appendix C: References 269

Index 271

About the Author

Chenyang Shi is a data science manager at a leading consulting firm, specializing in applying machine learning and data science to enhance marketing and commercialization forecasting for major pharmaceutical clients. He earned his Ph.D. from the Department of Applied Physics and Applied Mathematics at Columbia University (2015) and a master's in computer science with a focus on machine learning from Georgia Institute of Technology (2020). With over a decade of Python programming experience, Chenyang is the lead author of two peer-reviewed software programs, JRgui (published at *ACS Omega*) and xINTERPDF (*Journal of Applied Crystallography*), comprising over 7,500 lines of Python code. In his spare time, he enjoys playing chess, learning Japanese, following FC Bayern Munich, and spending time with his wife and two sons.

About the Technical Reviewer

Andrea Gavana has been programming Python for more than 20 years, dabbling with other languages since the late 1990s. He graduated from university with a master's degree in chemical engineering, and he is now a Master Development Planning Architect working for TotalEnergies in Copenhagen, Denmark. Andrea enjoys programming at work and for fun, and he has been involved in multiple open source projects, all Python-based. One of his favorite hobbies is Python coding, but he is also fond of cycling, swimming, and cozy dinners with family and friends. This is his fifth book as a technical reviewer.

Acknowledgments

I still remember that very moment one and a half years ago: I stood in front of my whiteboard, wrote down the names of the algorithms I knew, and said to myself, "Wait, maybe I can write a book myself." Since then, I have dedicated my spare time to writing this book, and it was quite a remarkable journey.

I would like to thank Prof. Eric Vigoda and Prof. David Goldsman. The great courses I took from both at Georgia Tech, i.e., "Introduction to Graduate Algorithms" and "Simulation," inspired a couple of chapters in the book. The excellent "Design and Analysis of Algorithms" and "Introduction to Algorithms" classes from MIT OpenCourseWare have introduced numerous curious learners worldwide, including myself, to the wonderful world of computer algorithms. Various great academic and industry books on the same topic have taught me the foundation of the algorithms. Last but not least, under the influence of my son, Gilbert, my recent obsession with chess has led to the last chapter of the book.

The book would not have been possible without the support from the wonderful staff members at Apress. I would like to thank Managing Director Welmoed Spahr, Acquisitions Editor Celestin John, Development Editor Jim Markham, and Coordinating Editor Gryffin Winkler. I am also grateful to Technical Reviewer Andrea Gavana for his in-depth comments for improving the book. Lastly, I would like to thank my family for their support and patience while I was writing the book.

Introduction

The computer algorithms are the bedrock for the success of any IT professionals (software engineers or data scientists alike), yet they seem intimidating for many at first glance. They are intimidating because they are not easy and often cleverly designed. Simply memorizing the pseudocode/code is a recipe for frustration. Also, the fact that there are so many different algorithms often overwhelms the newcomers. I, like many others, realized the importance of algorithms quite early and have gone through various learning practices such as solving (thousands of) coding problems at online judge websites, taking university algorithm classes, and reading algorithm books written by university professors and industry experts. Despite all these efforts, it was a bit strange that I still felt "not good enough on algorithms." It is this feeling that urges me to reflect on how to find an effective way of learning algorithms.

First, we need to acknowledge that algorithms are many and we cannot learn all of them. Instead, we should master the classic ones, which are the foundations for other modern or complex algorithms. We need to really understand the classic ones. Rote memorization leads nowhere. The academic algorithm books are great resources, but, in my experience, sometimes they tend to be too abstract and concise to follow. In contrast, some industry books are either oversimplified or just display the code snippets without explaining how they are come up with.

This book aims to bridge that gap. It covers major classic algorithms such as Greedy, Dynamic Programming, Breadth-First Search, and Depth-First Search, relates them to daily objects, and explains them from the ground-up. Real-life examples such as chess or business travels help the readers build intuition gradually with concrete examples. All algorithms are implemented in Python from scratch which can be used as future references.

There is no shortcut for mastering the algorithms. However, learning them with a fun yet easy-to-follow resource will make this journey pleasant – that is the purpose of the book.

INTRODUCTION

How This Book Is Organized

Each chapter of the book introduces one major type of algorithm and explains it with ample examples from easy to advanced. At the end of each chapter, a practical application of the algorithm discussed in the chapter is shown. All examples come with coding snippets written in Python from scratch.

Specifically, Chapter 1 introduces recursion, its fundamentals, and its application in a binary tree. Chapter 2 turns attention to divide-and-conquer where Merge Sort, Quick Sort, and Fast Fourier Transform are discussed in detail. Chapter 3 covers the Greedy method and its application in compressing data (Huffman coding). Chapter 4 focuses on Dynamic Programming (DP), a generic way to devise a DP solution, and its application in content-aware image resizing (seam carving). Chapter 5 explores the famous RSA Cryptosystem and various math fundamentals to understand RSA including the greatest common divisor and primality test. Chapter 6 changes the direction a bit and delves into more data science-themed Monte Carlo methods. It introduces random number generation, tests of the independence and uniformity of the computer-generated number sequences, and various applications of the Monte Carlo method, ranging from solving integrals to simulating the endemic. Chapter 7 discusses five important algorithms with a fictitious example of a travelling consultant and the ten most populous cities in the United States. The algorithms examined are Simulated Annealing, Genetic Algorithm, Dijkstra's Algorithm, Gradient Descent, and K-means Clustering. Chapter 8 solves a variety of chess-inspired problems such as Knight's Tour and Eight Queens and explains various algorithms such as Breadth-First Search, Depth-First Search, Backtracking, and Monte Carlo Tree Search.

Appendix A reviews the key concepts of the Python programming language. Appendix B helps readers set up a code environment for running the code snippets on their local machine. All references used in the book are listed in Appendix C.

Source Code Listings

The source code listed in the book can be downloaded by visiting the book's GitHub page at https://github.com/Apress/Mastering-Algorithms-with-Python.

CHAPTER 1

Recursion

We encounter the idea of recursion very often in our daily lives without even knowing it. We have (grand) parents, and after a certain time, we will likely become (grand) parents ourselves. When we press the Delete button to delete a folder on a computer, the operating system checks if the folder contains subfolders and if any subfolder contains its own subfolders. The check is done recursively until every subfolder is detected at the deepest level. In computer science, recursion is an elegant technique to break down a complex problem that has repeated subproblems. The recursive code thus written is concise and intuitive. In this chapter, we will embark on a journey to learn the basics of recursion through a variety of practical examples.

Basics of Recursion

When I was a kid, I enjoyed playing with the Russian doll I received as a gift from my mother. I was impressed to see that the smaller doll kept popping up from the bigger one and they all looked alike except for the size. Also, as a kid, I often asked my mother to tell me a story before sleep. Inspired by the Russian doll, I guess she could have told a story like this: Once there was a hill. On top of the hill, there was a temple. Inside the temple lived an old monk. And the old monk told a story to his apprentice. The story goes like this. *Once there was a hill. On top of the hill, there was a temple. Inside the temple lived an old monk. And the old monk told a story to his apprentice...*

CHAPTER 1 RECURSION

That would have been a long, endless story and perhaps a boring one. Well. It might be. But both cases allure us to talk about the recursion in computer science. To implement a recursion algorithm, one must keep three things in mind:

(1) *The recursion function must have a base case.*

(2) *The recursion function must change its state and move toward the base case.*

(3) *The recursion function must call itself recursively.*

Let us take a simple example of calculating the factorial of an integer n. A recursive implementation of the factorial function is shown in Listing 1-1.

Listing 1-1. Implement a factorial function using recursion

```
1.  def factorial(n):
2.      if n == 1 or n == 0:
3.          return 1
4.      return factorial(n - 1) * n
```

Though simple, it does satisfy the three conditions we just mentioned. It does have a base case, that is, when n is 0 or 1, it returns 1. The state of the factorial function does change by decreasing n by 1 each time. Finally, we do see the factorial function gets called inside itself.

Let us now examine what gets calculated in a sequential order. Suppose $n = 5$. As shown in Figure 1-1, factorial(5) is first called, but to evaluate it, we still need factorial(4).

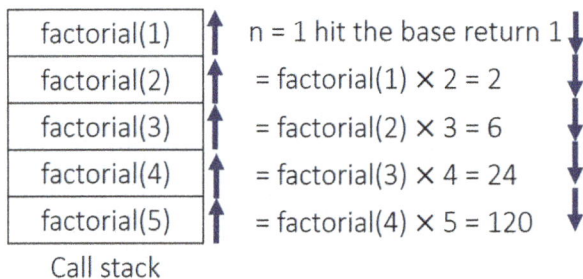

Figure 1-1. *The call stack of a factorial function*

Therefore, we temporarily put factorial(5) in a *call stack*. The same process applies to factorial(4), factorial(3), and factorial(2). Finally, at factorial(1), we hit the base case where we know the value of factorial(1) is 1. With the value of factorial(1) figured out, we can now evaluate factorial(2), which is factorial(1)× 2 = 2. And in a sequential fashion, we obtain values for factorial(3), factorial(4), and finally factorial(5).

Imagine what would happen if we forget to write a base condition. The new calculations will keep piling up in the call stack since *n* can always be decreased by 1. The program will get stuck and run forever. This will cause a stack overflow error, such as RecursionError: maximum recursion depth exceeded in comparison in Python. Here is an anecdote on this: A programmer's wife asked her husband for an errand. "While you are out, buy some tomatoes." He never went home, and the world runs out of tomatoes. Obviously, the poor wife forgot to specify the base case.

Simple Recursion Examples

Let us now practice recursion with more examples. Suppose you are given a nonnegative integer *n* (i.e., an integer greater than or equal to 0) and you are tasked with finding the sum of all nonnegative integers up to *n*. Following the design principle of the factorial case discussed previously, we can first define a function for summation, say, sum_n_integers(n). Then we shall consider the recursive relation between sum_n_integers(n) and sum_n_integers (n-1). Obviously, sum_n_integers (n)= sum_n_integers (n-1)+ n. On top of that, we need to specify the base case. See lines 1 to 6 in Listing 1-2.

Next, let us look at the variant of the original problem: How to find the sum of an *array* of integers instead? Again, the key here is to figure out how the input parameter gets updated each time. Since the input is an array of integers, we can divide the array into two parts, i.e., the first number and the rest of the array or the last number and the rest of the array. Either way, the input array gets reduced by one in size each time, and when its size becomes 1, we return the only element in the array. Lines 8–11 and 13–16 in Listing 1-2 implement it in two ways.

Listing 1-2. Recursion functions for a sum of integers

```python
def sum_n_integers(n):
    """Given input n, sum all nonnegative integers up to n
    """
    if n == 0 or n == 1:
        return n
    return sum_n_integers(n - 1) + n

def sum_arr_v1(nums):
    if len(nums) == 1:
        return nums[0]
    return nums[0] + sum_arr_v1(nums[1:])

def sum_arr_v2(nums):
    if len(nums) == 1:
        return nums[-1]
    return nums[-1] + sum_arr_v2(nums[:-1])

if __name__ == "__main__":
    assert sum_n_integers(5) == 15
    assert sum_arr_v1([1,2,3,4,5]) == 15
    assert sum_arr_v2([1,2,3,4,5]) == 15
```

It is worth mentioning that for these simpler examples, it is perhaps more straightforward to implement and debug them using an iterative way with a `for` or `while` loop. However, a recursive function could be more intuitive and concise for more complex problems, as we shall see in the following sections.

Number of Paths in a Grid

Consider an $m \times n$ grid. You start from the top left and want to go to the bottom right. You are only allowed to go either down or right, one step at each move. How many unique ways can you find?

To begin with, let us draw an example grid of, say, 7×4; see Figure 1-2. Since we start from the top left, we can assign coordinates to each cell of the grid. For example, the top left cell is at (1, 1) and the bottom right cell is at (7,4), etc. To count the unique ways to reach the goal cell, let us take a step back by looking at the number of ways to reach an arbitrary cell (x, y). It can only be reached either from the cell to the left or the one above it, since we are only allowed to make rightward or downward moves.

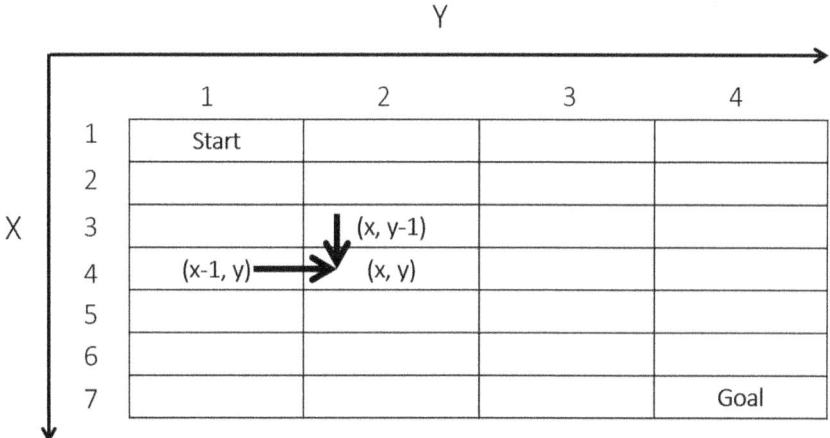

Figure 1-2. *A grid of 7×4 and possible previous moves at a cell (x, y)*

Therefore, we can write down the recursive relation as follows:

$$Count(x,y) = Count(x-1,y) + Count(x,y-1)$$

Next, we need to figure out the base cases. There are essentially two base cases, that is, when either *x* or *y* is 1 (see Figure 1-3). In both cases, there is only one way to reach the goal. The base cases therefore are *Count*(*x*,1)=*Count*(1, *y*) = 1.

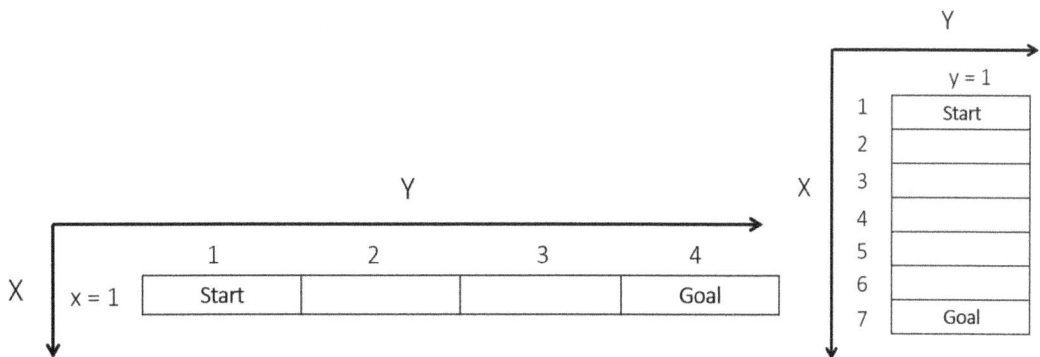

Figure 1-3. *The base case when x= 1 or y = 1*

We now have enough information to solve the problem. The code is in Listing 1-3.

Listing 1-3. Number of unique paths in a grid by recursion

```
1.  def count_unique_paths(m, n):
2.      if m == 1 or n == 1:
3.          return 1
4.      return count_unique_paths(m-1, n) + count_unique_paths(m, n-1)
5.
6.  if __name__ == "__main__":
7.      print (count_unique_paths(7,4))
```

In this book, we run the code using IPython, an interactive Python shell. The advantage of using it is that we can check the values of intermediate parameters interactively. After running the program, there are 84 unique ways to go from top left to bottom right for the given problem.

```
In [1]: run Listing_1_3_number_unique_paths.py
84
```

H-Tree

A fractal is an infinitely repeated pattern that is self-similar across different scales. There are many natural fractals such as Romanesco broccoli, tree branches, ice, snow, and rivers. Let us now construct a fractal called an H-tree with the help of a computer. As the name suggests, it is called H-tree because it has a basic motif of an H-like shape (see Figure 1-4).

CHAPTER 1 RECURSION

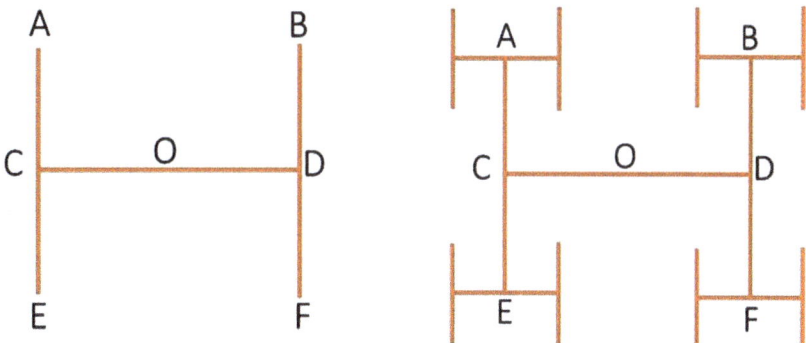

Figure 1-4. *Examples of H-trees at different levels: levels 1 and 2*

To begin, and at level 1, we draw an H with points A, B, C, D, E, F, O where O is the center point. The length of CD equals to that of AE and BF. Next, at level 2, we draw a new H pattern with A, B, E, F as the center points, respectively. And the side length of this new H pattern is reduced by half. And the pattern continues.

Due to this repeated nature, we can leverage recursion to draw H-trees on a computer. The recursion stops when the desired level is achieved. Inside the recursion function, we can keep track of the coordinates of points A, B, C, D, E, F, and O, which are calculated using a length parameter, and update the coordinates values upon a change of the level. For visualization, we can use the matplotlib package to draw a line to connect two points. The code is shown in Listing 1-4. At lines 4–5, the helper function draw_line is defined. Lines 8–9 specify the stopping condition. Lines 29–30 show that the level and length parameters get updated at each recursion call. The amount by which the length is reduced is controlled by the factor parameter. Here, the default value of factor is 4, i.e., reduce the length by half at each iteration.

CHAPTER 1 RECURSION

Listing 1-4. The recursion code for drawing an H-tree

```python
import math
import matplotlib.pyplot as plt
plt.figure()
def draw_line(x1, y1, x2, y2):
    plt.plot([x1, x2], [y1, y2], color = 'r', lw = 2)

def draw_h_tree(x0, y0, length, level, factor):
    if level == 0:
        return

    coord_c_x = x0 - length / 2.
    coord_c_y = y0
    coord_d_x = x0 + length /2.
    coord_d_y = y0

    coord_a_x = x0 - length / 2.
    coord_a_y = y0 + length / 2.
    coord_e_x = x0 - length / 2.
    coord_e_y = y0 - length / 2.
    coord_b_x = x0 + length / 2.
    coord_b_y = y0 + length / 2.
    coord_f_x = x0 + length / 2.
    coord_f_y = y0 - length / 2.

    draw_line(coord_c_x, coord_c_y, coord_d_x, coord_d_y)
    draw_line(coord_a_x, coord_a_y, coord_e_x, coord_e_y)
    draw_line(coord_b_x, coord_b_y, coord_f_x, coord_f_y)

    length /= math.sqrt(factor)
    level -= 1
    draw_h_tree(coord_a_x, coord_a_y, length, level, factor)
    draw_h_tree(coord_b_x, coord_b_y, length, level, factor)
    draw_h_tree(coord_e_x, coord_e_y, length, level, factor)
    draw_h_tree(coord_f_x, coord_f_y, length, level, factor)

if __name__ == "__main__":
    draw_h_tree(0, 0, 2, 5, 4)
    plt.tight_layout()
    plt.show()
```

Shown in Figure 1-5 are examples of H-trees at levels 3, 4, and 5.

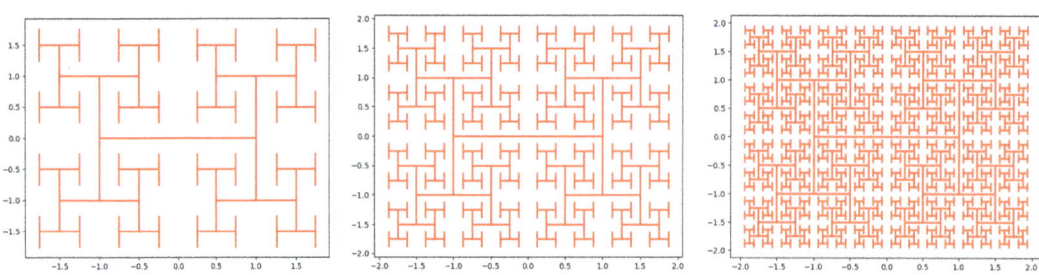

Figure 1-5. *Computer art of an H-tree at levels 3, 4, and 5*

Tower of Hanoi

The legend of the Tower of Hanoi tells a story about the Kashi Vishwanath Temple in India. The Hindu temple houses three giant poles and 64 golden disks. The priests there were continuously moving disks among poles, one disk at a time. Based on the ancient prophecy, when the last disk is moved, the world would end. Based on the legend, the French mathematician Edouard Lucas developed the puzzle of the Tower of Hanoi (see Figure 1-6). The goal of the puzzle is to move all disks from the start pole to the target pole, subject to three rules:

(1) Only one disk can be moved at a time.

(2) Only the disk on top of the piles can be moved.

(3) A larger disk may not be put on top of a smaller disk.

Figure 1-6. *Starting positions of the Tower of Hanoi*

Suppose there are *n* disks in the starting positions. Mathematically, it can be proven that it requires at least $2^n - 1$ steps to move all disks from the start pole to the target pole. If the priests in the legend can complete moving one disk in one second, it would require ~585 billion years to finish the task (as a reference, the age of the universe is ~13.8 billion years). Fortunately for us, the world will not end any time soon.

Now, let us turn our attention to figuring out the exact moves of disks with the help of a computer. The nature of the puzzle certainly yells at us to use recursion to solve it, but it is not obvious where to start. Never mind, let us start simple. Suppose there is only one disk: How do we move one disk from the first pole to the last? The answer is simple – we just move it directly in one step. How about two disks? We must use the second pole as an auxiliary pole and do it in the following three steps.

(1) Move the smaller disk from the first pole to the second pole.

(2) Move the larger disk from the first pole to the third pole.

(3) Move the smaller disk from the second pole to the third pole.

CHAPTER 1　RECURSION

Let us now attempt to generate the steps for n disks. At first glance, it seems not immediately clear, as it would require many intermediate steps to move disks around. However, let us group the disks into two piles : the first pile is the top $n-1$ disks, and the second is the largest one at the bottom. Think in terms of pile, rather than the individual disk. In this case, we would do it in three steps, as shown in Figure 1-7 below.

(1)　Move the $n-1$ disks from the first pole to the second pole (Step 1 to Step 2).

(2)　Move the largest disk from the first pole to the third pole (Step 2 to Step 3).

(3)　Move the $n-1$ disks from the second pole to the third pole (Step 3 to Finish).

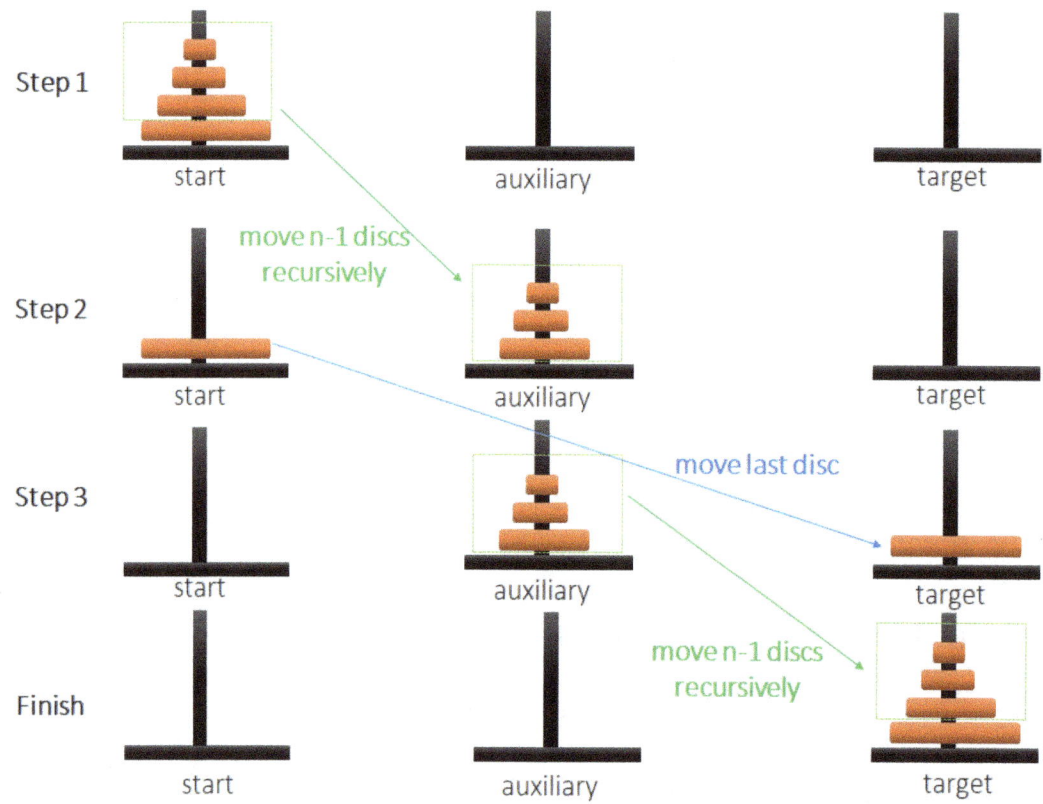

Figure 1-7. *A strategy to move n disks from the start to the target pole*

CHAPTER 1 RECURSION

What we propose for *n* disks resembles the two disks case, except that we will need to further figure out how to move $n - 1$ disks from the first pole to the second and from the second to the third pole. However, we can do it later and recursively using the same logic. Here we have successfully reduced the problem of moving *n* disks to moving $n - 1$ disks. We will do this repeatedly until we hit the base case where there is only one disk left.

Let us go about coding a solution. We can define a function `tower_of_hanoi` with input parameters of `num_disks, start_pole, auxililary_pole,` and `target_pole` where the latter three describe the purpose of each pole more accurately than simply calling them first, middle, and last poles. In Listing 1-5, we first write down the base case at lines 2–3, i.e., when there is only one disk, we move it from the start pole to the target pole. At lines 5–7, we move the piles of disks in three steps as discussed above. First, we move $n - 1$ disks from the start pole to the auxiliary pole with the help of the target pole. Then, we move the largest disk from the start pole to the target pole. Finally, we move again $n - 1$ disks from the auxiliary pole to the target pole, with the help of the start pole. To our surprise, the code is quite simple, which is exactly the beauty of recursion.

Listing 1-5. The recursive code to solve the Tower of Hanoi

```
1.  def tower_of_hanoi(num_disks, start_pole, auxililary_pole, target_pole):
2.      if num_disks == 1:
3.          print (f"Move disk 1 from {start_pole} to {target_pole}")
4.      else:
5.          tower_of_hanoi(num_disks - 1, start_pole, target_pole, auxiliary_pole)
6.          print (f"Move disk {num_disks} from {start_pole} to {target_pole}")
7.          tower_of_hanoi(num_disks - 1, auxiliary_pole, start_pole, target_pole)
8.
9.  if __name__ == "__main__":
10.     tower_of_hanoi(4, "A", "B", "C")
```

Let us try our problem for moving four disks. The 15-step instructions are printed out and shown below. We can see the first seven steps are dedicated to moving the top three disks from the start to the central pole, followed by a single step that moves the largest disc #4 from A to C, and followed by again seven steps to move the top three disks from the central pole to the destination.

CHAPTER 1 RECURSION

```
In [2]: run Listing_1_5_tower_of_hanoi.py
Move disk 1 from A to B
Move disk 2 from A to C
Move disk 1 from B to C
Move disk 3 from A to B
Move disk 1 from C to A
Move disk 2 from C to B
Move disk 1 from A to B
Move disk 4 from A to C
Move disk 1 from B to C
Move disk 2 from B to A
Move disk 1 from C to A
Move disk 3 from B to C
Move disk 1 from A to B
Move disk 2 from A to C
Move disk 1 from B to C
```

Application

The binary tree is an important data structure in computer science and finds application in various real-world problems. In Chapter 8, we will discuss in detail how we can leverage trees to solve various chess-inspired problems. In this section, we will take an initial look at a binary tree and learn how to use recursion to do a traversal of the tree.

A classic binary tree is illustrated in Figure 1-8. It is an upside-down tree compared with the trees we see in our daily lives.

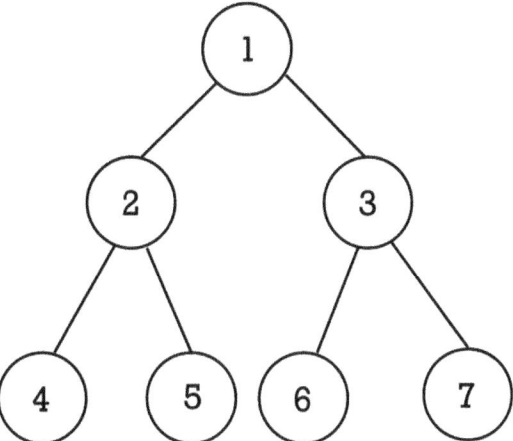

Figure 1-8. *A computer representation of a binary tree*

Each circle in the illustration is called a tree node which stores the value associated with the node. In the current example, each node stores an integer value, but it can store other types of information (e.g., a tuple). The top node is by convention called the *root* node. Each node in a binary tree can have up to two child nodes. In the example, the root node has two children – its left child of node 2 and right child of node 3. The nodes at the bottom, i.e., nodes 4, 5, 6, 7, have no children and are thus called *leaf* nodes. Note that each node in the example has either 0 or 2 children. In a real application, it can have any of 0, 1, or 2 children.

The recursive nature of a binary tree can be seen in Figure 1-9 below. The tree has essentially three components, i.e., root, left subtree, and right subtree. At the top level, the root is node 1. The left subtree is another tree that consists of nodes 2, 4, 5, whereas the right subtree is comprised of nodes 3, 6, 7. For the left subtree, its root is node 2, the left subtree is node 4 (with no children), and the right subtree is node 5 (also with no children). The right subtree rooted at node 3 shares the same traits as its left counterpart.

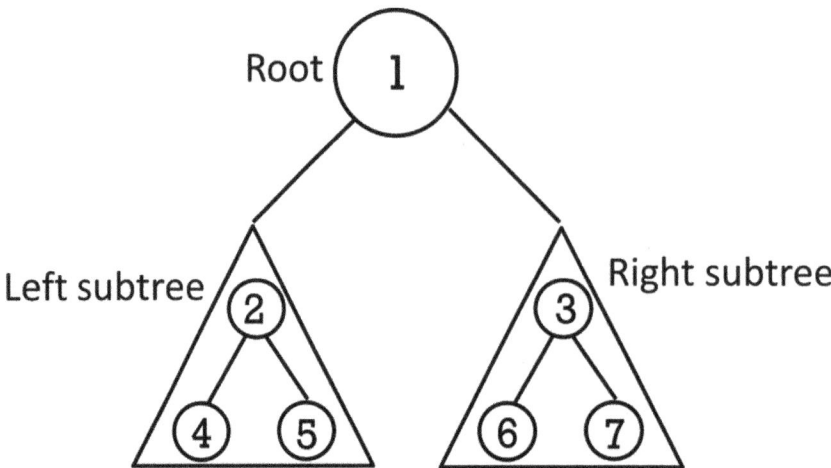

Figure 1-9. *A binary tree is recursive*

One important traversal of a binary tree is pre-order traversal where it explores the tree in the order of root, left subtree, and right subtree. In our example, the pre-order traversal yields a sequence of integers in the order of 1 → 2 → 4 → 5 → 3 → 6 → 7. Pre-order traversal is the foundation for the Depth-First Search (DFS) algorithm which we will deep dive into in Chapter 8. Let us now implement the pre-order traversal with recursion.

To represent a binary tree in Python, for convenience, one typically uses a Python class as shown in lines 1–5 in Listing 1-6. It has an __init__ constructor with value, left child, and right child initialized. Sometimes, one can also add a parent attribute to keep track of the parent of the current node, but it is optional. And the tree we have seen above can be constructed using code at lines 18–24. At the end of the day, we are left with a root node, i.e., TreeNode(1), and can use it to access other nodes.

Listing 1-6. Pre-order traversal of a binary tree using recursion

```
1.  class TreeNode:
2.      def __init__(self, value):
3.          self.value = value
4.          self.left = None
5.          self.right = None
6.
7.  def pre_order_traversal(root):
8.      sequence = []
9.      def preorder_helper(node):
10.         if node:
11.             sequence.append(node.value)
12.             preorder_helper(node.left)
13.             preorder_helper(node.right)
14.     preorder_helper(root)
15.     return sequence
16.
17. if __name__ == "__main__":
18.     root = TreeNode(1)
19.     root.left = TreeNode(2)
20.     root.right = TreeNode(3)
21.     root.left.left = TreeNode(4)
22.     root.left.right = TreeNode(5)
23.     root.right.left = TreeNode(6)
24.     root.right.right = TreeNode(7)
25.     print("Preorder traversal of the tree:", pre_order_traversal(root))
```

The code for pre-order traversal is at lines 7–15 in Listing 1-6. Since we have decided to use recursion for this task, we define a helper function `preorder_helper` within the main function `pre_order_traversal` which calls itself at lines 12 and 13. The helper function takes in a `node` as an input parameter and uses a `sequence` to store the integers. Following the order of exploration, i.e., root, left subtree, and right subtree, at line 11, we collect its value and save it to the `sequence` since it is at the root node; at line 12, we recursively explore the left subtree, whereas at line 13, we explore the right subtree in a recursive fashion. All these explorations happen only when the root node is not empty (i.e., line 10). If, for example, the traversal hits the children of leaf nodes, which contain null values, the exploration will skip those and move on to other non-null nodes. As expected, the code returns the desired sequence of numbers.

```
In [3]: run Listing_1_6_application_preorder.py
Preorder traversal of the tree: [1, 2, 4, 5, 3, 6, 7]
```

CHAPTER 1 RECURSION

In addition to a pre-order traversal, there are other traversals such as in-order traversal and post-order traversal. To perform an in-order traversal, the left subtree is explored first, then the root, and finally the right subtree. In comparison, the post-order traversal explores the tree in the order of left subtree → right subtree → root. To implement in-order/post-order traversals recursively, we can largely reuse the pre-order traversal code – we only need to tweak the order of explorations of the tree (i.e., lines 11–13 in Listing 1-6). The code for in-order and post-order traversals is shown in Listing 1-7.

Listing 1-7. In-order and post-order traversals of a binary tree using recursion

```
1.  def in_order_traversal(root):
2.      sequence = []
3.      def inorder_helper(node):
4.          if node:
5.              inorder_helper(node.left)
6.              sequence.append(node.value)
7.              inorder_helper(node.right)
8.      inorder_helper(root)
9.      return sequence
10.
11. def post_order_traversal(root):
12.     sequence = []
13.     def postorder_helper(node):
14.         if node:
15.             postorder_helper(node.left)
16.             postorder_helper(node.right)
17.             sequence.append(node.value)
18.     postorder_helper(root)
19.     return sequence
```

```
In [4]: run Listing_1_7_application_inorder_postorder.py
Inorder traversal of the tree: [4, 2, 5, 1, 6, 3, 7]
Postorder traversal of the tree: [4, 5, 2, 6, 7, 3, 1]
```

Summary

In this first chapter, we learn the recursion, a technique foundational to many complex problems with repeated patterns. We learn the three basic steps, i.e., (1) define a base case, (2) find the recursive relation, and (3) recursively call the same function with state changes toward the base case. With these basics in mind, we can avoid the stack overflow issues when designing a recursive program. We also learn how a call stack works behind a recursive program. We then consolidate our understanding of recursion by looking at several examples and the real-world application of traversing a binary tree.

It is worth mentioning that most of the problems solvable by recursion can also be solved by using an iterative method. The iterative method is memory efficient as it does not require calling the same function repeatedly and putting intermediate operations onto a call stack. In comparison, the recursion method is more concise and easy to follow, significantly reducing the overhead of reading the code. Depending on the problem, it is up to the readers to pick up the more appropriate technique.

CHAPTER 2

Divide and Conquer

The idea of divide-and-conquer is ubiquitous in our daily lives. When we pick up a new human language, we split our efforts into learning four basic subjects of a language, i.e., speaking, writing, reading, and listening. When a team of developers work on building a modern software program, they often divide the tasks: some members focus on back-end logic development, some on front-end User Interface (UI) design, some on the database, while others focus on product deployment using modern cloud technology. Divide-and-conquer is also a fundamental idea in computer science: it breaks down a complex problem into smaller problems (divide), attacks the subproblems separately (conquer), and combines the individual solutions to arrive at a final solution (combine). In this chapter, we will learn divide-and-conquer through a variety of examples, from guessing a number using binary search, merge sort/quick sort, through multiplication of two integers, to the Fast Fourier Transform. We will leverage the recursion technique we learned in Chapter 1 and apply it to implement divide-and-conquer solutions.

Guess a Number

Two friends Alice and Bob are playing a game.

Alice: "Let us play a game of guessing numbers. I have one number from 1 to 100 in my mind. Can you guess it?"

Bob: "Well, that is 1 out of 100 probabilities."

Alice: "But you can ask me if it is greater or smaller than X, and I will say yes or no. How many questions do you need to nail it?"

Bob: "Well, if I ask if it is greater than 50 and your answer is yes, then the number is within [51, 100] range. Or if the answer is no, it is within [1, 49]. Each time I ask a question, I can get rid of half of the numbers. Since $2^7 = 128 > 100$, I will need at most seven questions to find the number!"

CHAPTER 2   DIVIDE AND CONQUER

Bob is indeed correct. The search algorithm that narrows down the search space by half at a time is called *binary search*. The action of a binary search on finding a number is shown in Figure 2-1.

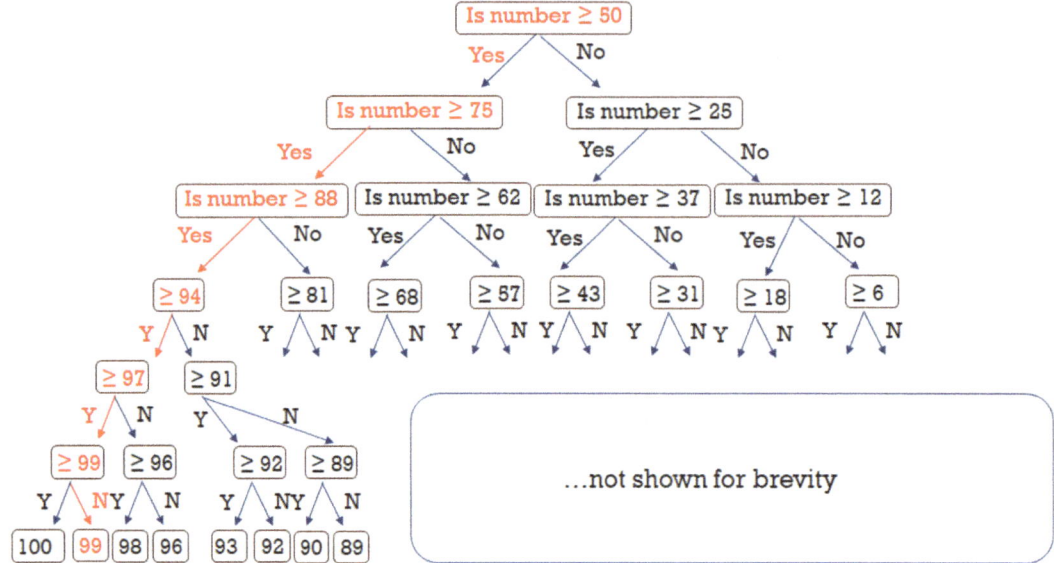

Figure 2-1. *The binary search tree diagram for guessing a number*

We can use an iterative method with a `while` loop to implement it (see Listing 2-1). The binary search is an example of a divide-and-conquer algorithm, and it has an efficient time complexity of O(log N) where N is the total number of elements. In the example below, it would take at most 6 guesses to guess 99.

Listing 2-1. Binary search for a number iteratively

```python
1.  def guess_number(lower_bound, upper_bound, num):
2.      # expand the bounds by 1 to avoid getting stuck in infinite loops
3.      lower_bound -= 1
4.      upper_bound += 1
5.      num_guesses = 1
6.      guess = (lower_bound + upper_bound) // 2
7.      print (f"initial guess -->{guess}")
8.      while guess != num:
9.          if guess > num:
10.             upper_bound = guess
11.         elif guess < num:
12.             lower_bound = guess
13.         else:
14.             print (f"Guessed it, the number is {guess}")
15.         guess = (lower_bound + upper_bound) // 2
16.         print (f"guess -->{guess}")
17.         num_guesses += 1
18.     print (f"it takes {num_guesses} guesses to guess {num}")
19.
20. if __name__ == "__main__":
21.     lower_bound = 1
22.     upper_bound = 100
23.     num = 99
24.     guess_number(lower_bound, upper_bound, num)
```

```
In [1]: run Listing_2_1_guess_number.py

initial guess -->50

guess -->75

guess -->88

guess -->94

guess -->97

guess -->99

it takes 6 guesses to guess 99
```

Merge Sort

Binary search in the previous example is one use case of the generic divide-and-conquer algorithm that breaks a complex problem into smaller parts, processes them individually, and combines the results to reach the final result. Let us see how we can use divide-and-conquer to sort an array of integers. For example, we have an array of integers [5, -1, 0, 3, 2]; how should we go about sorting it?

CHAPTER 2 DIVIDE AND CONQUER

One way is to pick up the first element, 5, and compare it with its neighbor, -1. Since it is bigger than its neighbor, we will swap it with its neighbor, and the array becomes [-1, 5, 0, 3, 2]. We repeat it three more times until 5 reaches the end of the array which becomes [-1, 0, 3, 2, 5]. Then we repeat the process for -1, 0, 3, and 2, respectively. We will need another swap of 3 and 2, and the array will be sorted. This is the process of the Bubble Sort as each number moves from left to right like a bubble (see Figure 2-2). Let us examine how many unit operations we need for Bubble Sort. In the worst case, we will need 4 + 3 + 2 + 1 = 10 unit operations. To generalize to an array of size N, we will need (N-1) + (N-2) + ... + 2 + 1 = (N-1) × N / 2 times of operations. The time complexity asymptotes to N^2, and it is not very efficient. On the plus side, there is no additional space required because we just swap elements in the original array with no additional array created.

There is another sorting algorithm named Insertion Sort. It resembles how we arrange the cards in our hands when playing poker. Consider these numbers as poker cards. How shall we arrange them? The first card we receive is 5; we just hold it in our hand. The next one we get is -1; since it is smaller than 5, we put it to the left of 5. Then 0 arrives; it will be sitting between -1 and 5. Next, 3 arrives; it will be put between 0 and 5. Finally, we will put 2 between 0 and 3. Same as Bubble Sort, in the worst case, one will need to compare a pair of numbers 1 + 2 + 3 + 4 = 10 times. That is also an $O(N^2)$ algorithm.

There is also a Selection Sort algorithm. We start with the first element 5, find the minimum of the rest of the array [-1, 0, 3, 2], and swap with it if 5 is bigger. So, the array becomes [-1, 5, 0, 3, 2]. Repeat it for the second element; it becomes [-1, 0, 5, 3, 2], then [-1, 0, 2, 3, 5]. The last round does not change the result. Again, this is also an $O(N^2)$ algorithm. But all these three algorithms are in place without the need for additional space.

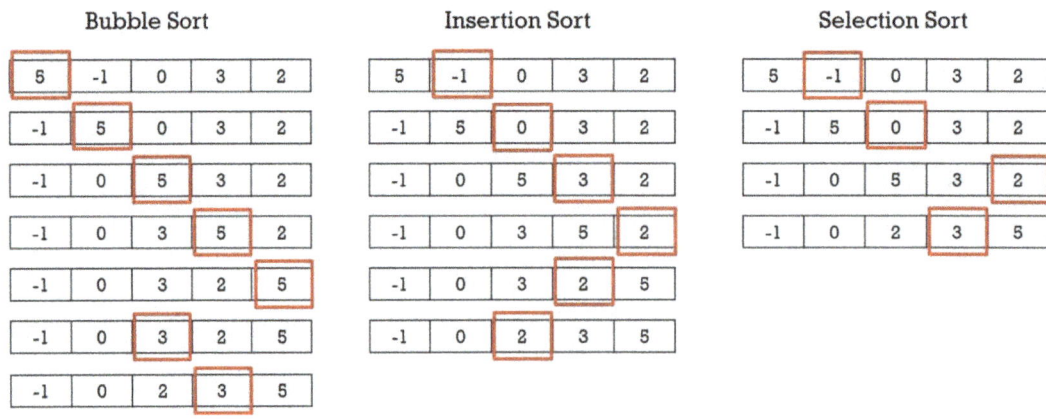

Figure 2-2. *Illustrations of sorting an array using Bubble/Insertion/Selection Sort*

The code implementations of Bubble/Insertion/Selection Sorts are in Listing 2-2.

Listing 2-2. Code implementations of three naïve sorting algorithms

```python
def selection_sort(nums):
    def find_min_index(arr):
        min_idx = None
        min_val = float("inf")
        for idx, num in enumerate(arr):
            if num < min_val:
                min_idx, min_val = idx, num
        return min_idx, min_val

    i = 0
    while i < len(nums):
        min_idx, min_val = find_min_index(nums[i:])
        if nums[i] > min_val:
            nums[i], nums[min_idx + i] = nums[min_idx + i], nums[i]
        i += 1
    return nums

def bubble_sort(nums):
    for i in range(len(nums)):
        for j in range(len(nums) - 1 - i):
            if nums[j] > nums[j+1]:
                nums[j], nums[j+1] = nums[j+1], nums[j]
    return nums

def insertion_sort(nums):
    for i in range(1, len(nums)):
        j = i
        while j > 0:
            if nums[j] < nums[j-1]:
                nums[j], nums[j-1] = nums[j-1], nums[j]
            j -= 1
    return nums

if __name__ == "__main__":
    unsorted_arr_1 = [5, -1, 0, 3, 2]
    sorted_arr_1 = selection_sort(unsorted_arr_1)
    print(sorted_arr_1)

    unsorted_arr_2 = [5, -1, 0, 3, 2]
    bubble_sort(unsorted_arr_2)
    print(unsorted_arr_2)

    unsorted_arr_3 = [5, -1, 0, 3, 2]
    insertion_sort(unsorted_arr_3)
    print(unsorted_arr_3)
```

```
In [2]: run Listing_2_2_selection_bubble_insertion_sort.py

[-1, 0, 2, 3, 5]

[-1, 0, 2, 3, 5]

[-1, 0, 2, 3, 5]
```

We can certainly sort an array of integers with a more efficient algorithm such as a Merge Sort algorithm.

Use the same array [5, -1, 0, 3, 2] as an example; starting with the original array, we divide it into two parts. Since the length of the array is 5, an odd number, we can decide that the first part has a length of 2, the second half 3. We continue to divide the left half, [5, -1], into two parts, i.e., [5] and [-1]. We do the same for the right half, [0, 3, 2], into two parts, [0] and [3, 2]. [3, 2] will be further divided into [3] and [2]. The reason we recursively break down the array by half is that at the end of the splitting, we have the smallest array with a single element, such as [5], [-1], [0], [3], or [2], which are sorted by default.

With these sorted subarrays, we can merge them in a bottom-up fashion, layer by layer. For example, [5] and [-1] will be combined as [-1, 5]; [3] and [2] will be merged as [2, 3], which will be further combined with [0] to arrive at [0, 2, 3]. Finally merging [-1, 5] and [0, 2, 3], we have a sorted array [-1, 0, 2, 3, 5].

Do not forget the three basic elements when writing a recursive function: (1) define a base case to avoid stack overflow, (2) define a function which will be called itself inside the body of the function, and (3) the parameter of the function needs to be updated in the recursive case, which makes it edge toward the base case and finally exit the recursion.

Also, when merging two sorted arrays, one can use a two-pointer approach to iterate through both array elements step-by-step (see the `merge_lists` function in Listing 2-3). During each comparison, the smaller element will be saved to an auxiliary array, and its pointer will be advanced one step. We repeat this until we reach the end of the array. Do not forget the elements from the array where the pointer still stays in the middle. Concatenate the elements past the pointer to the auxiliary array (Listing 2-3).

CHAPTER 2 DIVIDE AND CONQUER

Listing 2-3. Implementation of the Merge Sort

```
1.  def merge_lists(l1, l2):
2.      res = []
3.      i = 0
4.      j = 0
5.      while i < len(l1) and j < len(l2):
6.          if l1[i] <= l2[j]:
7.              res.append(l1[i])
8.              i += 1
9.          else:
10.             res.append(l2[j])
11.             j += 1
12.     res += l1[i:]
13.     res += l2[j:]
14.     return res
15.
16. def merge_sort(arr):
17.     length = len(arr)
18.     if length == 1 or length == 0:
19.         return arr
20.     mid_point_idx = length // 2
21.     left_part = merge_sort(arr[:mid_point_idx])
22.     print ("left part -->", left_part)
23.     right_part = merge_sort(arr[mid_point_idx:])
24.     print ("right part -->", right_part)
25.     sorted_arr = merge_lists(left_part, right_part)
26.     print ("merge sorted arr -->", sorted_arr)
27.     return sorted_arr
28.
29. if __name__ == "__main__":
30.     unsorted_arr = [5, -1, 0, 3, 2]
31.     sorted_arr = merge_sort(unsorted_arr)
32.     print (sorted_arr)
```

For our own curiosity, let us print out the intermediate steps for merging and reconstructing a binary tree for Merge Sort. As shown in Figure 2-3, the function finishes processing the left subtree (a → b → c) and then the right subtree (d → e → f → g → h) and then merges the left subtree and the right subtree to update the root (c → h → i).

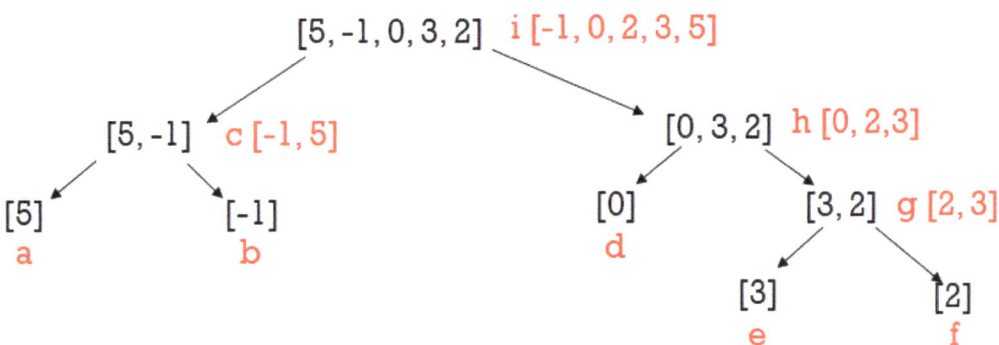

Figure 2-3. The tree illustration of a Merge Sort process

25

CHAPTER 2   DIVIDE AND CONQUER

```
In [3]: run Listing_2_3_merge_sort.py
left part --> [5]
right part --> [-1]
merge sorted arr --> [-1, 5]
left part --> [-1, 5]
left part --> [0]
left part --> [3]
right part --> [2]
merge sorted arr --> [2, 3]
right part --> [2, 3]
merge sorted arr --> [0, 2, 3]
right part --> [0, 2, 3]
merge sorted arr --> [-1, 0, 2, 3, 5]
[-1, 0, 2, 3, 5]
```

The way we write our recursive code at lines 21, 23, and 25 (where we explore the left part first, then the right part, and finally merge the left and right parts) dictates that it is a pre-order traversal of the tree.

Let us examine the time complexity. We break down the array recursively by half. The height of the tree will be O(log N). At each layer, we merge the sorted arrays, which has a linear time O(N). The final time complexity will be O(NlogN). As for the space complexity, we used the auxiliary array to collect the sorted results. Since we have N elements, the space complexity will be O(N). Compared with Bubble Sort, Insertion Sort, and Selection Sort, Merge Sort is quicker but at the expense of additional space.

Quick Sort

Quick Sort is another efficient algorithm for sorting. Let us use the same array [5, -1, 0, 3, 2] as an example. Similar to Merge Sort, in Quick Sort, the array is recursively broken into smaller ones. Unlike Merge Sort that splits the array in half, Quick Sort designates a *pivot* and uses that pivot to divide the array into three parts, i.e., the array with numbers smaller than or equal to the pivot, the pivot array (with a single element), and the array with numbers greater than the pivot. To choose a pivot, we can randomly pick a number in the array as a pivot or, even simpler, pick the first element as a pivot.

If we choose the first number as the pivot, the original array [5, -1, 0, 3, 2] will be broken into [-1, 0, 3, 2], **[5]**, and []. In the next round, [-1, 0, 3, 2] will be divided into [], **[-1]**, and [0, 3, 2]. Then [0, 3, 2] becomes [], **[0]**, and [3, 2]. [3, 2] becomes [2], **[3]**, and []. See Figure 2-4 below; the pivot is highlighted in blue.

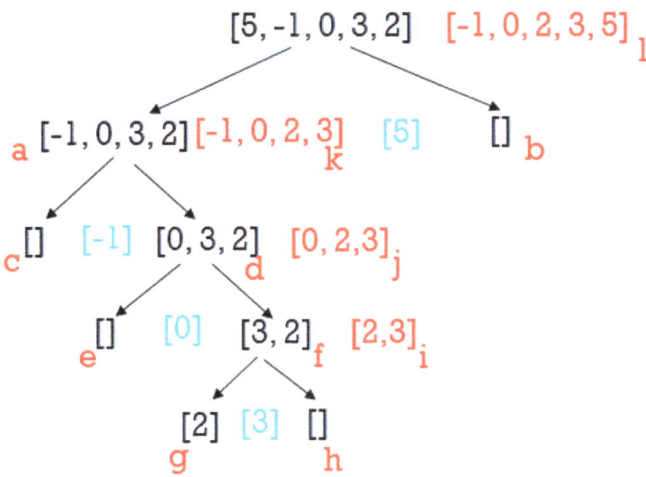

Blue is the pivot number; red is sorted subarray

Figure 2-4. *The tree illustration of a Quick Sort process*

Similar to Merge Sort, once we have a single-element array, by definition, it is sorted. What we need to do next is to merge them together, i.e., concatenate [left] + [pivot] + [right], bottom-up, and in a recursive fashion, to arrive at the sorted array.

The code implementation of Quick Sort is similar to that of Merge Sort (Listing 2-4).

Listing 2-4. Implementation of the Quick Sort

```
1.  def quick_sort(arr):
2.      length = len(arr)
3.      if length == 1 or length == 0:
4.          return arr
5.      pivot_num = arr[0]
6.      left_part = [num for num in arr[1:] if num <= pivot_num]
7.      print ("left part -->", left_part)
8.      right_part = [num for num in arr[1:] if num > pivot_num]
9.      print ("right part -->", right_part)
10.     sorted_arr = quick_sort(left_part) + [pivot_num] + quick_sort(right_part)
11.     print ("quick sorted arr -->", sorted_arr)
12.     return sorted_arr
13.
14. if __name__ == "__main__":
15.     unsorted_arr = [5, -1, 0, 3, 2]
16.     sorted_arr = quick_sort(unsorted_arr)
17.     print (sorted_arr)
```

CHAPTER 2 DIVIDE AND CONQUER

```
In [4]: run Listing_2_4_quick_sort.py
left part --> [-1, 0, 3, 2]
right part --> []
left part --> []
right part --> [0, 3, 2]
left part --> []
right part --> [3, 2]
left part --> [2]
right part --> []
quick sorted arr --> [2, 3]
quick sorted arr --> [0, 2, 3]
quick sorted arr --> [-1, 0, 2, 3]
quick sorted arr --> [-1, 0, 2, 3, 5]
[-1, 0, 2, 3, 5]
```

For the time complexity, we see a similar tree diagram in Figure 2-4 as in Figure 2-3, with an average height of log (N). In the average case, the time will be O(N log N). In terms of space complexity, we have used an auxiliary array, so the space complexity will be O(N).

Unlike Merge Sort where the array is broken into halves, here in Quick Sort, the sizes of the smaller arrays can be skewed. Consider this special scenario of an array [-1, 0, 2, 3, 5], where all numbers are already sorted. In such a case, the tree diagram will become extremely unbalanced. The height of the tree is not log(N) but N (see Figure 2-5). In sum, the time complexity for Quick Sort is on average O(NlogN), but in the worst case, it becomes $O(N^2)$.

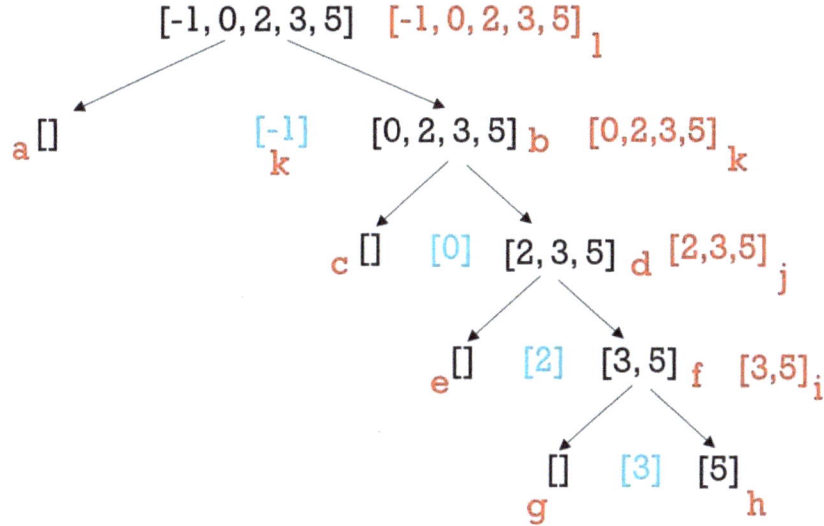

* Blue is the pivot number; red is sorted subarray

Figure 2-5. *The tree illustration of a Quick Sort for an already-sorted array*

```
In [5]: run Listing_2_4_quick_sort_special_case.py
left part --> []
right part --> [0, 2, 3, 5]
left part --> []
right part --> [2, 3, 5]
left part --> []
right part --> [3, 5]
left part --> []
right part --> [5]
quick sorted arr --> [3, 5]
quick sorted arr --> [2, 3, 5]
quick sorted arr --> [0, 2, 3, 5]
quick sorted arr --> [-1, 0, 2, 3, 5]
[-1, 0, 2, 3, 5]
```

CHAPTER 2   DIVIDE AND CONQUER

Multiplication of Two Positive Integers

Let us continue our journey with divide-and-conquer by looking at the problem of multiplying two positive n-bit integers, say P and Q. The integers can be represented in binary format. For example, let P =11 which is $(1011)_2$ and Q = 9 which is $(1001)_2$. And we are tasked with finding the product of $(1011)_2$ and $(1001)_2$. Using the elementary-school multiplication technique, this would require 4×4 multiplication and seven addition operations for this example, yielding $(1100011)_2$, which is 99 (Figure 2-6). The time complexity is dominated by the multiplication step and asymptotes to $O(n^2)$ with n being the number of bits for the integers.

$$
\begin{array}{r}
(1011)_2 \\
\times \quad (1001)_2 \\
\hline
(1011)_2 \\
(0000)_2 \\
(0000)_2 \\
(1011)_2 \\
\hline
= \quad (1100011)_2
\end{array}
$$

Figure 2-6. *Multiplying two binary numbers using basic math*

Can we do better than the grade-school technique? Let us break each number into two equal parts based on the number of bits, and see if we can reconstruct the original number using both parts.

If breaking the number $(1011)_2$ into two equal parts, the left part will be $(10)_2$ and the right part will be $(11)_2$. And $(1011)_2 = (10)_2 \times 2^2 + (11)_2$. In general, for an n-bit integer P, it can be reconstructed by

$$P = P_L 2^{n/2} + P_R$$

Now do the same breakdown for the other integer Q, and see what the multiplication leads to. The derived result is shown below:

$$P = P_L 2^{n/2} + P_R,\ Q = Q_L 2^{n/2} + Q_R$$

$$P \times Q = (P_L 2^{n/2} + P_R) \times (Q_L 2^{n/2} + Q_R)$$

$$= P_L Q_L 2^n + 2^{n/2}(P_L Q_R + P_R Q_L) + P_R Q_R \tag{1}$$

We still need a total of four multiplication steps for cross products of both parts of P and Q. It does not seem to improve relative to our naïve approach above. Yes, in its current form, it does not improve. The key idea is that the multiplication is expensive, but the addition is cheap time-wise. Maybe we can reduce the two multiplications in the middle term of Equation (1) to one multiplication? Observe:

$$(P_L + P_R) \times (Q_L + Q_R) = P_L Q_L + (P_L Q_R + P_R Q_L) + P_R Q_R.$$

Then the middle term in (1) can be obtained by

$$(P_L Q_R + P_R Q_L) = (P_L + P_R) \times (Q_L + Q_R) - P_L Q_L - P_R Q_R$$

And plug this into the original Equation (1), we have:

$$P \times Q = P_L Q_L 2^n + 2^{n/2}\big((P_L + P_R) \times (Q_L + Q_R) - P_L Q_L - P_R Q_R\big) + P_R Q_R$$

Let us denote $A = P_L Q_L$, $B = P_R Q_R$, $C = (P_L + P_R) \times (Q_L + Q_R)$, then

$$P \times Q = A \times 2^n + 2^{n/2}(C - A - B) + B \tag{2}$$

Indeed, we now only need to evaluate three multiplications instead of four.

If we recursively break down the integers into two parts and at each level evaluate the product for each part by finding its own A, B, C, we shall have a more efficient algorithm than $O(n^2)$. Suppose the number of operations needed is $T(n)$ and n is the number of bits for each integer. Then

$$T(n) = 3 \times T\left(\frac{n}{2}\right) + O(n)$$

where $O(n)$ is the time required for piecing together A, B, C using unit operations in Equation (2).

By master theorem [1], which says if $T(n) = aT\left(\frac{n}{b}\right) + O(n^d)$ for some constants a>0, b>1, d≥0, then

CHAPTER 2   DIVIDE AND CONQUER

$$T(n) = \begin{cases} O(n^d) \text{ if } d > log b^a \\ O(n^d log n) \text{ if } d = log b^a \\ O(n^{log b^a}) \text{ if } d < log b^a \end{cases}$$

Plug in $a = 3$, $b = 2$, and $d = 1$; we have $T(n) = O(n^{log b^a}) = O(n^{log 2^3}) \cong O(n^{1.58})$. This is indeed more efficient than the naïve method, which requires a $O(n^2)$

Let us go over a concrete example; for example, use the same 11×9 example. Since both integers have four bits, they can be divided each into two equal parts. As shown in Figure 2-7, to calculate the product of 11 and 9, we need values for A, B, and C as defined in Equation (2), where $A = (10)_2 \times (10)_2$, $B = (11)_2 \times (01)_2$, and $C = ((10)_2 + (11)_2) \times ((10)_2 + (01)_2)$, respectively.

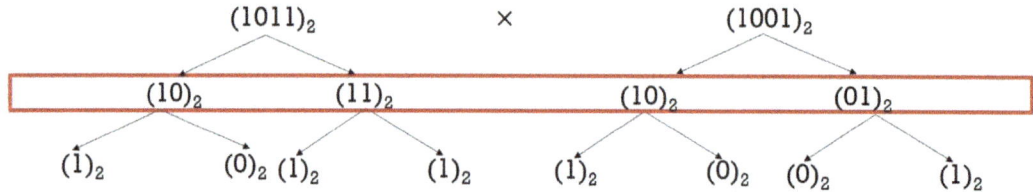

Figure 2-7. *Diagram for the multiplication of two binary numbers*

Let us calculate A and B; see Figure 2-8. We obtain the values for A and B recursively by further splitting them to single digits (note the A', B', and C' in Figure 2-8 are operated on single bits). When *we only have a single bit left, we simply calculate their product and return the value.* In the end, we get A = 2×2 = 4 and B = 3×1=3, respectively.

CHAPTER 2 DIVIDE AND CONQUER

Calculate A

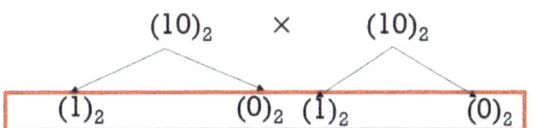

$P_L = (1)_2 = 1$, $P_R = (0)_2 = 0$, $Q_L = (1)_2 = 1$, $Q_R = (0)_2 = 0$, $n = 2$
$A' = P_L \times Q_L = 1$, $B' = P_R \times Q_R = 0$, $C' = (P_L + P_R) \times (Q_L + Q_R) = 1$
$2 \times 2 = (10)_2 \times (10)_2 = A' \times 2^n + 2^{n/2} \times (C'-A'-B') + B' = 1 \times 2^2 + 2^1 \times (1-1-0) + 0 = 4$

Calculate B

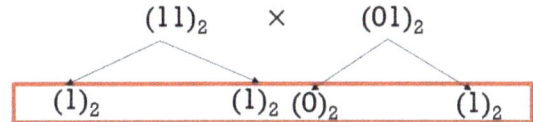

$P_L = (1)_2 = 1$, $P_R = (0)_2 = 1$, $Q_L = (0)_2 = 0$, $Q_R = (1)_2 = 1$, $n = 2$
$A' = P_L \times Q_L = 0$, $B' = P_R \times Q_R = 1$, $C' = (P_L + P_R) \times (Q_L + Q_R) = 2$
$3 \times 1 = (10)_2 \times (01)_2 = A' \times 2^n + 2^{n/2} \times (C'-A'-B') + B' = 0 \times 2^2 + 2^1 \times (2-0-1) + 1 = 3$

Figure 2-8. *Detailed procedures to calculate A and B in the given example*

The tricky part is for calculating C (Figure 2-9).

Calculate C = $((10)_2 + (11)_2) \times ((10)_2 + (01)_2) = (101)_2 \times (11)_2$

```
      (101)₂       ×       (11)₂
       /  \                / \
    (10)₂  (1)₂ (1)₂     (1)₂
```

Figure 2-9. *An initial attempt to calculate C*

After summing up the left and right parts of integer P, we get $(101)_2$ with three bits. It is not obvious how to divide it into two halves. Also, the summed counterpart for Q is $(11)_2$ with two bits, which is different from three bits. This makes us wonder: For the algorithm to work, do we require both input integers with an equal even number of bits?

CHAPTER 2   DIVIDE AND CONQUER

Ideally, we aim for a more generic multiplication algorithm that works for any pair of positive integers. Also, even if the integer has an even number of bits, during recursion, it could still have an odd number of bits. For example, if we start with a number with six bits, then during the next round of recursion, it will be reduced to three bits.

Here is a way to deal with this. Given two integers P and Q, with numbers of bits n_1, and n_2, respectively.

- Find $n = max(n_1, n_2)$.

- If n is odd, add 1, else do nothing.

- Pad zeros to the left of P and Q, respectively, to make the length equal to n.

This way, at each time, we are guaranteed to have an even number of bits for both integers which can be divided by 2. Let us try this new method to recalculate C with $(101)_2 \times (11)_2$. The process is displayed in Figure 2-10. It works ! It gives the correct value for 5×3.

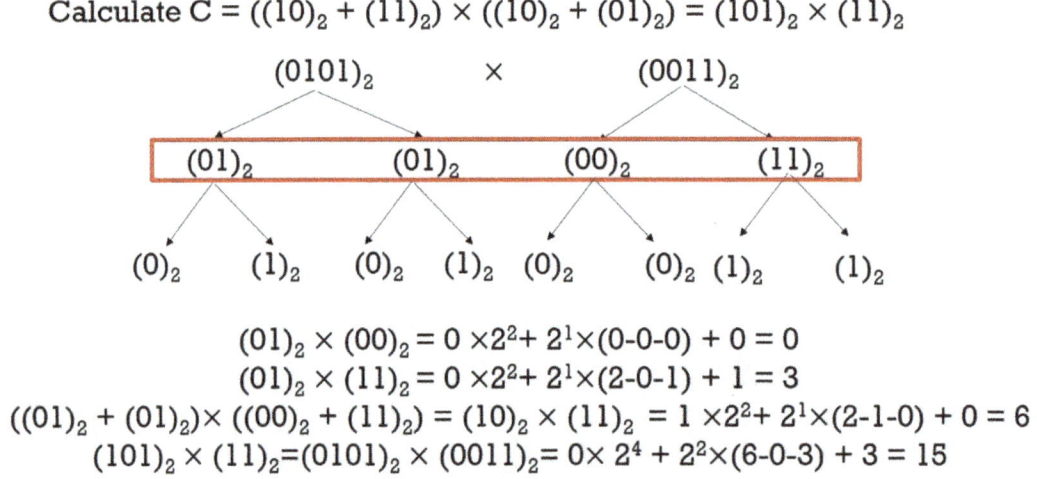

Calculate $C = ((10)_2 + (11)_2) \times ((10)_2 + (01)_2) = (101)_2 \times (11)_2$

$(01)_2 \times (00)_2 = 0 \times 2^2 + 2^1 \times (0-0-0) + 0 = 0$
$(01)_2 \times (11)_2 = 0 \times 2^2 + 2^1 \times (2-0-1) + 1 = 3$
$((01)_2 + (01)_2) \times ((00)_2 + (11)_2) = (10)_2 \times (11)_2 = 1 \times 2^2 + 2^1 \times (2-1-0) + 0 = 6$
$(101)_2 \times (11)_2 = (0101)_2 \times (0011)_2 = 0 \times 2^4 + 2^2 \times (6-0-3) + 3 = 15$

Figure 2-10. *An improved procedure to calculate C*

Now if we plug in A=4, B=3, and C=15 into Equation (2), we get $11 \times 9 = (1011)_2 \times (1001)_2 = 99$. See detailed calculation in Figure 2-11.

CHAPTER 2 DIVIDE AND CONQUER

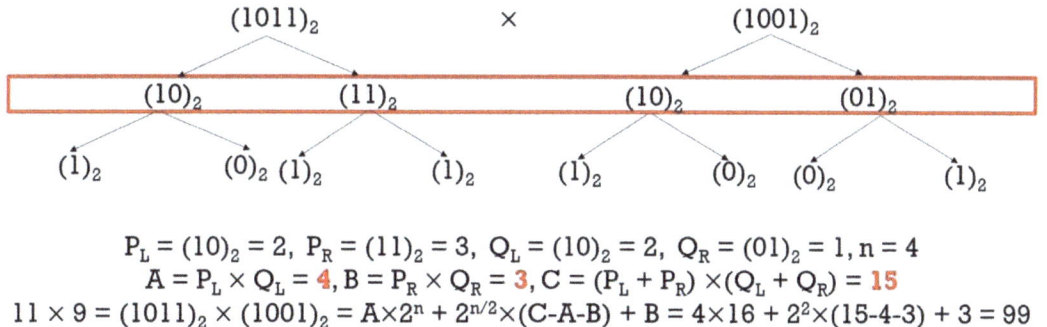

$P_L = (10)_2 = 2, P_R = (11)_2 = 3, Q_L = (10)_2 = 2, Q_R = (01)_2 = 1, n = 4$
$A = P_L \times Q_L = 4, B = P_R \times Q_R = 3, C = (P_L + P_R) \times (Q_L + Q_R) = 15$
$11 \times 9 = (1011)_2 \times (1001)_2 = A \times 2^n + 2^{n/2} \times (C-A-B) + B = 4 \times 16 + 2^2 \times (15-4-3) + 3 = 99$

Figure 2-11. *The calculation of 11× 9 by leveraging results from binary numbers half of the original size recursively*

The code implementation is now straightforward; see Listing 2-5.

Listing 2-5. Multiplying two n-bit integers using recursion

```
def multiply_n_bits_integers(x, y):
    binary_x = bin(x)[2:]
    binary_y = bin(y)[2:]
    n_x = len(binary_x)
    n_y = len(binary_y)

    if n_x == 1 or n_y == 1:
        return x * y

    n = max(n_x, n_y)
    if n % 2 == 1:
        n += 1
    binary_x = binary_x.zfill(n)
    binary_y = binary_y.zfill(n)

    x_left = int(binary_x[: n//2], 2)
    x_right = int(binary_x[n //2: ], 2)
    y_left = int(binary_y[:n//2], 2)
    y_right = int(binary_y[n//2: ], 2)
    A = multiply_n_bits_integers(x_left, y_left)
    B = multiply_n_bits_integers(x_right, y_right)
    C = multiply_n_bits_integers(x_left + x_right, y_left + y_right)
    return 2**n * A + 2**(n // 2) * (C - A - B) + B

if __name__ == "__main__":
    print (multiply_n_bits_integers(11, 9) == 11 * 9)
    print (multiply_n_bits_integers(123, 45678) == 123 * 45678)
```

Let us test our code with more examples. As expected, it works for both examples 11×9 and 123× 45678.

```
In [6]: run Listing_2_5_multiply_n_bit_numbers.py
True
True
```

Fast Fourier Transform

The next problem is about polynomial multiplication. Suppose we have two polynomials:

$$a(x) = -5 + 4x + 3x^2 + 2x^3 \text{ and } b(x) = -2 + 2x + 3x^2 + 5x^3.$$

The goal is to find the coefficients of their product $c(x)$.

The naïve approach would be calculating the cross-product term one by one and then regrouping based on the degree of the polynomial. It is the technique we learned in middle school. The process is as follows:

$$c(x) = \left(10 - 10x - 15x^2 - 25x^3\right) +$$

$$\left(-8x + 8x^2 + 12x^3 + 20x^4\right) +$$

$$\left(-6x^2 + 6x^3 + 9x^4 + 15x^5\right) +$$

$$\left(-4x^3 + 4x^4 + 6x^5 + 10x^6\right)$$

$$= 10 - 18x - 13x^2 - 11x^3 + 33x^4 + 21x^5 + 10x^6.$$

The calculation is correct. But how many elementary calculations did we just do? Well, there are four coefficients each from $a(x)$ and $b(x)$. So, the number of multiplications is 4 × 4 = 16. In addition, the regroup step for each degree of polynomial has a total of 1 + 2 + 3 + 4 + 3 + 2 + 1 = 15 additions. In general, if $a(x)$ and $b(x)$ each has N terms, the time complexity will be $O(N^2)$.

Naturally, the question is, can we do better than this? At first glance, it seems we cannot bypass the multiplication of the coefficients, which requires $O(N^2)$ and dictates the time. However, this is because we represent the polynomial as coefficient, such as [-5, 4, 3, 2] for $a(x)$ and [−2, 2, 3, 5] for $b(x)$; the time required is in the order of $O(N^2)$. But how about we represent the polynomial in *another form*? That is, instead of using coefficient representation, how about we represent it using values? For example, we know a linear line can be uniquely determined by two points. Likewise, a quadratic curve can be uniquely determined by three points. In general, a polynomial with a degree of *d* will be uniquely determined by *d + 1* points.

In value representation, we can represent $a(x)$ by arbitrary four points that sit on the curve, say $[(-2,-17),(-1,-8),(0,-5),(1,4)]$. Same for $b(x)$, we can choose $[(-2,-34),(-1,-6),(0,-2),(1,8)]$. Since the highest degree of polynomial is 6 for $c(x)$, to uniquely determine it, we will need seven points. Let us add three more points to values for $a(x)$ and $b(x)$. We have:

$$[(-3, -44), (-2, -17), (-1, -8), (0, -5), (1, 4), (2, 31), (3, 88)] \to a(x)$$
$$[(-3, -116), (-2, -34), (-1, -6), (0, -2), (1, 8), (2, 54), (3, 166)] \to b(x)$$

Calculating the points for $c(x)$ now becomes straightforward – we can multiply the y coordinates from $a(x)$ and $b(x)$ in linear time (see plots in Figure 2-12).

$$[(-3, 5104), (-2, 578), (-1, 48), (0, 10), (1, 32), (2, 1674), (3, 14608)] \to c(x)$$

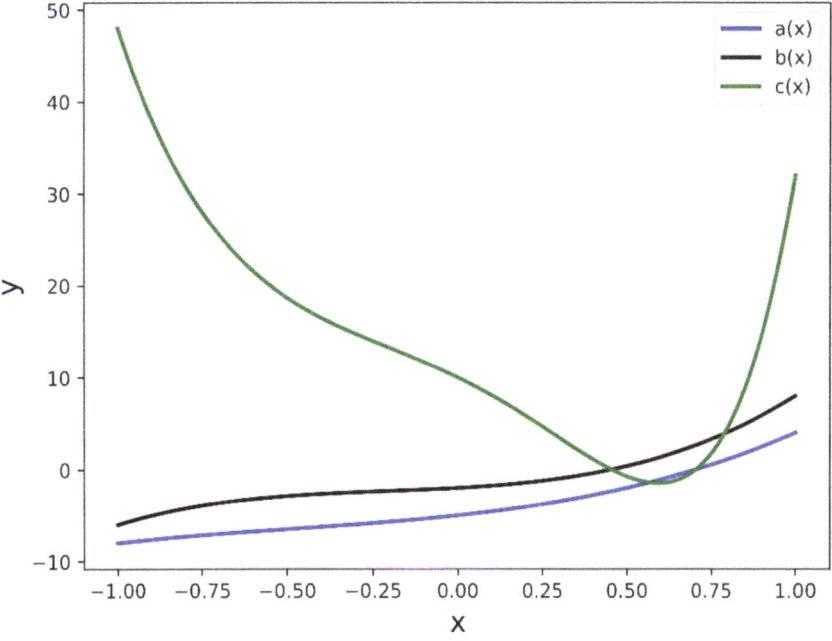

Figure 2-12. *Plots of a(x), b(x), and c(x) from -1 to 1*

CHAPTER 2   DIVIDE AND CONQUER

But wait! Although calculating the points for c(x) based on value representations of a(x) and b(x) takes linear time, to calculate the value representations for a(x) and b(x), each still takes $O(N^2)$ time. There seems to be no improvement over the naïve approach.

Previously, we arbitrarily chose x = [-3, -2, -1, 0, 1, 2, 3] for representing a(x) and b(x) perhaps for convenience. However, if we choose these x points wisely, the number of computations can be reduced. As a matter of fact, the time will become O(NlogN), which hints at divide-and-conquer!

Let us now focus on $a(x) = -5 + 4x + 3x^2 + 2x^3$. We know we will have to find four unique points to represent it. What if I tell you the four points chosen are $\omega^0, \omega^1, \omega^2, \omega^3$ where $\omega = e^{\frac{2\pi i}{n}} = e^{\frac{2\pi i}{4}}$. This is certainly out of nowhere, but let us just give it a try. In such case, $\omega^0 = 1$, $\omega^1 = i$, $\omega^2 = -1$, $\omega^3 = -i$. Let us plug in these points to a(x) and evaluate:

$$a(\omega^0) = -5 + 4(\omega^0) + 3(\omega^0)^2 + 2(\omega^0)^3 = 4$$

$$a(\omega^1) = -5 + 4(\omega^1) + 3(\omega^2)^2 + 2(\omega^3)^3 = -8 + 2i$$

$$a(\omega^2) = -5 + 4(\omega^2) + 3(\omega^2)^2 + 2(\omega^2)^3 = -8$$

$$a(\omega^3) = -5 + 4(\omega^3) + 3(\omega^3)^2 + 2(\omega^3)^3 = -8 - 2i$$

Rearrange it in matrix format:

$$\begin{bmatrix} a(\omega^0) \\ a(\omega^1) \\ a(\omega^2) \\ a(\omega^3) \end{bmatrix} = \begin{bmatrix} 1 & \omega^0 & \omega^0 & \omega^0 \\ 1 & \omega^1 & \omega^2 & \omega^3 \\ 1 & \omega^2 & \omega^4 & \omega^6 \\ 1 & \omega^3 & \omega^6 & \omega^9 \end{bmatrix} \begin{bmatrix} a_0 \\ a_1 \\ a_2 \\ a_3 \end{bmatrix}$$

You must be curious: Why do we pick up complex numbers $\omega^0, \omega^1, \omega^2, \omega^3$, and what are these values [4, −8 + 2i, −8, −8 − 2i]? These values are the Fourier transform of the coefficients of a(x). The complex numbers thus chosen are for a quick calculation of Fourier transform, a.k.a. the Fast Fourier Transform (FFT). The $\omega = e^{\frac{2\pi i}{n}}$ term is the nth root of unity, that is, it is the solution to $\omega^n = 1$. If there are two coefficients for $a(x)$ (N = 2), we would propose a value representation at $a(\omega^0)$ and $a(\omega^1)$ where $\omega = e^{\frac{2\pi i}{2}}$; likewise, for N = 4, we would use $a(\omega^0)$, $a(\omega^1)$, $a(\omega^2)$, and $a(\omega^3)$ where $\omega = e^{\frac{2\pi i}{4}}$, and for N = 8, we instead propose $a(\omega^0)$, ..., $a(\omega^7)$ where $\omega = e^{\frac{2\pi i}{8}}$. The evaluation of these ω values is summarized in Table 2-1 for N = 2, 4, and 8, respectively.

Table 2-1. *The choice of complex numbers for functions with 2, 4, and 8 coefficients, respectively*

	N= 2	N=4	N=8
ω^0	1	1	1
ω^1	−1	i	$\sqrt{2}/2(1+i)$
ω^2	-	−1	i
ω^3	-	$-i$	$-\sqrt{2}/2(1-i)$
ω^4	-	-	−1
ω^5	-	-	$-\sqrt{2}/2(1+i)$
ω^6	-	-	$-i$
ω^7	-	-	$\sqrt{2}/2(1-i)$

If we examine Table 2-1 closely, we notice that we do not need to calculate each power term of ω. In fact, we only need to compute the first half of the terms. For example, for N = 8, we only need $(\omega^0, \omega^1, \omega^2, \omega^3)$ since $(\omega^4, \omega^5, \omega^6, \omega^7)$ have just the opposite values. This property can be better visualized on a complex plane where it is easy to observe $\omega^j = -\omega^{j+n/2}$ where $j = \{0, 1, ..., n/2 - 1\}$. Moreover, all these ω values are the roots of $\omega^n = 1$ (Figure 2-13).

CHAPTER 2   DIVIDE AND CONQUER

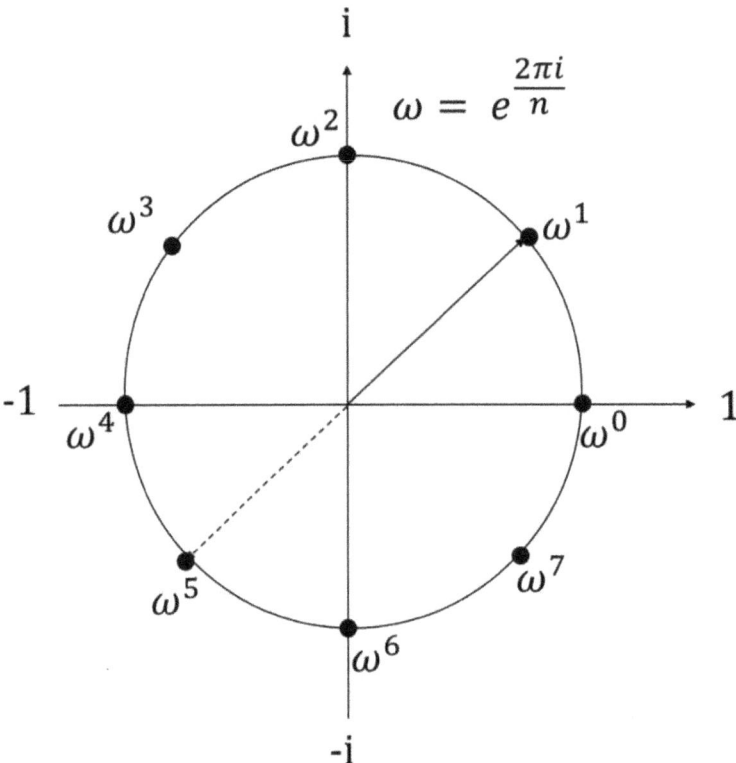

Figure 2-13. *nth root of unity in a complex plane (here n=8)*

The symmetry here encourages us to think of a divide-and-conquer algorithm where in each iteration we can cut the computations by half. Let us look at the previous example $a(x) = -5 + 4x + 3x^2 + 2x^3$ and see if we can devise such an algorithm. In the process as depicted in Figure 2-14, we group the even-degree polynomial terms and the odd-degree polynomial terms separately.

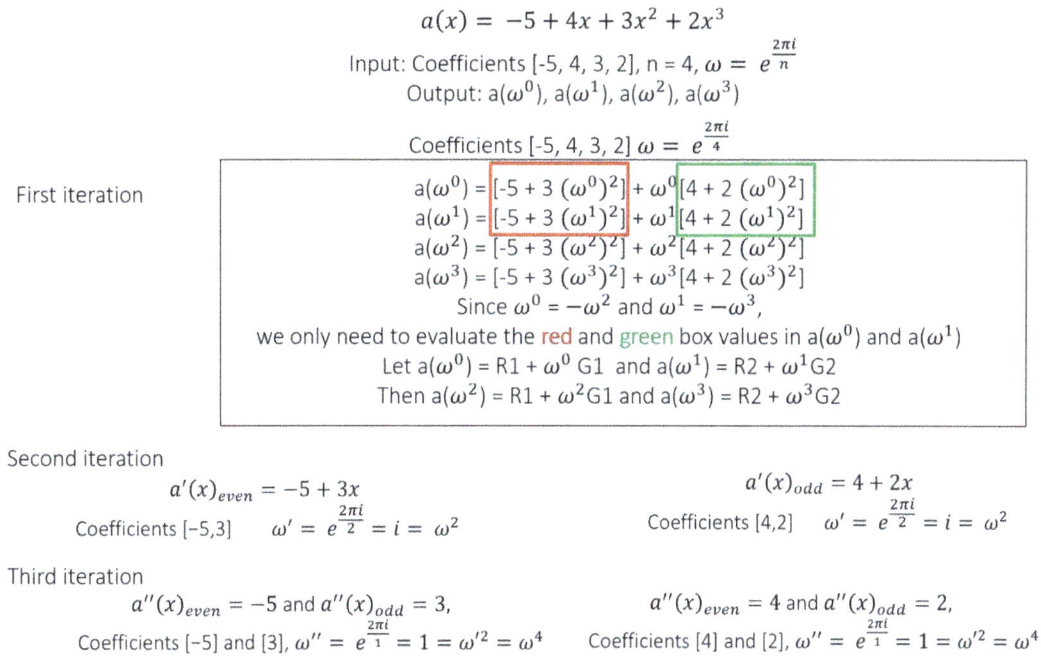

CHAPTER 2 DIVIDE AND CONQUER

$$a(x) = -5 + 4x + 3x^2 + 2x^3$$

Input: Coefficients [-5, 4, 3, 2], n = 4, $\omega = e^{\frac{2\pi i}{n}}$
Output: $a(\omega^0), a(\omega^1), a(\omega^2), a(\omega^3)$

Coefficients [-5, 4, 3, 2] $\omega = e^{\frac{2\pi i}{4}}$

First iteration

$a(\omega^0) = [-5 + 3\ (\omega^0)^2] + \omega^0[4 + 2\ (\omega^0)^2]$
$a(\omega^1) = [-5 + 3\ (\omega^1)^2] + \omega^1[4 + 2\ (\omega^1)^2]$
$a(\omega^2) = [-5 + 3\ (\omega^2)^2] + \omega^2[4 + 2\ (\omega^2)^2]$
$a(\omega^3) = [-5 + 3\ (\omega^3)^2] + \omega^3[4 + 2\ (\omega^3)^2]$
Since $\omega^0 = -\omega^2$ and $\omega^1 = -\omega^3$,
we only need to evaluate the red and green box values in $a(\omega^0)$ and $a(\omega^1)$
Let $a(\omega^0) = R1 + \omega^0\ G1$ and $a(\omega^1) = R2 + \omega^1 G2$
Then $a(\omega^2) = R1 + \omega^2 G1$ and $a(\omega^3) = R2 + \omega^3 G2$

Second iteration

$a'(x)_{even} = -5 + 3x$ $\qquad$ $a'(x)_{odd} = 4 + 2x$
Coefficients [-5,3] $\quad \omega' = e^{\frac{2\pi i}{2}} = i = \omega^2$ $\qquad$ Coefficients [4,2] $\quad \omega' = e^{\frac{2\pi i}{2}} = i = \omega^2$

Third iteration

$a''(x)_{even} = -5$ and $a''(x)_{odd} = 3$, $\qquad$ $a''(x)_{even} = 4$ and $a''(x)_{odd} = 2$,
Coefficients [-5] and [3], $\omega'' = e^{\frac{2\pi i}{1}} = 1 = \omega'^2 = \omega^4$ $\quad$ Coefficients [4] and [2], $\omega'' = e^{\frac{2\pi i}{1}} = 1 = \omega'^2 = \omega^4$

Figure 2-14. *The procedure to calculate Fourier coefficients of a(x): step 1, recursively break it down till it hits the base case (a top-to-bottom process)*

In the first iteration, we can write the expressions for $a(\omega^0)$, $a(\omega^1)$, $a(\omega^2)$, and $a(\omega^3)$ based on $\omega = e^{\frac{2\pi i}{4}}$. And by symmetry, we only need to evaluate values in red and green boxes in $a(\omega^0)$, $a(\omega^1)$ only, thus cutting the calculation by half. In the second iteration, we separate the calculation of Fourier coefficients into even and odd terms. Note here a'(x) becomes linear (not quadratic), and $\omega' = \omega^2$. Moving onto the third iteration, where we further divide the coefficient terms to a single value and thus reach the bottom of the recursion. It is time to return the value upward.

Once we hit the bottom of the split, it is time to return the values (Figure 2-15).

CHAPTER 2 DIVIDE AND CONQUER

Return the FFT values upwards

$a''(x)_{even} = -5$ and $a''(x)_{odd} = 3$,
Coefficients [-5] and [3], $\omega'' = e^{\frac{2\pi i}{1}} = 1 = \omega'^2 = \omega^4$
$a''(\omega''^0)_{even} = -5 \quad a''(\omega''^0)_{odd} = 3$

$a''(x)_{even} = 4$ and $a''(x)_{odd} = 2$,
Coefficients [4] and [2], $\omega'' = e^{\frac{2\pi i}{1}} = 1 = \omega'^2 = \omega^4$
$a''(\omega''^0)_{even} = 4 \quad a''(\omega''^0)_{odd} = 2$

$a'(x)_{even}(\omega'^0) = a''(\omega''^0)_{even} + (\omega')^0 a''(\omega''^0)_{odd} = -5 + 3 = -2$
$a'(x)_{even}(\omega'^1) = a''(\omega''^0)_{even} - (\omega')^0 a''(\omega''^0)_{odd} = -5 - 3 = -8$

$a'(x)_{odd}(\omega'^0) = a''(\omega''^0)_{even} + (\omega')^0 a''(\omega''^0)_{odd} = 4 + 2 = 6$
$a'(x)_{odd}(\omega'^1) = a''(\omega''^0)_{even} - (\omega')^0 a''(\omega''^0)_{odd} = 4 - 2 = 2$

$a(\omega^0) = a'(x)_{even}(\omega'^0) + (\omega)^0 a'(x)_{odd}(\omega'^0) = -2 + (i)^0 \times 6 = 4$
$a(\omega^2) = a'(x)_{even}(\omega'^0) - (\omega)^0 a'(x)_{odd}(\omega'^0) = -2 - (i)^0 \times 6 = -8$
$a(\omega^1) = a'(x)_{even}(\omega'^1) + (\omega)^1 a'(x)_{odd}(\omega'^1) = -8 + (i)^1 \times 2 = -8 + 2i$
$a(\omega^3) = a'(x)_{even}(\omega'^1) - (\omega)^1 a'(x)_{odd}(\omega'^1) = -8 - (i)^1 \times 2 = -8 - 2i$

Figure 2-15. *The procedure to calculate Fourier coefficients of a(x): step 2, recursively return the values upward (a bottom-to-top process)*

At the third layer, since there is only one coefficient, we return the Fourier coefficient to be of the same value. Next, we return to the second layer, and we obtain the [-2, -8] and [6, 2] for even and odd term Fourier coefficients, respectively. Lastly, we arrive at the top layer and evaluate the final Fourier coefficients for the polynomial $a(x)$, for which we get $[4, -8 + 2i, -8, -8 - 2i]$.

This is quite a journey. The reason that recursion can keep going is that for nth root of unity, if we square the roots, half of the roots still have opposite values of the rest half; the same property holds just as those before squaring. For example, for N=8, we have ω^0, $\omega^1, \omega^2, \omega^3, \omega^4, \omega^5, \omega^6, \omega^7$ where the first four terms have opposite values of the last four. If we square the first four terms, they become $\omega^0, \omega^2, \omega^4, \omega^6 \to (1, i, -1, i)$ where the first half terms (ω^0, ω^2) have opposite values of the second half (ω^4, ω^6). If we keep squaring the first two terms, i.e., (ω^0, ω^2), we have $\omega^0, \omega^4 \to (1, -1)$; it has the same property. It is this nice property from root of unity that enables us to reduce the computation by half and achieve a O(NlogN) algorithm.

The Fast Fourier Transform (FFT) algorithm can now be written as the following pseudocode [2] in Figure 2-16. We recursively divide the coefficients into even and odd terms. Pay attention to the for loop where we piece together the Fourier coefficients of even and odd terms.

```
FFT(p)
Inputs: coefficients p = (p₀, p₁, .. pₙ₋₁) for polynomial P(x)
        w is nth root of unity and n is the power of 2
Output: P(w⁰), P(w¹), ..., P(wⁿ⁻¹)
    n = length of p
    if n = 1, return P(1)
    w = e^(2πi/n)
    let p_even = (p₀, p₂, ..., pₙ₋₂) and p_odd = (p₁, p₃, ..., pₙ₋₁)
    P_even(w⁰), P_even(w²), ..., P_even(wⁿ⁻²) = FFT(p_even)
    P_odd(w⁰), P_odd(w²), ..., P_odd(wⁿ⁻²) = FFT(p_odd)
    For j = 0 → n/2 – 1:
        P(wʲ) = P_even(w^(2j)) + wʲ P_odd(w^(2j))
        P(w^(j+n/2)) = P(-wʲ) = P_even(w^(2j)) - wʲ P_odd(w^(2j))
    Return P(w⁰), P(w¹), ..., P(wⁿ⁻¹)
```

Figure 2-16. Pseudocode for implementing Fast Fourier Transform

Back to our original problem where we need to find the coefficients of the product of two polynomials $a(x)$ and $b(x)$. We now can find the Fourier coefficients for both polynomials and then do a dot product of these Fourier coefficients to get the value representation of $c(x)$. But the remaining problem is how do we transform back from Fourier coefficients to normal coefficients. For that, we can do an Inverse Fast Fourier Transform (IFFT). Recall the matrix form of FFT for $a(x)$ where $\omega = e^{\frac{2\pi i}{n}} = e^{\frac{2\pi i}{4}}$.

$$\begin{bmatrix} a(\omega^0) \\ a(\omega^1) \\ a(\omega^2) \\ a(\omega^3) \end{bmatrix} = \begin{bmatrix} 1 & \omega^0 & \omega^0 & \omega^0 \\ 1 & \omega^1 & \omega^2 & \omega^3 \\ 1 & \omega^2 & \omega^4 & \omega^6 \\ 1 & \omega^3 & \omega^6 & \omega^9 \end{bmatrix} \begin{bmatrix} a_0 \\ a_1 \\ a_2 \\ a_3 \end{bmatrix}$$

CHAPTER 2 DIVIDE AND CONQUER

We now need to find the inverse of the Discrete Fourier Transform (DFT) matrix. It turns out the inverse is much like the original DFT matrix, with the exponent term multiplied by -1. Also, do not forget the normalization factor $1/n$, and here $\omega = e^{\frac{-2\pi i}{n}} = e^{\frac{-2\pi i}{4}}$.

$$\begin{bmatrix} a_0 \\ a_1 \\ a_2 \\ a_3 \end{bmatrix} = \left(\begin{bmatrix} 1 & \omega^0 & \omega^0 & \omega^0 \\ 1 & \omega^1 & \omega^2 & \omega^3 \\ 1 & \omega^2 & \omega^4 & \omega^6 \\ 1 & \omega^3 & \omega^6 & \omega^9 \end{bmatrix}^{-1} \begin{bmatrix} a(\omega^0) \\ a(\omega^1) \\ a(\omega^2) \\ a(\omega^3) \end{bmatrix} \right) = \frac{1}{n} \left(\begin{bmatrix} 1 & \omega^0 & \omega^0 & \omega^0 \\ 1 & \omega^{-1} & \omega^{-2} & \omega^{-3} \\ 1 & \omega^{-2} & \omega^{-4} & \omega^{-6} \\ 1 & \omega^{-3} & \omega^{-6} & \omega^{-9} \end{bmatrix} \begin{bmatrix} a(\omega^0) \\ a(\omega^1) \\ a(\omega^2) \\ a(\omega^3) \end{bmatrix} \right)$$

To calculate the coefficients for $c(x)$, since the highest degree of polynomial for $a(x)$ and $b(x)$ is 3, which implies that the highest degree of polynomial for $c(x)$ is 6, it requires seven coefficients to represent $c(x)$. Since the FFT/IFFT algorithm works on power of 2 number of coefficients, we will settle on eight coefficients. This means we will have to pad $a(x)$ and $b(x)$ with four zeros to the right.

We can now implement the FFT and IFFT in code, and use both to compute the coefficients for $c(x)$; see Listing 2-6. The Fourier coefficients for $a(x)$ and $b(x)$ are $[4, -8 + 2i, -8, -8 - 2i]$ and $[8, -5 - 3i, -6, -5 + 3i]$, respectively. The coefficients for $c(x)$ are $[10, -18, -13, -11, 33, 21, 10, 0]$, which agrees with our calculation by hand, i. e., $10 - 18x - 13x^2 - 11x^3 + 33x^4 + 21x^5 + 10x^6$.

CHAPTER 2   DIVIDE AND CONQUER

Listing 2-6. The code for FFT and IFFT

```python
from cmath import sqrt
from math import e, pi
i = sqrt(-1)

def fast_fourier_transform(Xn):
    N = len(Xn)
    if N == 1:
        return Xn
    w = e**(2 * pi * i / N)
    X_even, X_odd = Xn[::2], Xn[1::2]
    Y_even, Y_odd = fast_fourier_transform(X_even), fast_fourier_transform(X_odd)
    Y = [0] * N
    for j in range(N // 2):
        Y[j] = Y_even[j] + w**j * Y_odd[j]
        Y[j + N // 2] = Y_even[j] - w**j * Y_odd[j]
    return Y

def IFFT_helper(Xn):
    N = len(Xn)
    if N == 1:
        return Xn
    
    w = e**(-2 * pi * i / N)
    X_even, X_odd = Xn[::2], Xn[1::2]
    Y_even, Y_odd = IFFT_helper(X_even), IFFT_helper(X_odd)
    Y = [0] * N
    for j in range(N // 2):
        Y[j] = Y_even[j] + w**j * Y_odd[j]
        Y[j + N // 2] = Y_even[j] - w**j * Y_odd[j]
    return Y

def inverse_fourier_transform(Xn):
    return [val / (len(Xn)) for val in  IFFT_helper(Xn)]

if __name__ == "__main__":
    a_x = [-5, 4, 3, 2]
    b_x = [-2, 2, 3, 5]
    print (fast_fourier_transform(a_x))
    print (fast_fourier_transform(b_x))
    
    # calculate the polynomial multiplication
    a_x_pad_zeros = a_x + [0] * len(a_x)
    b_x_pad_zeros = b_x + [0] * len(b_x)
    A_x = fast_fourier_transform(a_x_pad_zeros)
    B_x = fast_fourier_transform(b_x_pad_zeros)
    C_x = [A_x[i] * B_x[i] for i in range(len(A_x))]
    c_x = inverse_fourier_transform(C_x)
    print (c_x)
```

CHAPTER 2   DIVIDE AND CONQUER

In [7]: run Listing_2_6_fourier_transform_fft_ifft.py

[(4+0j), (-8+2j), (-8+0j), (-8-2j)]

[(8+0j), (-5-3j), (-6+0j), (-5+3j)]
[(9.999999999999996+8.881784197001252e-16j),
(-18.000000000000007+1.9906700292510374e-15j),
(-13.000000000000002+0j), (-11.000000000000004-
6.584023997008495e-16j), (33-8.881784197001252e-16j),
(21.000000000000007-1.5620436495494636e-15j), (10.000000000000
002+0j), 2.297760199992757e-16j]

Application

The FFT algorithm is one of the most ingenious algorithms. It is named one of the ten most important algorithms in the 20th century by the *Computing in Science & Engineering* magazine [3]. Its ingenuity lies in the following aspects:

(1) Represent the polynomial by values instead of coefficients.

(2) Evaluate the polynomials at points of opposite values, which leverages the symmetry properties of odd/even functions to cut the computations by half.

(3) Represent values via the nth root of unity. Squaring these roots maintains the +/- pair properties, thus enabling the recursion to continue.

(4) The inverse Fourier transform is largely the same as the Fourier transform.

The Fourier transform technique is ubiquitous in all disciplines of science and engineering. The author's PhD thesis investigates the atomic structure of nanoscale materials using the Fourier transform of high-energy X-ray collected at US national laboratories [4]. The Fourier transform of the X-ray scattering signal yields the atomic pair distribution function (PDF), which is a plot of probability density as a function of atomic separation distance. The PDF technique is suitable for studying the aperiodic material such as amorphous materials that lack long-range structure.

Let us apply FFT and IFFT to some simple sine/cosine waves, say, a mixture of three waves.

$$T_1 = 20 \times \sin(2\pi \times 5t)$$

CHAPTER 2   DIVIDE AND CONQUER

$$T_2 = 50 \times \cos(2\pi \times 15t)$$

$$T_3 = 100 \times \cos(2\pi \times 25t)$$

$$T = T_1 + T_2 + T_3$$

We can quickly plot the curve and apply the FFT to it (Figure 2-17).

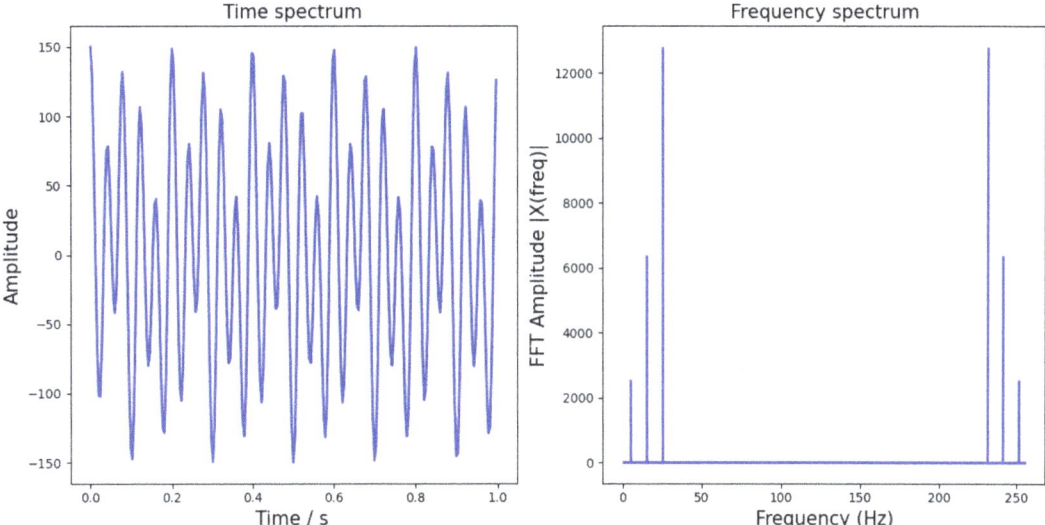

Figure 2-17. *The original mixed signal and its Fourier transformed signal*

After Fourier transforming the time signal, in the frequency domain, we can see distinct delta-function-like peaks at 5, 15, and 25 Hz, which is expected. But at 231, 241, and 251 Hz, we see the mirror peaks. What are they? The discrete Fourier transform signal is symmetric at half of the sampling rate (at line 5 of Listing 2-7, the sampling rate is set at $256=2^8$), which is called the Nyquist frequency or the folding frequency, and it is 128 Hz in the example. As we observed, 5 Hz and 251 Hz, 15 and 241 Hz, and 25 and 231 Hz are all symmetric around 128 Hz. But these higher frequency waves occupy the same sampled values as their low-frequency counterpart and thus do not provide additional information. As such, we can safely discard these signals above the Nyquist frequency.

We can implement the high-/low-pass filter using Fourier techniques (Figure 2-18). The high-pass filter is a filter that only permits signals that are above the cutoff frequency, whereas a low-pass filter only allows the signals with frequencies below a certain cutoff to pass. In the high-pass filter, we set the high-pass cutoff to 20 Hz, only allowing signal 3 (with a frequency of 25 Hz) to pass. And in the low-pass filter, the cutoff is set at 6 Hz so that only signal 1 with a frequency of 5 Hz can pass. Due to symmetry, we only plot the frequency below half of the sampling rate. We then apply the inverse Fourier transform to both filtered signals to reconstruct the signals in the time domain. As expected, the magnitudes and frequencies match values derived from previous mathematical formulas.

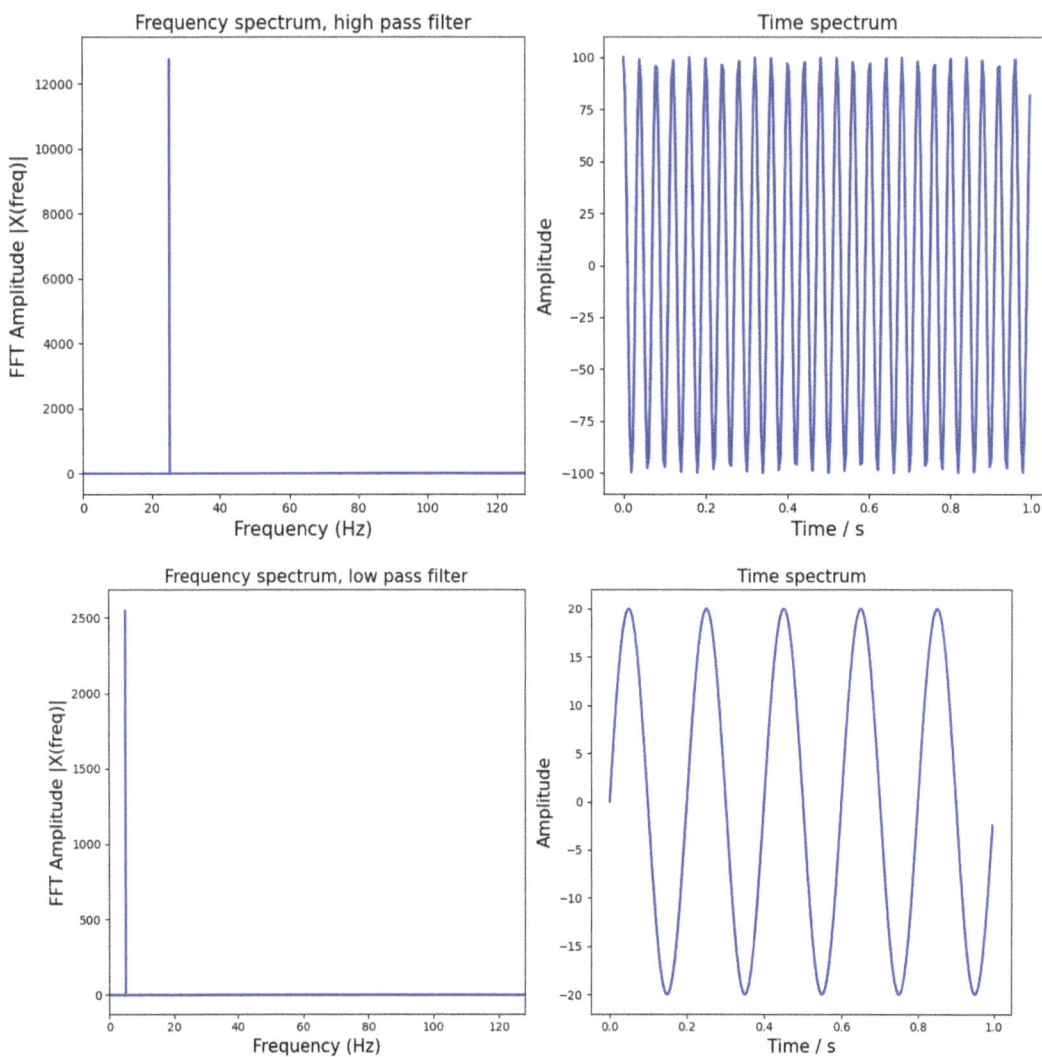

Figure 2-18. The signals filtered using high- and low-pass filters and reconstructions using IFFT

CHAPTER 2 DIVIDE AND CONQUER

Listing 2-7. FFT and low-/high-pass filters of a time signal

```
1.  from Listing_2_6_fourier_transform_fft_ifft import fast_fourier_transform,
    inverse_fourier_transform
2.  import numpy as np
3.  import matplotlib.pyplot as plt
4.
5.  def generate_time_signal(sampling_rate = 256):
6.      sampling_interval = 1.0/sampling_rate
7.      t = np.arange(0,1,sampling_interval)
8.
9.      frequency_1, frequency_2, frequency_3 = 5, 15, 25
10.     amplitude_1, amplitude_2, amplitude_3 = 20, 50, 100
11.     T1 = amplitude_1 * np.sin(2*np.pi*frequency_1*t)
12.     T2 = amplitude_2 * np.cos(2*np.pi*frequency_2*t)
13.     T3 = amplitude_3 * np.cos(2*np.pi*frequency_3*t)
14.     T = T1 + T2 + T3
15.     return t, T, sampling_rate
16.
17. def convert_signal_to_frequency_domain():
18.     t, T, sampling_rate = generate_time_signal()
19.     plt.figure(figsize = (12, 6))
20.     plt.subplot(121)
21.     plt.plot(t, T, 'b-', lw=2)
22.     plt.xlabel("Time / s", fontsize = 15)
23.     plt.ylabel('Amplitude', fontsize = 15)
24.     plt.title("Time spectrum", fontsize = 15)
25.
26.     F=np.array(fast_fourier_transform(T))
27.     # calculate the frequency
28.     N = len(F)
29.     n = np.arange(N)
30.     frequency = n/(N/sampling_rate)
31.
32.     plt.subplot(122)
33.     markerline, stemlines, baseline = plt.stem(frequency, np.abs(F), 'b',
            markerfmt="", basefmt="-b")
34.     plt.setp(stemlines, 'linewidth', 2)
35.     plt.setp(baseline, 'linewidth', 2)
36.     plt.xlabel('Frequency (Hz)', fontsize = 15)
37.     plt.ylabel('FFT Amplitude |X(freq)|', fontsize = 15)
38.     plt.title("Frequency spectrum", fontsize = 15)
39.     plt.tight_layout()
40.     plt.show()
41.
42. def low_high_pass_filter(cutoff_frequency, mode = "low_pass"):
43.     t, T, sampling_rate = generate_time_signal()
44.     F=np.array(fast_fourier_transform(T))
45.     # calculate the frequency
46.     N = len(F)
47.     n = np.arange(N)
48.     frequency = n/(N/sampling_rate)
49.     # set frequency at right half to 0
50.     F[N//2:] = 0
```

49

CHAPTER 2   DIVIDE AND CONQUER

```
51.
52.      # high pass and low pass
53.      if mode == "low_pass":
54.          F[(frequency > cutoff_frequency)] = 0
55.      else:
56.          F[(frequency < cutoff_frequency)] = 0
57.
58.      T = 2 * np.array(inverse_fourier_transform(F))
59.
60.      plt.figure(figsize = (12, 6))
61.      plt.subplot(121)
62.      markerline, stemlines, baseline = plt.stem(frequency, np.abs(F), 'b',
         markerfmt=" ", basefmt="-b")
63.      plt.setp(stemlines, 'linewidth', 2)
64.      plt.setp(baseline, 'linewidth', 2)
65.      plt.xlim([0, frequency[N//2]])
66.      plt.xlabel('Frequency (Hz)', fontsize = 15)
67.      plt.ylabel('FFT Amplitude |X(freq)|', fontsize = 15)
68.      plt.title("Frequency spectrum, {} filter".format(' '.join(mode.split('_'))),
         fontsize = 15)
69.
70.      plt.subplot(122)
71.      plt.plot(t, T, 'b-', lw=2, label = "Filtered waves")
72.      plt.xlabel("Time / s", fontsize = 15)
73.      plt.ylabel('Amplitude', fontsize = 15)
74.      plt.title("Time spectrum", fontsize = 15)
75.      plt.tight_layout()
76.      plt.show()
77.
78. if __name__ == "__main__":
79.      convert_signal_to_frequency_domain()
80.      low_high_pass_filter(cutoff_frequency = 20, mode = "high_pass")
81.      low_high_pass_filter(cutoff_frequency = 6, mode = "low_pass")
```

Summary

This chapter applies the recursion knowledge we learned in the previous chapter to leverage the divide-and-conquer algorithm to break complex problems into smaller, manageable subproblems, before arriving at the final solution. We start off by introducing the binary search algorithm that narrows down the search space by half at each step, resulting in an efficient logarithmic time complexity. We then review various sorting algorithms, from less time-efficient Bubble Sort, Selection Sort, and Insertion Sort to more efficient ones including Merge Sort and Quick Sort. Next, we shift our focus to the multiplication of two integers. Instead of a naïve $O(n^2)$ solution, by reducing the total multiplications from 4 to 3 and leveraging the divide-and-conquer idea, we have arrived at a more efficient

$O(n^{1.58})$ solution. Finally, we learn the Fast Fourier Transform (FFT) that is regarded as one of the most important algorithms of the 20th century. The key to a successful divide-and-conquer algorithm in FFT is the ingenious leverage of the complex plane and symmetry of points lying on the same plane. The FFT algorithm plays a fundamental role in signal/image processing and many other science and engineering fields.

CHAPTER 3

Greedy Algorithm

When we play chess, we calculate extensively to find the "strongest" move on each of our turns. We hope that by spotting these most accurate moves step-by-step, we will beat our opponent eventually. This shares the similarity with the Greedy Algorithm in computer science in that both try to find the local best solution at each intermediate step, and a combination of these local best solutions *may* lead to a global optimum solution. In chess, if we are bothered by the local best move too much, we could overlook the brilliant tactics of a sequence of forcing moves (such as a queen sacrifice) that win us the game. Same for the Greedy Algorithm, a succession of local best solutions does not guarantee a global optimum solution. However, the Greedy Algorithm is still an important algorithm that excels at finding quick, approximate solutions to complex problems that would otherwise require an exponential time algorithm. In this chapter, we will dive deep into the Greedy Algorithm with a selection of examples.

Coin Change

Suppose we have unlimited supplies of coins with various denominations such as 1, 2, 5, 10, 20, 50, 100, 1000. Our task is to find the minimum number of coins that make up a given amount. To use the minimum number of coins, intuitively, we would pick up the coin with the largest value that is no bigger than the asked amount. For example, if the given amount is 125. We would first try 100. The target amount is then reduced to 25. Next, we will choose 20 and then 5. In total, three coins are needed.

Believe it or not, we just exercised a Greedy Algorithm on the coin change problem. A Greedy Algorithm is often applied to optimization problems, such as finding the minimum or maximum of certain parameters while subject to constraints. It works by making optimal local decisions at each stage in the hope of achieving a globally optimal solution. The Greedy Algorithm is intuitive, efficient, and easy to implement. But there is no guarantee of optimality depending on the specific problems.

CHAPTER 3 GREEDY ALGORITHM

In the example of finding the global minimum value, a Greedy Algorithm (e.g., hill climbing) would just compare the current value with its neighboring values and decide the next move. In the simplified picture in Figure 3-1, starting with the current position (marked as a triangle), it would go to the local valley. However, the optimum value is at the valley to the right (marked as a star). Despite this non-optimality, as you shall see in the subsequent sections, the Greedy Algorithm can find an approximate solution for some quite complicated problems which otherwise require an exponential solution (i.e., Build TV Towers).

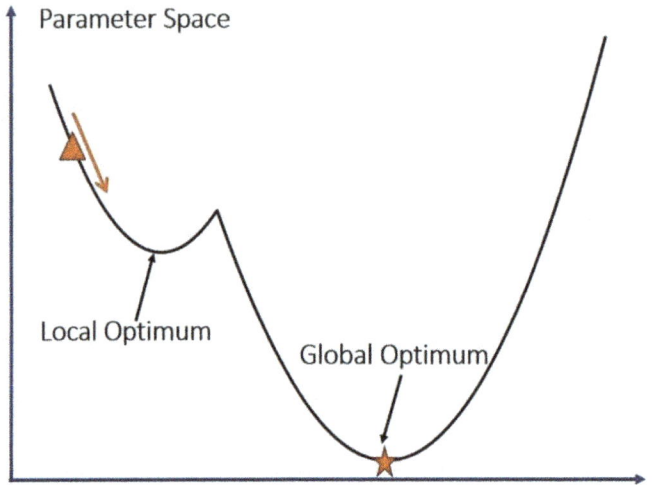

Figure 3-1. *The Greedy Algorithm may get stuck in a local optimum*

Before we move on, let us code the coin change up (Listing 3-1).

Listing 3-1. Coin change problem

```python
1.  def coin_change(coins, amount):
2.      num_coins = 0
3.      coins.sort()
4.      max_coin_index = len(coins) - 1
5.      while amount:
6.          while True:
7.              if coins[max_coin_index] > amount:
8.                  max_coin_index -= 1
9.              else:
10.                 break
11.         amount -= coins[max_coin_index]
12.         num_coins += 1
13.     return num_coins
14.
15. if __name__ == "__main__":
16.     coins = [1,2,5,10,20,50,100,1000]
17.     amount_1 = 70
18.     amount_2 = 122
19.     amount_3 = 2035
20.     assert(coin_change(coins, amount_1) == 2)
21.     assert(coin_change(coins, amount_2) == 3)
22.     assert(coin_change(coins, amount_3) == 5)
```

Class Scheduling

Let us turn our attention to the class scheduling problem. As students, at the beginning of each semester, we need to decide which classes to take. Given the schedule for the classes in one day shown in Table 3-1, which classes shall we choose such that we can take **as many classes as possible**? Suppose we are equally interested in any class. In a typical school day, the class begins at 9:00 a.m. and ends at 3:00 p.m whereas 11:30 a.m. to 12:00 p.m. is the lunch break.

Table 3-1. The schedule for a typical school day

Subject	Art	Literature	Math	Physics	History	Biology	Latin
Start time	9:30 a.m.	12:00 p.m.	8:00 a.m.	9:00 a.m.	8:30 a.m.	2:00 p.m.	12:30 p.m.
End time	11:30 a.m.	1:30 p.m.	10:00 a.m.	10:00 a.m.	9:30 a.m.	3:00 p.m.	2:00 p.m.

Using the default order of the subjects in the table, if we pick Art, we can choose Literature next, since Art ends before Literature starts. After that, we can only squeeze in Biology. Thus, we can select three classes in total. But is this the optimal solution? It seems the answer is no; we can still take History before Art, making it four in total.

Perhaps we will need to sort the subjects first. We have two choices here: either to sort by start time or end time. End time seems more reasonable – if we know when a class finishes, we can compare the end time with the start time of the next class. In this way, we can decide whether we can take the next class or not. Sorting the start time cannot help us make such decisions.

Let us now sort the table by the end time (Table 3-2). Based on Table 3-2, we can now start with History, and then Art, Literature, and finally Biology.

Table 3-2. *The schedule for a typical school day, sorted by end time*

Subject	History	Math	Physics	Art	Literature	Latin	Biology
Start time	8:30 a.m.	8:00 a.m.	9:00 a.m.	9:30 a.m.	12:00 p.m.	12:30 p.m.	2:00 p.m.
End time	9:30 a.m.	10:00 a.m.	10:00 a.m.	11:30 a.m.	1:30 p.m.	2:00 p.m.	3:00 p.m.

This is the Greedy Algorithm once again. At each step, we pick the class that ends the soonest which is the locally optimal solution. By repeating the step and combining locally optimal solutions, we can find a globally optimal solution. Though seems simple, it is indeed the optimal solution for the class scheduling problem.

In the code implementation (Listing 3-2) for the class scheduling problem, we used a helper function `convert_am_pm_to_mins` to convert a timestamp (e.g., 11:30 am) into minutes, which was used in the `sort` function at line 10. It is sorted by end time, and start time is used as a tiebreaker. The `reverse=True` flag is used such that at line 11, after the `pop` operation, the class that ends soonest is retrieved. The results are expected – the four classes are History, Art, Literature, and Biology.

Listing 3-2. Code for class scheduling problem

```python
1.  def convert_am_pm_to_mins(time_stamp):
2.      hour, minutes = time_stamp.split()[0].split(":")
3.      am_pm = time_stamp.split()[1]
4.      hour, minutes = int(hour), int(minutes)
5.      return hour * 60 + minutes if am_pm == "am" else (hour % 12 + 12) * 60 + minutes
6.
7.  def max_class_scheduling(class_schedules):
8.      classes_selected = []
9.      # sort classes by end time
10.     class_schedules.sort(key = lambda s: (convert_am_pm_to_mins(s[2]),
        convert_am_pm_to_mins(s[1])), reverse=True)
11.     first_class, _, cur_class_end_time = class_schedules.pop()
12.     classes_selected.append(first_class)
13.     while class_schedules:
14.         next_class, next_class_start_time, next_class_end_time = class_schedules.pop()
15.         if convert_am_pm_to_mins(cur_class_end_time) <= convert_am_pm_to_mins(next_
            class_start_time):
16.             classes_selected.append(next_class)
17.             cur_class_end_time = next_class_end_time
18.     return classes_selected
19.
20. if __name__ == "__main__":
21.     schedules = [("Art", "9:30 am", "11:30 am"),
22.                  ("Literature", "12:00 pm", "1:30 pm"),
23.                  ("Math", "8:00 am", "10:00 am"),
24.                  ("Physics", "9:00 am", "10:00 am"),
25.                  ("History", "8:30 am", "9:30 am"),
26.                  ("Biology", "2:00 pm", "3:00 pm"),
27.                  ("Latin", "12:30 pm", "2:00 pm")]
28.     print (max_class_scheduling(schedules))
```

In [1]: run Listing_3_2_class_scheduling.py

['History', 'Art', 'Literature', 'Biology']

Jumping Frog

Given an array of nonnegative integers, a frog is initially at the first index of the array. Each element in the array represents the maximum jump length at that position. Determine if the frog can reach the last index.

To attack the problem, let us explore it with a couple of examples. Let us say the array is [2, 3, 1, 1, 4]. The frog can jump one step from index 0 to 1, then three steps to the last index 4. As another example, with the array of [3, 2, 1, 0, 4], the frog can arrive at index 3 no matter what. But since its jump length is 0, the poor frog can never reach the last index. The question is whether the frog can reach the last index. For that, we can initialize a Boolean array (with default values `False`) that tells if the frog can reach the current index.

CHAPTER 3　GREEDY ALGORITHM

If yes, the value is changed to True. In the end, we just return the last entry of the Boolean array. Figure 3-2 shows the reachable state for the frog, step-by-step, for [2, 3, 1, 1, 4], and the code implementation is in Listing 3-3.

	Jump length	2	3	1	1	4
	Index	0	1	2	3	4
	Is reachable	False	False	False	False	False
	Jump length	2	3	1	1	4
At index 0	Index	0	1	2	3	4
	Is reachable	True	True	True	False	False
	Jump length	2	3	1	1	4
At index 1	Index	0	1	2	3	4
	Is reachable	True	True	True	True	True
	Jump length	2	3	1	1	4
At index 2	Index	0	1	2	3	4
	Is reachable	True	True	True	True	True
	Jump length	2	3	1	1	4
At index 3	Index	0	1	2	3	4
	Is reachable	True	True	True	True	True

Figure 3-2. *An initial attempt on the jumping frog example of [2, 3, 1, 1, 4]: keep track of the reachable state at each step*

Listing 3-3. A naïve solution for jumping frog

```
def frog_jump(jump_lengths):
    n = len(jump_lengths)
    is_reachable = [False]*n
    for i in range(n - 1): # we do not care about the last index
        for j in range(i, i + jump_lengths[i] + 1):
            is_reachable[j] = True
    return is_reachable[-1]

if __name__ == "__main__":
    assert frog_jump([2,3,1,1,4])==True
    assert frog_jump([3,2,1,0,4])==False
```

CHAPTER 3   GREEDY ALGORITHM

The approach certainly works but is not most time-efficient. The nested for loop returns an O(n²) time complexity. Perhaps we can do better than this by being a bit *greedier* here. At line 5, in the second for loop in Listing 3-3, we check for **all** reachable indexes, thus increasing the time complexity. Let us keep track of the *maximum reachable index* at each step.

(1) If the current maximum reachable index is no less than the last index, we return True right away.

(2) If the current maximum reachable index is smaller than the next index, we return False, since there is no way to reach the next index.

In Figure 3-3, the example for [2, 3, 1, 1, 4], the program stops right after checking the first two indexes and returns True.

	Jump length	2	3	1	1	4
	Index	0	1	2	3	4
	Max reachable Index	None	None	None	None	None
	Jump length	2	3	1	1	4
At index 0	Index	0	1	2	3	4
	Max reachable Index	2	None	None	None	None
	Jump length	2	3	1	1	4
At index 1	Index	0	1	2	3	4
	Max reachable Index	2	4	None	None	None

Figure 3-3. *An improved solution for the jumping frog example of [2, 3, 1, 1, 4]: keep track of the maximum reachable index at each step*

On the other hand, for the [3, 2, 1, 0, 4], where the frog cannot reach the final position, we check all indexes. Since the maximum reachable index never reaches 4, we return False.

59

CHAPTER 3 GREEDY ALGORITHM

	Jump length	3	2	1	0	4
	Index	0	1	2	3	4
	Max reachable Index	None	None	None	None	None
At index 0	Jump length	3	2	1	0	4
	Index	0	1	2	3	4
	Max reachable Index	3	3	3	3	None
At index 1	Jump length	3	2	1	0	4
	Index	0	1	2	3	4
	Max reachable Index	3	3	None	None	None
At index 2	Jump length	3	2	1	0	4
	Index	0	1	2	3	4
	Max reachable Index	3	3	3	None	None
At index 3	Jump length	3	2	1	0	4
	Index	0	1	2	3	4
	Max reachable Index	3	3	3	3	None

Figure 3-4. *An improved solution for the jumping frog example of [3, 2, 1, 0, 4]: keep track of the maximum reachable index at each step*

This gives us a linear time O(n) complexity; see code in Listing 3-4.

Listing 3-4. An improved solution for jumping frog

```python
def frog_jump(jump_lengths):
    n = len(jump_lengths)
    max_reachable_indexes = [-1]*n
    for i in range(n - 1): # we do not care the last index
        max_reachable_index = i + jump_lengths[i]
        max_reachable_indexes[i] = max(max_reachable_indexes[i], max_reachable_index)
        if max_reachable_index >= n - 1:
            return True
        if max_reachable_index < i + 1:
            return False

if __name__ == "__main__":
    assert frog_jump([2,3,1,1,4])==True
    assert frog_jump([1,1,1,1,4])==True
    assert frog_jump([3,2,1,0,4])==False
```

A by-product of the current Greedy Algorithm is the minimum number of steps needed to reach the final index. We can obtain this by looking at the *maximum reachable indexes* array, where the number of **distinct** (positive) values in the array is equivalent to the number of minimum steps needed. For example, in [2, 3, 1, 1, 4], we have 2 and 4; thus, the frog needs two steps to reach the goal.

Build TV Towers

Suppose there are five neighborhoods in the city named A, B, C, D, and E, respectively. The local TV broadcasting company plans to build TV towers that would cover all neighborhoods. As illustrated in Figure 3-5, it is obvious that multiple towers are needed. The costs of building towers are listed in Table 3-3.

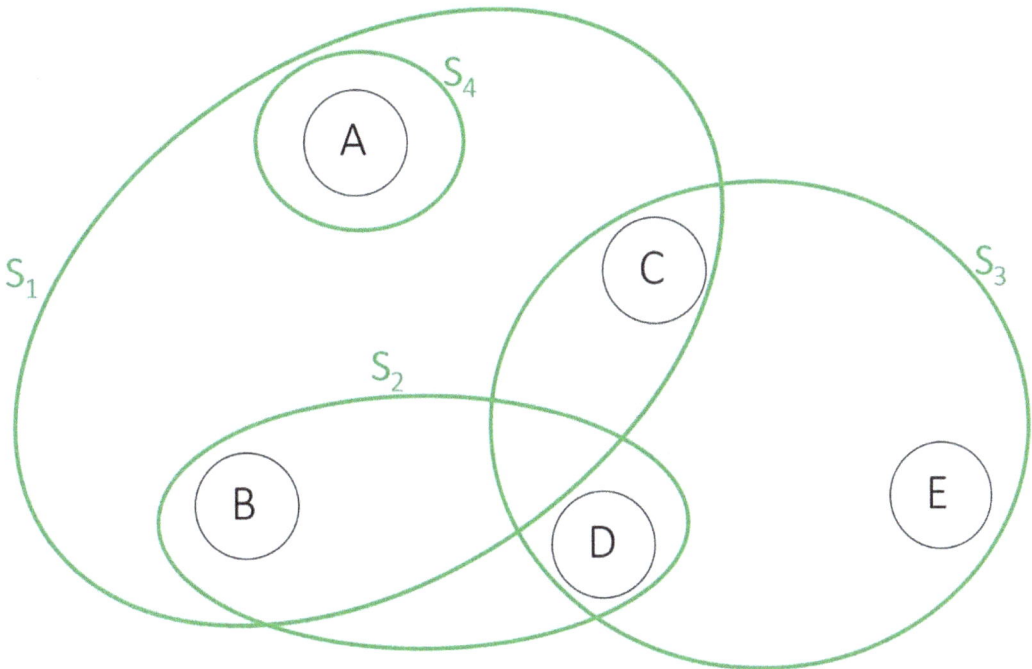

Figure 3-5. *The coverage of TV towers for the community. The green eclipse shows the coverage of each TV tower*

CHAPTER 3 GREEDY ALGORITHM

Table 3-3. *The coverage and the cost of TV towers*

Neighborhood Set Number	Neighborhoods Covered	Cost of Building Tower (million $)
S_1	A, B, C	10
S_2	B, D	15
S_3	C, D, E	12
S_4	A	5

What is the minimum cost to build a TV tower such that it can cover all neighborhoods?

A naïve approach would be to try all combinations of four TV towers, and check if it satisfies the conditions that

(1) The union of the selected towers covers all neighborhoods.

(2) The building cost is minimized.

For the current problem, here are the specific combinations of options to test. We can try the single set S_1, S_2, S_3, S_4; union of two sets, i.e., $\{S_1, S_2\}$, $\{S_1, S_3\}$, $\{S_1, S_4\}$, $\{S_2, S_3\}$, $\{S_2, S_4\}$, $\{S_3, S_4\}$; and union of three sets, $\{S_1, S_2, S_3\}$, $\{S_1, S_2, S_4\}$, $\{S_1, S_3, S_4\}$, $\{S_2, S_3, S_4\}$, and finally, combine all sets $\{S_1, S_2, S_3, S_4\}$. That is in total $C_4^1 + C_4^2 + C_4^3 + C_4^4 = 15$ combinations of subsets to test. In general, if we have n sets, the total number of combinations would be $C_n^1 + C_n^2 + \ldots + C_n^{n-1} + C_n^n$, which evaluates to $2^n - 1$. That would require exponential time to check all choices of subsets. Obviously, brute force approach fails quickly with increasing n, and we need a better approach.

Instead of a brute force method, here is the Greedy Algorithm for solving the current problem, a.k.a., the Set Cover problem.

(1) Start with an empty set I.

(2) For each set S_i, calculate the cost per new element, that is, $Cost(S_i)/|S_i - I|$.

(3) Add the set S_j with the minimum cost per new element to I, i.e., $I \cup S_j$, record cost, $Cost(S_j)$.

(4) Repeat (2) and (3) until the set I has all elements.

(5) Return the total cost.

Let us try the proposed algorithm on the current problem.

(1) In the first iteration, $I = \{\}$.

   a. The new elements are A, B, C. Cost per new element from S_1 is 10 / 3.

   b. The new elements are B, D. Cost per new element from S_2 is 15 / 2.

   c. The new elements are C, D, E. Cost per new element from S_3 is 12 / 3.

   d. The new element is A. Cost per new element from S_4 is 5 / 1.

   We pick S_1 and $I = I \cup S_1 = \{A, B, C\}$ and record the cost of 10.

(2) In the second iteration, $I = \{A, B, C\}$.

   a. The new element is D. Cost per new element from S_2 is 15 / 1.

   b. The new elements are D, E. Cost per new element from S_3 is 12 / 2.

   c. No new element from S_4. Cost per new element from S_4 is $5 / 0 = \infty$.

   We pick S_2 and $I = I \cup S_3 = \{A, B, C, D, E\}$ and record the cost of 12.

Since I has all the elements, we stop the program and return the total cost of $10 + 12 = 22$. Compared with another possible coverage using S_2, S_3, and S_4, which requires a total cost of $15 + 12 + 5 = 32$, the Greedy Algorithm solution seems optimal.

For the current problem, the Greedy Algorithm does give the best solution. As we know by this point, this is not always guaranteed. The Greedy solution for the current Set Cover problem is polynomial in time and not far from the optimal solution.

The code implementation is shown in Listing 3-5. The time complexity is $O(mn)$ where m and n are the number of sets and the total number of neighborhoods, respectively.

Listing 3-5. Build TV towers greedily

```python
1.  def build_tv_towers(sets_and_costs):
2.      I = set()
3.      all_neighbors = set()
4.      for cur_set, _ in sets_and_costs:
5.          all_neighbors |= cur_set
6.      total_cost = 0
7.      selected_sets = []
8.      while I != all_neighbors:
9.          per_new_element_costs = []
10.         for cur_set, cur_cost in sets_and_costs:
11.             new_element_set = cur_set - I
12.             if new_element_set:
13.                 per_new_element_costs.append((cur_cost / len(new_element_set), cur_set,
                        cur_cost))
14.         min_cost, new_set, cur_cost = min(per_new_element_costs, key = lambda x: x[0])
15.         total_cost += cur_cost
16.         I |= new_set
17.         selected_sets.append(new_set)
18.         sets_and_costs.remove((new_set, cur_cost))
19.     return total_cost, selected_sets
20.
21. if __name__ == "__main__":
22.     sets_and_costs = [({"A", "B", "C"}, 10),
23.                       ({"B", "D"}, 15),
24.                       ({"C", "D", "E"}, 12),
25.                       ({"A"}, 5)]
26.     print (build_tv_towers(sets_and_costs))
```

In [2]: run Listing_3_5_build_tv_towers.py

(22, [{'C', 'A', 'B'}, {'D', 'E', 'C'}])

Minimum Spanning Tree: Kruskal's Algorithm

A remote island country consists of seven islands named A to G which are connected by bridges. The lengths of the bridges are labelled in Figure 3-6. To save cost, the state council has decided to keep only necessary bridges such that (1) all islands are reachable from any starting position and (2) the total length of the bridges is the smallest. How to determine and keep only the essential bridges?

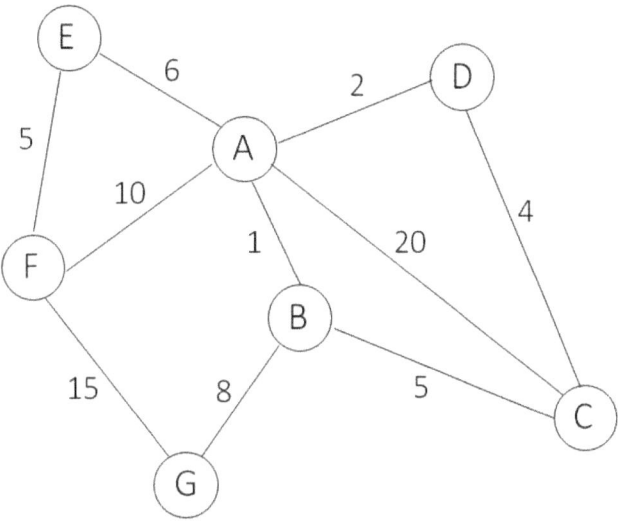

Figure 3-6. *The map of seven islands connected by bridges*

We can recast it as a graph problem. We are given an *undirected* graph since there is no one-way traffic. We are tasked with removing several edges of the graph such that the total weight of the graph is the minimum. In other words, we need to find a sub-graph or, more precisely, a tree from the original graph and make sure all nodes are reachable from any starting node. In computer science, this tree is called the *Minimum Spanning Tree (MST)*.

Let us attempt a solution with our intuition. If we must guess, we will keep the bridge between A and B since the length of the bridge between A and B is only 1, the smallest of all bridges. It will be most cost-effective to keep it to connect two islands. By the same logic, we will keep the bridge between A and D and D and C. Thus, we are building the network that connects A, B, C, and D. Here, we do not need to keep the bridge between B and C as C can be reached from B, using a route B → A → D → C. In other words, we are not expecting any *cycles* in the final network.

Moving on, we will keep bridges between A and E, B and G, and E and F. We exclude the bridges between A–F and F–G because they are among the longest (i.e., 10 and 15, respectively). And the final network is shown in Figure 3-7, and the total connected length of the bridge is 26.

CHAPTER 3 GREEDY ALGORITHM

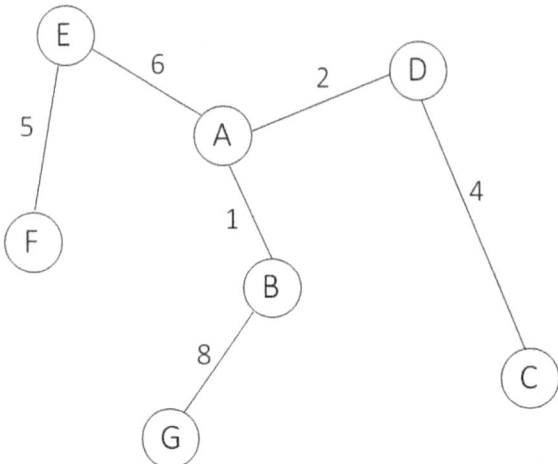

Figure 3-7. *A proposed bridge network based on intuition*

The idea behind our approach is essentially Kruskal's algorithm, published by Joseph Kruskal in 1956 [5]. Kruskal's algorithm is a Greedy Algorithm, and it starts by sorting all edges by weight. We repeatedly pick the edge with the smallest weight to build the MST. We discard the edge that forms a cycle, and we stop when all nodes are included in the MST. See the below diagram for more details. Note that although the edge lengths between B and C and E and F are both 5, we discard that of B and C, because it will form a cycle connecting A, B, C, and D.

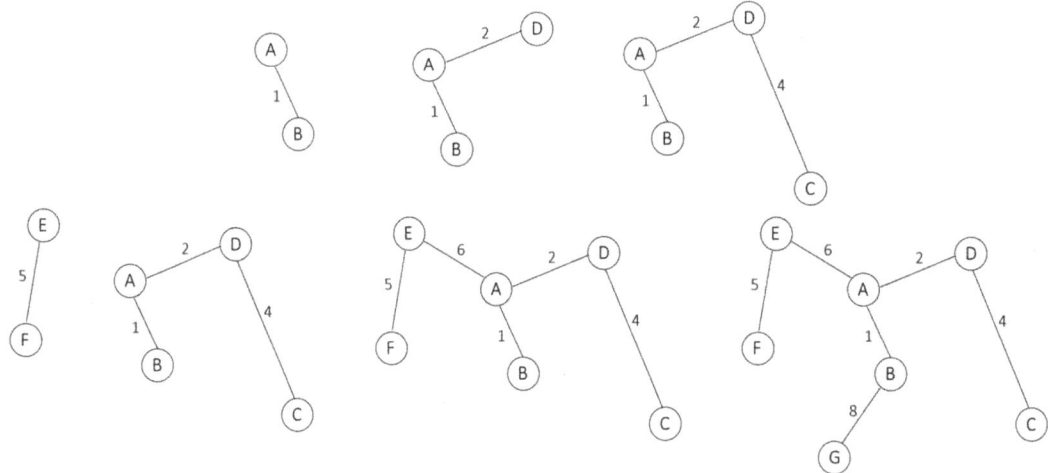

Figure 3-8. *A step-by-step illustration of finding MST using Kruskal's algorithm*

66

CHAPTER 3   GREEDY ALGORITHM

The algorithm is intuitive. Let us now try to code it up. In Listing 3-6, we decide to use the adjacency list to represent the graph. What we need is the `distance_lst` that stores the edge lengths between pairs of nodes. We sort them at line 2 in reverse order such that the smallest edge appears at the end of the list, which will be popped out first at line 6. At line 3, we initialize a `visited` parameter to keep track of the nodes that have been visited. From lines 5–10, we iteratively build the MST where at each step we pick a pair of nodes with the shortest distance and push them to the `paths` only if neither of them has been visited before. From lines 12–16, we print out the path to the console.

Listing 3-6. An initial attempt at the island problem using Kruskal's algorithm

```
1.  def minimum_spanning_tree_kruskal(distance_lst, nodes):
2.      distance_lst.sort(key = lambda t: t[2], reverse=True)
3.      visited = set()
4.      paths = []
5.      while len(visited) < len(nodes):
6.          node_1, node_2, distance = distance_lst.pop()
7.          if not (node_1 in visited and node_2 in visited):
8.              paths.append((node_1, node_2, distance))
9.              visited.add(node_1)
10.             visited.add(node_2)
11.     # print path
12.     total_distance = 0
13.     for node_1, node_2, distance in paths:
14.         total_distance += distance
15.         print (node_1, "-->", node_2, "--", distance)
16.     print (f"Shortest total distance is {total_distance}")
17.     return paths
18.
19. if __name__ == "__main__":
20.     nodes = ["A", "B", "C", "D", "E", "F", "G"]
21.     distance_lst = [("A", "B", 1), ("A", "C", 20), ("A", "D", 2), ("A", "E", 6),
        ("A", "F", 10),
22.                     ("B", "C", 5), ("B", "G", 8),
23.                     ("C", "D", 4),
24.                     ("E", "F", 5),
25.                     ("F", "G", 15)]
26.
27.     print (minimum_spanning_tree_kruskal(distance_lst, nodes))
```

Let us check the output from this code. It is missing the edge between A and E!

67

CHAPTER 3   GREEDY ALGORITHM

```
In [3]: run Listing_3_6_mst_kruskal_initial.py
A --> B -- 1
A --> D -- 2
C --> D -- 4
E --> F -- 5
B --> G -- 8
Shortest total distance is 20
[('A', 'B', 1), ('A', 'D', 2), ('C', 'D', 4), ('E', 'F', 5), ('B', 'G', 8)]
```

Why is that? I suspect our logic to detect the cycle is a bit problematic at line 7. It does prevent the addition of edge BC, since both nodes have been visited at this stage; see Figure 3-9.

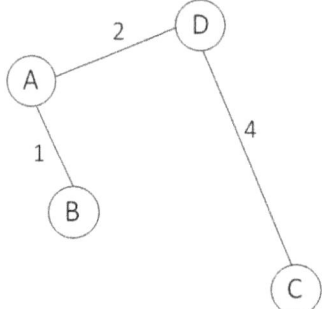

Figure 3-9. *Adding edge BC would form a cycle*

But it also prevents adding edge AE! After we construct a partial tree as shown in Figure 3-10, both nodes A and E are already in `visited`! It seems our logic to detect a cycle is oversimplified.

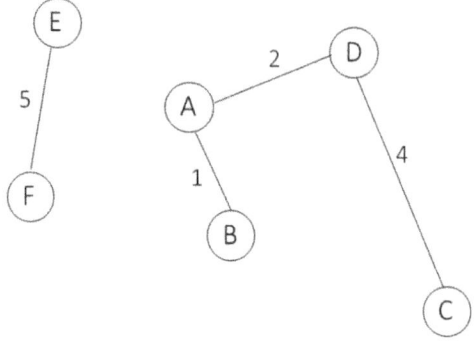

Figure 3-10. *Given a partial tree like this, we cannot construct the edge AE*

CHAPTER 3 GREEDY ALGORITHM

We need a more robust way to detect the cycle. A simple yet elegant data structure required here is called Union Find. Let us see how Union Find works by going through the tree-building steps one more time.

(0) At step 0 or before we build an MST, we have seven disconnected groups, A to G, whose parents are also A to G, respectively. The size of each group is 1 to begin with (Table 3-4).

Table 3-4. Initial setup of seven groups

Parent	A	B	C	D	E	F	G
Node	A	B	C	D	E	F	G
Size	1	1	1	1	1	1	1

(1) We plan to connect A and B. But before doing that, we check if doing so will form a cycle. We check the parents of A and B, and we see they have distinct parents. We proceed to connect them (Figure 3-11).

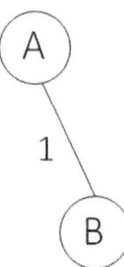

Figure 3-11. Connect nodes A and B

After connecting A and B, we update the table. Now both A and B have the same parent A, and the sizes are updated to 2 for both, since they are within the same group of size 2 (Table 3-5).

Table 3-5. An update of seven groups

Parent	A	A	C	D	E	F	G
Node	A	B	C	D	E	F	G
Size	2	2	1	1	1	1	1

(2) We will add edge AD (Figure 3-12). Since A and D have different parents, we proceed to do so and update the table (Table 3-6).

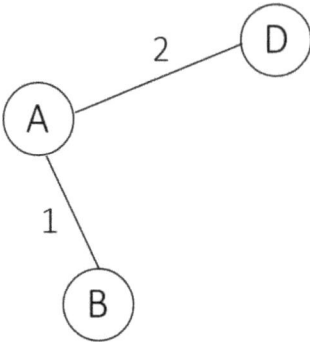

Figure 3-12. *Add edge AD*

Table 3-6. *An update of seven groups*

Parent	A	A	C	A	E	F	G
Node	A	B	C	D	E	F	G
Size	3	3	1	3	1	1	1

(3) Same for adding edge DC (Figure 3-13). We add it and update the table (Table 3-7).

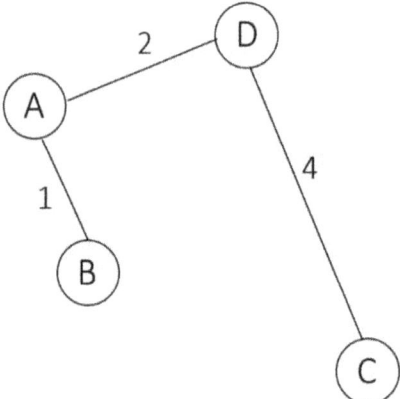

Figure 3-13. *Add edge AD*

Table 3-7. *An update of seven groups*

Parent	A	A	A	A	E	F	G
Node	A	B	C	D	E	F	G
Size	4	4	4	4	1	1	1

(4) We attempt to add edge BC, but according to Table 3-7, both B and C have the same parent A, meaning they are within the same group. Therefore, this addition is rejected (Figure 3-14).

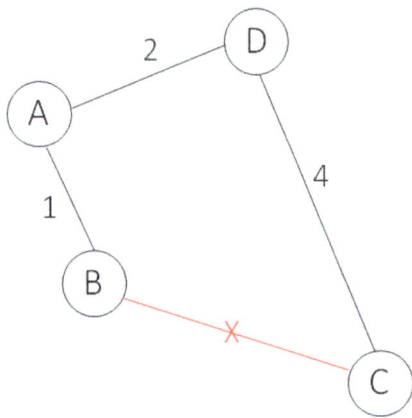

Figure 3-14. *No addition of BC, as it forms a cycle*

(5) By the same logic, we can add edge EF (Figure 3-15).

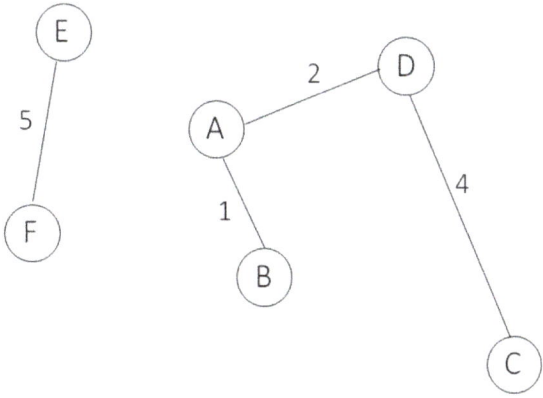

Figure 3-15. *Add edge EF*

CHAPTER 3 GREEDY ALGORITHM

And the table is updated (Table 3-8).

Table 3-8. *An update of seven groups*

Parent	A	A	A	A	E	F	G
Node	A	B	C	D	E	F	G
Size	4	4	4	4	2	2	1

(6) Next, we add edge AE (Figure 3-16) and update the table (Table 3-9). When merging both groups A and E, since the size of group A (4) is bigger than E (2), group E will be incorporated into group A.

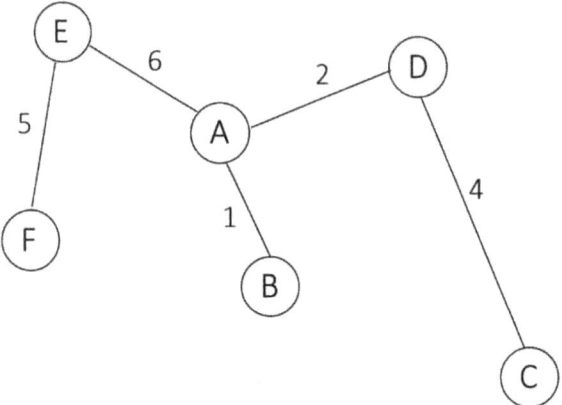

Figure 3-16. *Add edge AE*

Table 3-9. *An update of seven groups*

Parent	A	A	A	A	A	A	G
Node	A	B	C	D	E	F	G
Size	6	6	6	6	6	6	1

(7) Finally, we incorporate edge BG to complete the construction of MST (Figure 3-17).

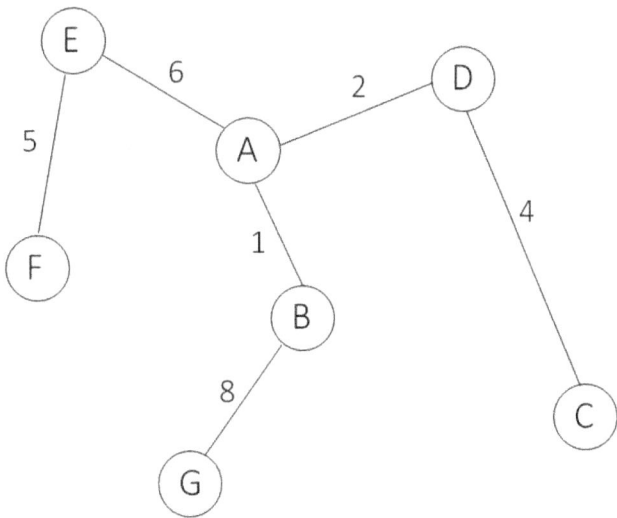

Figure 3-17. *Add edge BG to complete the MST*

And the final table is complete with a single group of size 7 (Table 3-10).

Table 3-10. *A final table of seven groups*

Parent	A	A	A	A	A	A	A
Node	A	B	C	D	E	F	G
Size	7	7	7	7	7	7	7

We can implement the Union Find as a Python class (see Listing 3-7). Without losing generality, instead of naming each node by letters, we track nodes by index numbers starting from 0. That is what we do at lines 5 and 6 where by default the parent of each node is itself and the size is 1. The find method recursively finds the parent of a node, whereas the union method combines the two groups of nodes by merging the smaller group into the bigger one.

Listing 3-7. An implementation of Union Find

```
1.  from collections import defaultdict
2.  import string
3.  class UnionFind:
4.      def __init__(self, size):
5.          self.parent = [i for i in range(size + 1)]
6.          self.size = [1 for i in range(size + 1)]
7.
8.      def find(self, x):
9.          if self.parent[x] != x:
10.             self.parent[x] = self.find(self.parent[x])
11.         return self.parent[x]
12.
13.     def union(self, x, y):
14.         px, py = self.find(x), self.find(y)
15.         if px == py:
16.             return px
17.
18.         if self.size[px] > self.size[py]:
19.             px, py = py, px
20.
21.         # component y is bigger than component x
22.         self.parent[px] = py
23.         self.size[py] += self.size[px]
24.         return py
```

With the help of the `UnionFind` class to avoid the cycle, the code for Kruskal's is straightforward; see Listing 3-8. The code to avoid forming a cycle is at lines 10–12 where the parents of the current pair of nodes are compared. If both nodes share the same parent, we reject the addition of the current edge.

CHAPTER 3 GREEDY ALGORITHM

Listing 3-8. An implementation of Kruskal's algorithm using Union Find

```
1.  def minimum_spanning_tree_kruskal(graph, distance_lst):
2.      num_nodes = len(graph)
3.      union_find = UnionFind(num_nodes)
4.      distance_lst.sort(key = lambda t: t[2], reverse=True)
5.      visited = set()
6.      paths = []
7.      while len(visited) < num_nodes:
8.          node_1, node_2, distance = distance_lst.pop()
9.          # make sure joining node_1, node_2 not forming a cycle
10.         node_1_parent = union_find.find(node_1)
11.         node_2_parent = union_find.find(node_2)
12.         if node_1_parent != node_2_parent:
13.             union_find.union(node_1, node_2)
14.             paths.append((node_1, node_2, distance))
15.             visited |= {node_1, node_2}
16.
17.     # print path
18.     total_distance = 0
19.     uppercase_letters = string.ascii_uppercase
20.     for node_1, node_2, distance in paths:
21.         total_distance += distance
22.         print (uppercase_letters[node_1], "-->", uppercase_letters[node_2], "--",
                distance)
23.     print (f"Shortest total distance is {total_distance}")
24.     return paths
25.
26. if __name__ == "__main__":
27.     distance_lst = [(0, 1, 1), (0, 2, 20), (0, 3, 2), (0, 4, 6), (0, 5, 10),
28.                     (1, 2, 5), (1, 6, 8),
29.                     (2, 3, 4),
30.                     (4, 5, 5),
31.                     (5, 6, 15)]
32.
33.     graph = defaultdict(list)
34.     for node_1, node_2, distance in distance_lst:
35.         graph[node_1].append((node_1, node_2, distance))
36.         graph[node_2].append((node_2, node_1, distance))
37.
38.     print (minimum_spanning_tree_kruskal(graph, distance_lst))
```

After executing the code, it returns the desired MST with an expected total weight of 26.

```
In [4]: run Listing_3_7_and_3_8_mst_kruskal_improved.py
A --> B -- 1
A --> D -- 2
C --> D -- 4
E --> F -- 5
A --> E -- 6
B --> G -- 8
Shortest total distance is 26
[(0, 1, 1), (0, 3, 2), (2, 3, 4), (4, 5, 5), (0, 4, 6), (1, 6, 8)]
```

CHAPTER 3 GREEDY ALGORITHM

In terms of the time complexity of Kruskal's, it is dominated by the step of sorting all edges, which is O(ElogE) where E is the number of edges.

Minimum Spanning Tree: Prim's Algorithm

Another way to find the minimum spanning tree of an undirected graph is through Prim's algorithm [6]. Here is how it works with the aid of illustrations in Figure 3-18.

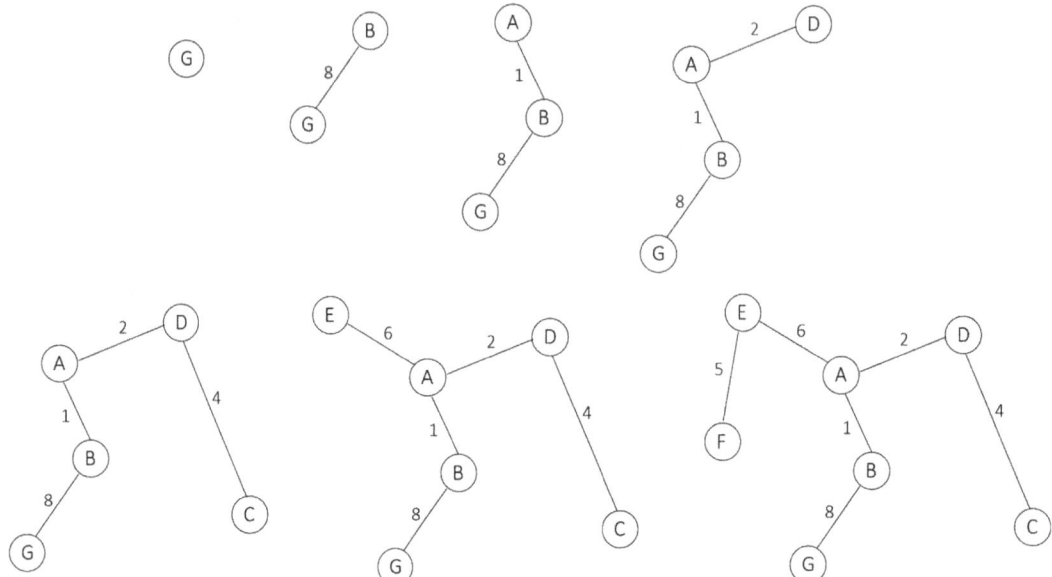

Figure 3-18. *A step-by-step illustration of Prim's algorithm*

(1) We randomly pick a node, in our example G.

(2) We connect it with its shortest distance neighbor, in this case B (not F, as the length of GF > GB).

(3) We then treat B and G as a single group and find its shortest distance neighbor, in this case A.

(4) By the same logic, we incorporate D.

(5) We incorporate C. The group now has members of A, B, C, D, G.

(6) We avoid connecting B and C, since both nodes have already been visited.

(7) We extend the group by including E.

(8) We complete the MST by including the last missing node F.

This is another Greedy Algorithm. It builds MST by successively adding nodes, whereas Kruskal's by adding edges. Let us code MST using Prim's algorithm. In Listing 3-9, from lines 25-38, we represent the graph using adjacency lists (see `graph` at IPython console output [6] below). In the crucial step (6) listed above, it avoids forming a cycle by checking whether the nodes have been visited or not. This can be done by tracking a set of visited nodes, e.g., at lines 6 and 13–14, in Listing 3-9. The challenge lies in the implementation of *treating various nodes as a single group and finding its shortest distance neighbor*. A naïve way would be combining all neighbors' adjacency lists into a Python list and sorting it every time a node is included in the MST; see below at lines 18–19 in Listing 3-9.

Listing 3-9. A naïve implementation of Prim's algorithm

```python
from collections import defaultdict
import random
random.seed(1234)

def minimum_spanning_tree_prim(graph, nodes):
    visited = set()
    start_node = random.choice(nodes)
    neighbors = graph[start_node].copy()
    paths = []
    while len(visited) < len(nodes):
        for i in range(len(neighbors) -1, -1, -1):
            start_node, next_node, next_distance = neighbors[i]
            if start_node in visited and next_node in visited:
                continue
            break
        if (start_node, next_node, next_distance) not in paths and (next_node, start_node, next_distance) not in paths:
            paths.append((start_node, next_node, next_distance))
        neighbors.extend(graph[next_node])
        neighbors.sort(key = lambda t: t[2], reverse = True)
        visited.add(start_node)
        start_node = next_node
    return paths

if __name__ == "__main__":
    nodes = ["A", "B", "C", "D", "E", "F", "G"]
    distance_lst = [("A", "B", 1), ("A", "C", 20), ("A", "D", 2), ("A", "E", 6),
                    ("A", "F", 10),
                    ("B", "C", 5), ("B", "G", 8),
                    ("C", "D", 4),
                    ("E", "F", 5),
                    ("F", "G", 15)]
    graph = defaultdict(list)
    for node_1, node_2, distance in distance_lst:
        graph[node_1].append((node_1, node_2, distance))
        graph[node_2].append((node_2, node_1, distance))

    # sort the neighbors by distance
    for node in graph:
        graph[node].sort(key = lambda t: t[2], reverse = True)

    print (minimum_spanning_tree_prim(graph, nodes))
```

Although time-inefficient, it does return the desired result.

```
In [5]: run Listing_3_9_mst_prim_initial.py
[('G', 'B', 8), ('B', 'A', 1), ('A', 'D', 2), ('D', 'C', 4), ('A', 'E', 6),
('E', 'F', 5)]
In [6]: graph
Out[6]:
defaultdict(list,
            {'A': [('A', 'C', 20),
                   ('A', 'F', 10),
                   ('A', 'E', 6),
                   ('A', 'D', 2),
                   ('A', 'B', 1)],
             'B': [('B', 'G', 8), ('B', 'C', 5), ('B', 'A', 1)],
             'C': [('C', 'A', 20), ('C', 'B', 5), ('C', 'D', 4)],
             'D': [('D', 'C', 4), ('D', 'A', 2)],
             'E': [('E', 'A', 6), ('E', 'F', 5)],
             'F': [('F', 'G', 15), ('F', 'A', 10), ('F', 'E', 5)],
             'G': [('G', 'F', 15), ('G', 'B', 8)]})
```

We can improve the code by making several changes.

(1) To address the concern of finding the shortest distance neighbor of the current group of nodes, we can define auxiliary parameters, such as min_edge_length_dict and paths_dict where the former tracks the minimum edge length coming out of the current node and the latter tracks the parent of the current node.

(2) Use a min heap instead of using sort. We push the neighbors of the current node into the heap if, and only if, the neighbor node has not been visited and it has a shorter edge length than the previous distance value stored in min_edge_length_dict. We retrieve the neighbor node and edge length from the heap each time.

(3) Combining (1) and (2), we bypass the need to sort all edges every time. Instead, we push to the min heap only the necessary edges that would improve the minimum edge length for neighbor nodes.

CHAPTER 3 GREEDY ALGORITHM

These auxiliary parameters do make our lives easier. At line 14 in Listing 3-10, we stop the while loop once we have visited all nodes. We pop a node from the min heap and then push its neighbors to the heap that satisfies the conditions at line 21. If both conditions are satisfied, we record min edge lengths for the nodes and the path (lines 22, 24), respectively.

Listing 3-10. An improved version of Prim's algorithm

```
1.  from collections import defaultdict
2.  import random
3.  import heapq
4.
5.  random.seed(1234)
6.  def minimum_spanning_tree_prim(graph, nodes):
7.      cur_node = random.choice(nodes)
8.      visited = set()
9.      min_edge_length_dict = {node: float("inf") for node in nodes}
10.     min_heap = []
11.     heapq.heappush(min_heap, min(graph[cur_node]))
12.     paths_dict = {node: None for node in nodes} # {child: parent}
13.
14.     while len(visited) < len(nodes):
15.         # pop from min heap
16.         distance, cur_node, neighbor_node = heapq.heappop(min_heap)
17.         visited.add(cur_node)
18.
19.         # push to min heap
20.         for distance, cur_node, neighbor_node in graph[cur_node]:
21.             if neighbor_node not in visited and distance < 
                    min_edge_length_dict[neighbor_node]:
22.                 min_edge_length_dict[neighbor_node] = distance
23.                 heapq.heappush(min_heap, (distance, neighbor_node, cur_node))
24.                 paths_dict[neighbor_node] = (cur_node, distance)
25.
26.     # print path
27.     total_distance = 0
28.     for child_node in nodes:
29.         if paths_dict[child_node]:
30.             parent_node, distance = paths_dict[child_node]
31.             total_distance += distance
32.             print (child_node, "-->", parent_node, "--", distance)
33.     print (f"Shortest total distance is {total_distance}")
34.     return paths_dict
35.
36. if __name__ == "__main__":
37.     nodes = ["A", "B", "C", "D", "E", "F", "G"]
38.     distance_lst = [("A", "B", 1), ("A", "C", 20), ("A", "D", 2), ("A", "E", 6),
                        ("A", "F", 10),
39.                     ("B", "C", 5), ("B", "G", 8),
40.                     ("C", "D", 4),
41.                     ("E", "F", 5),
42.                     ("F", "G", 15)]
43.     graph = defaultdict(list)
44.     for node_1, node_2, distance in distance_lst:
45.         graph[node_1].append((distance, node_1, node_2))
46.         graph[node_2].append((distance, node_2, node_1))
47.
48.     print (minimum_spanning_tree_prim(graph, nodes))
```

```
In [7]: run Listing_3_10_mst_prim_improved.py
A --> B -- 1
B --> G -- 8
C --> D -- 4
D --> A -- 2
E --> A -- 6
F --> E -- 5
Shortest total distance is 26
{'A': ('B', 1), 'B': ('G', 8), 'C': ('D', 4), 'D': ('A', 2), 'E': ('A', 6), 'F': ('E', 5),
'G': None}
```

Let us now examine the time complexity of Prim's algorithm. Building the adjacency list takes O(E), where E is the number of edges. Each edge is processed at most once, and operations on the heap take O(logV) time, where V is the number of vertices. The overall time complexity is O((V+E)logV).

Application

When we send files via email, we can compress the files to save space. One Greedy Algorithm for information compression is Huffman coding, named after American mathematician David Huffman. Let us see how Huffman coding works. Suppose we write our message with only eight characters "ABCDabcd" (in real life, we use 26 uppercase/lowercase letters). For this, we can encode each character using a binary number, either 0 or 1, where three bits are required to store each character; see Table 3-11.

CHAPTER 3 GREEDY ALGORITHM

Table 3-11. Using a binary encoding to encode different characters

Character	Binary Coding	Frequency
A	000	50
B	001	30
C	010	15
D	011	10
a	100	40
b	101	20
c	110	5
d	111	8

Suppose in our message, different characters appear at different frequencies (last column in Table 3-11). In the example, we will need a total of (50 + 30 + 15 + 10 + 40 + 20 + 5 + 8) × 3 = 534 bits to store the message. Can we do better than this?

As we observe, "A" and "a" appear most often. We could have saved more space if we had encoded them with two bits or fewer. Huffman proposed a way to encode them by constructing a binary tree or a Huffman Tree. Here are the detailed steps (Figure 3-19).

CHAPTER 3 GREEDY ALGORITHM

Initial state   A: 50, B: 30, C: 15, D: 10, a: 40, b:20, c: 5, d:8

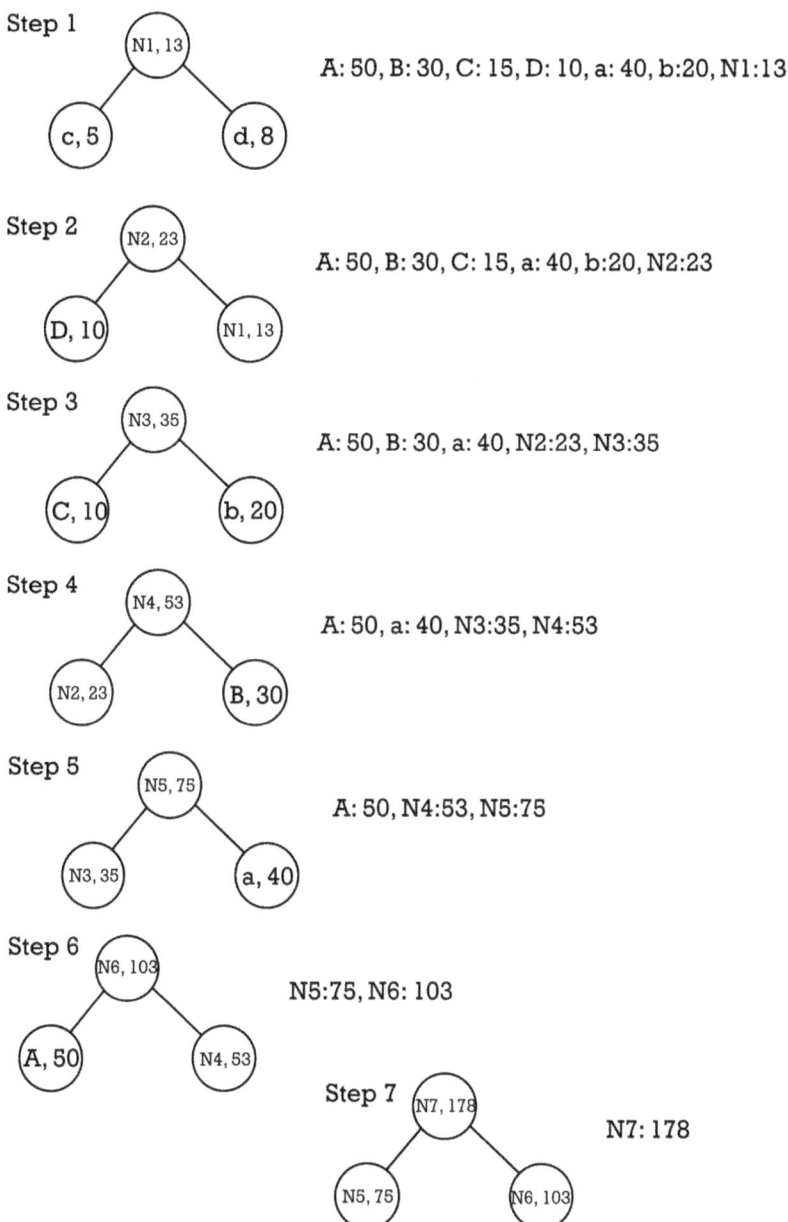

Figure 3-19. *The steps to construct a Huffman Tree*

CHAPTER 3   GREEDY ALGORITHM

At the initial stage, we list out the characters and their frequencies in a dictionary format. In Step 1, we pick two characters with the least frequencies ("c" and "d" in the example) and construct a tree stump with a dummy parent node "N1" whose value is the summed frequencies of its children. Here, each node stores the name and the frequency of the current character. We replace "c" and "d" with "N1" in the dictionary. Steps 2–7 repeat the same process as Step 1. After Step 7, we get a root node of N7 with a total frequency of 178.

We can construct the Huffman Tree by piecing together the tree stumps from Steps 1 to 7; see Figure 3-20.

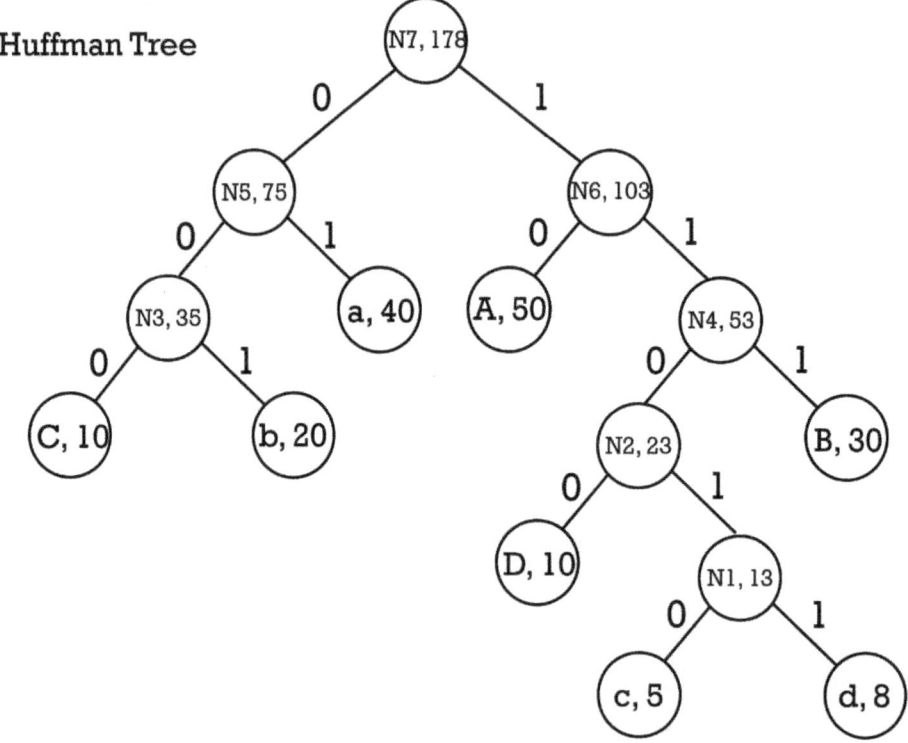

Figure 3-20. *The Huffman Tree for the current example*

Each character is now at the leaf node of the tree. In addition, we put 0 on the left edge and 1 on the right edge. To find the encoding for the character, we concatenate 0s and 1s while doing a root-to-leaf traversal. For example, "A" is "10"; "D" is "1100". The Huffman coding for "ABCDabcd" is listed in Table 3-12.

Table 3-12. *Using the Huffman coding to encode different characters*

Character	Binary Coding	Huffman Coding	Frequency
A	000	10	50
B	001	111	30
C	010	000	15
D	011	1100	10
a	100	01	40
b	101	001	20
c	110	11010	5
d	111	11011	8

As expected, for the most frequent characters "A" and "a", their Huffman coding requires two bits only. Using Huffman coding, we can store the message with (2×50 + 3×30 + 3×15 + 4×10 + 2×40 + 3×20 + 5×5 + 5×8)=480 bits, that is, ~10% reduction in size compared to the original binary coding with 534 bits.

Let us now implement the Huffman coding (Listing 3-11). We do it in two steps. First, we construct a Huffman Tree using a function construct_huffman_tree. The function input is frequency_dict, a dictionary that stores the characters and their corresponding frequencies. We start with the definition of a TreeNode from lines 2 to 7. Since each time we pick two nodes with the least frequencies, we resort to the heap data structure. At lines 12–13, we construct such a min heap where each element is a tuple of frequency, name, and TreeNode. In the while loop at line 15, we keep taking out two nodes from the heap, creating their parent node, and pushing it to the heap. The loop stops when the size of the heap is 1; that is, we are left with only the root node.

In the second step, we retrieve the encoding for each character. By looking at the illustration of the Huffman Tree in Figure 3-20, we notice the characters are at leaf nodes. Essentially, for each character, we want to find a root-to-leaf path which can be done with the help of a stack data structure. Interested readers may refer to *Chapter 8* for more detailed explanations.

Listing 3-11. The code implementation of Huffman coding

```python
1.  from heapq import heapify, heappop, heappush
2.  class TreeNode:
3.      def __init__(self, name, value):
4.          self.name = name
5.          self.value = value
6.          self.left = None
7.          self.right = None
8.
9.  # {"A": 50, "B": 30, "C": 15, "D": 10, "a": 40, "b": 20, "c": 5, "d": 8}
10. def construct_huffman_tree(frequency_dict):
11.     # construct the heap
12.     heap = [(frequency, name, TreeNode(name, frequency)) for name, frequency in frequency_dict.items()]
13.     heapify(heap)
14.     count = 1
15.     while len(heap) > 1:
16.         freq_1, _, node_1 = heappop(heap)
17.         freq_2, _, node_2 = heappop(heap)
18.         parent_freq = freq_1 + freq_2
19.         parent_name = f"N_{count}"
20.         parent_node = TreeNode(parent_name, parent_freq)
21.         parent_node.left = node_1
22.         parent_node.right = node_2
23.         heappush(heap, (parent_freq, parent_name, parent_node))
24.         count += 1
25.     root_node = heap[0][2]
26.     return root_node
27.
28. def retrieve_new_encoding(root_node):
29.     new_encoding_dict = {}
30.     stack = [(root_node, "")]
31.     while stack:
32.         node, encoding = stack.pop()
33.         if not node.left and not node.right:
34.             new_encoding_dict[node.name] = encoding
35.         if node.right:
36.             stack.append((node.right, encoding + '1'))
37.         if node.left:
38.             stack.append((node.left, encoding + '0'))
39.     return new_encoding_dict
40.
41. if __name__ == "__main__":
42.     freq_dict = {"A": 50, "B": 30, "C": 15, "D": 10, "a": 40, "b": 20, "c": 5, "d": 8}
43.     root_node = construct_huffman_tree(freq_dict)
44.     new_encoding_dict = retrieve_new_encoding(root_node)
45.     print (new_encoding_dict)
```

After running the program, the Huffman coding for each character is printed out. It is worth mentioning that in real applications, both parties should have access to the Huffman Tree so that it will be easy to encode and decode the message.

```
In [8]: run Listing_3_11_application_huffman_coding.py

{'C': '000', 'b': '001', 'a': '01', 'A': '10', 'D': '1100', 'c': '11010', 'd': '11011', 'B': '111'}
```

Summary

In this chapter, we learn about the Greedy Algorithm. It is an intuitive algorithm that attempts to find the global optimum solution by piecing together the locally best choice at each step. Most of the examples in this chapter are chosen such that they can be solved optimally using the Greedy Algorithm (except for Build TV Towers). It is not often the case. Nonetheless, the Greedy Algorithm still plays an important role in finding approximate solutions to complex problems that otherwise require exponential time algorithms (e.g., Build TV Towers, a.k.a. Set Cover Problem). In the next chapter, we will learn Dynamic Programming (DP). Similar to the Greedy Algorithm, we can use it to solve optimization problems, but it has an important difference: while the Greedy Algorithm relies on each single local best choice to hope for a global solution, the DP looks at all past choices to find the overall best combination so far, which often leads to an optimal solution.

CHAPTER 4

Dynamic Programming

In this chapter, we are going to learn Dynamic Programming. The gist of Dynamic Programming is to solve the overlapping subproblems, cache the results, and reuse these results to find a solution. This is different from the divide-and-conquer introduced in Chapter 2 which divides the problem into a series of individual and *nonoverlapping* subproblems. Dynamic Programming utilizes the idea of recursion in Chapter 1 and caches the intermediate results. It can be used to find the optimal solution for certain problems where the Greedy Algorithm in Chapter 3 can only find an approximate solution. In the chapter, we use a "bottom-up" approach to cache the results by storing them in a one-dimensional table or multidimensional tables. Let us get started!

Fibonacci Number

As an introductory example to this chapter, consider this problem. Suppose we have a pair of newborn rabbits. They mature in the second month and give birth to another pair of rabbits in the third month. Also, the newborns (one male and one female) mature in the second month and become parents to another pair. Assuming no rabbits die in this one year, how many rabbits in total after one year?

To attack this problem, let us make a table to help us. In Table 4-1, we keep track of the pairs of newborns and adults, respectively, and their sums are saved in the last column. In the first month, we only have a pair of newborns. In the second, the newborns mature into adults. In the third, the newly matured rabbits give birth to a pair of newborns. In the fourth, the same pair of parents gives birth to another pair of newborns. In the meantime, the newborns in the third month mature into adults. We can keep going like this and fill in the table till the 12th month. By the end of the year, there will be 144 pairs of rabbits in total!

CHAPTER 4　DYNAMIC PROGRAMMING

Table 4-1. *The growth of the rabbit family in a year*

Month	# Pair of Newborns	# Pair of Adults	Total # Pair of Rabbits
1	1	0	1
2	0	1	1
3	1	1	2
4	1	2	3
5	2	3	5
6	3	5	8
7	5	8	13
8	8	13	21
9	13	21	34
10	21	34	55
11	34	55	89
12	55	89	144

The total pair of rabbits form a sequence which is known as the *Fibonacci sequence*, named after the Italian mathematician Leonardo of Pisa, also known as Fibonacci. In mathematics, a 0th term is also introduced. Suppose $F(n)$ is the Fibonacci sequence, $F(0) = 0$. From Table 4-1, we can see $F(1) = 1$, $F(2) = F(1) + F(0) = 1$, $F(3) = F(2) + F(1) = 2$, $F(4) = F(3) + F(2) = 3$, ..., $F(12) = F(11) + F(10) = 89 + 55 = 144$. In general, $F(n) = F(n-1) + F(n-2)$ if $n \geq 2$, else 1.

Let us try to code a solution to find the nth Fibonacci number, applying the recursion knowledge learned in Chapter 1. The solution seems straightforward (Listing 4-1).

Listing 4-1. Find the Fibonacci sequence using recursion

```
# method 1: recursive
def fibonacci_recursive(n):
    if n == 0 or n == 1:
        return n
    return fibonacci_recursive(n - 1) + fibonacci_recursive(n - 2)
```

Using this code, let us find the 12th Fibonacci number to cross-check with our tabulated value. Sure enough, the program returns 144. The same as that in Table 4-1. How about the 20th number? It outputs 6765. Then the 50th? Well... The program gets stuck! It seems to be doing some heavy computation in the background!

Let us analyze exactly what is being computed. Instead of $F(50)$, let us analyze a smaller number, say, $F(6)$, as shown in Figure 4-1. Let us examine how many $F(n)$ are calculated.

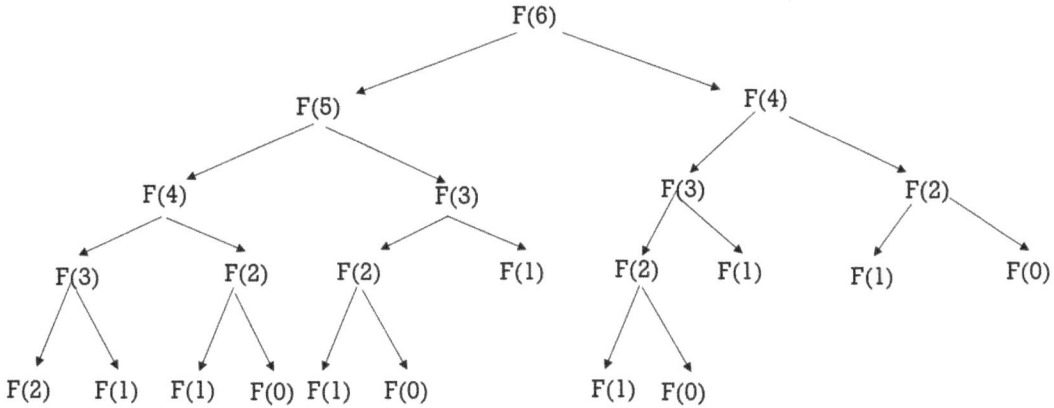

Figure 4-1. *The calculation tree for F(6), the sixth number of the Fibonacci sequence*

From the tree diagram, it is seen that $F(6)$ is computed once, $F(5)$ once, $F(4)$ twice, $F(3)$ three times, $F(2)$ five times, $F(1)$ seven times, and $F(0)$ four times. There are indeed a lot of redundant calculations! Ideally, each Fibonacci number needs to be calculated only once and is reused in calculating the next larger Fibonacci number. To improve the time efficiency of the solution, we can create an *array* to store the Fibonacci number one by one. The size of the array will be the Fibonacci number to be calculated plus 1 (plus 1 because we consider 0th number as well), and the array initially contains value 0 as default. We know the first two elements are $F(0) = 0$ and $F(1) = 1$. Then for $F(2)$ and onward, we just calculate it by adding up the previous two numbers (Listing 4-2).

CHAPTER 4 DYNAMIC PROGRAMMING

Listing 4-2. Implement the Fibonacci sequence using Dynamic Programming with an array

```
1.  # method 2: dynamic programming
2.  def fibonacci_dynamic_programming(n):
3.      if n == 0 or n == 1:
4.          return n
5.      arr = [0] * (n + 1)
6.      arr[1] = 1
7.      for i in range(2, n + 1):
8.          arr[i] = arr[i-1] + arr[i-2]
9.      return arr[n]
```

This way, each Fibonacci number is only calculated once, which is more efficient in terms of time. However, we have used an array to store the intermediate numbers. Since we are not interested in all Fibonacci numbers but the nth number, we can target a constant space here. To achieve this, we can define two parameters `fib_num_two_steps_back` and `fib_num_one_step_back` to store the intermediate numbers, bypassing the need to store all of them. See Listing 4-3 below.

Listing 4-3. Dynamic Programming with no extra space for Fibonacci

```
1.  # method 3: dynamic programming no extra space
2.  def fibonacci_dynamic_programming_no_extra_space(n):
3.      if n == 0 or n == 1:
4.          return n
5.      counter = 1
6.      fib_num_two_steps_back = 0
7.      fib_num_one_step_back = 1
8.      while counter < n:
9.          fib_num_current = fib_num_two_steps_back + fib_num_one_step_back
10.         fib_num_two_steps_back = fib_num_one_step_back
11.         fib_num_one_step_back = fib_num_current
12.         counter += 1
13.     return fib_num_current
```

Additionally, one can also derive a mathematical formula for the nth Fibonacci number based on the recursive relation, $F(n) = F(n-1) + F(n-2)$, using the characteristic function method. See the formula below.

$$F_n = \frac{\varphi^n - (-\varphi)^{-n}}{\sqrt{5}} = \frac{\varphi^n - (-\varphi)^{-n}}{2\varphi - 1}$$

$$\varphi = \frac{1 + \sqrt{5}}{2} \approx 1.6180339887\ldots$$

Notice the φ term is an irrational number. This is perhaps the reason that this formula was not discovered until 600 years after the Fibonacci sequence was published – because it is difficult to guess a formula with an irrational number. When using the formula, we need to round the result to get the Fibonacci number, which is an integer.

By the way, the φ term is also called the golden ratio, which frequently appears in art, architecture, and natural sciences. Let us now try the ratio of two subsequent Fibonacci numbers, say, $F(10)/F(9)$ and $F(100)/F(99)$.

$F(10)/F(9) = 55/34 = 1.6176$, and $F(100)/F(99) = 354224848179261915075 / 218922995834555169026 = 1.6180$.

For completeness, let us write a program for the fourth method to calculate the Fibonacci number (Listing 4-4).

Listing 4-4. Calculate the Fibonacci number using a mathematical expression

```
# method 4: mathematical expression
def fibonacci_mathematical_expression(n):
    phi = (1 + 5 ** 0.5) / 2
    numerator = phi ** n - (-phi)**(-n)
    denominator = 2 * phi - 1
    return numerator / denominator
```

Methods 2 and 3 use an algorithm named *Dynamic Programming (DP)*. It is an improvement over plain recursion (method 1) by storing the results of subproblems, so that we do not need to recompute them when needed later. This optimization reduces time complexities from exponential to polynomial. Let us see more examples of DP in the subsequent sections of this chapter.

The Generic Way of Designing a Dynamic Programming Solution

Let us look at two examples and learn how we would design a solution using DP. Here is the first one: given an array of numbers, calculate its prefix sum, $S(i)$, which is the sum of the first i items of an array. Suppose the array of interest is [-2, 1, -3, 4, -1, 2, 1, -5, 4]. We can calculate its prefix sum by summing up the first few items each time, as shown in Figure 4-2.

CHAPTER 4 DYNAMIC PROGRAMMING

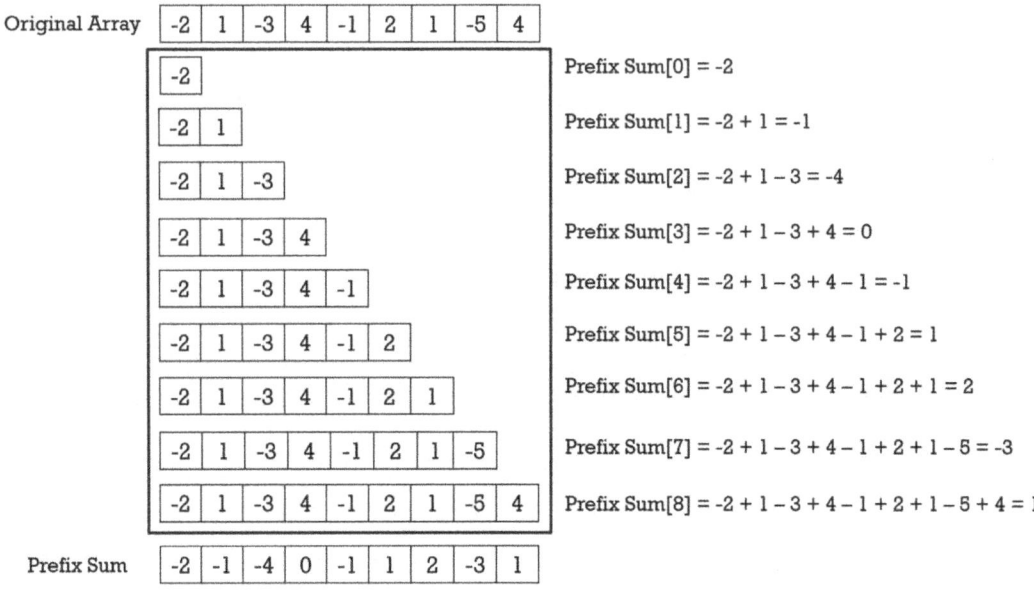

Figure 4-2. A naïve way to calculate the prefix sum of an array of integers

This follows the definition of prefix sum and gives the correct answer. But is it efficient? Not really. This would require a total number of $n(n + 1)/2$ evaluations, leading to $O(n^2)$ time complexity. We can see the same issue as the Fibonacci sequence that lots of duplicated calculations are done here. In Figure 4-2, the subsequent subarray is just one element larger than the preceding one, but the calculation is mostly repeated for both subarrays.

Let us take the chance to devise a DP solution. Here are the generic procedures for it.

- Write down the target in simple words.

- Find the recurrence relation for the target using previous results.

- Design and iteratively populate one-dimensional or higher-dimensional tables to store the intermediate results.

- In most cases, find the target either at the beginning or at the end of the table. In other cases, scan through the entire table for the desired target.

Let us apply the instructions to our prefix sum problem. First, in the current case, we want the prefix sum, $S(i)$, of an array of numbers $a_0, a_1, ..., a_i$. Then, we need to ask, can we find $S(i)$ in terms of $S(i-1), S(i-2), ... S(1), S(0)$, and/or $\{a_0, a_1, ..., a_i\}$? The answer is yes.

$S(i) = S(i-1) + a_i$. Based on this recurrence relation, we can construct a one-dimensional table and fill the numbers one by one. This approach is both linear in time and space (Figure 4-3 and Listing 4-5).

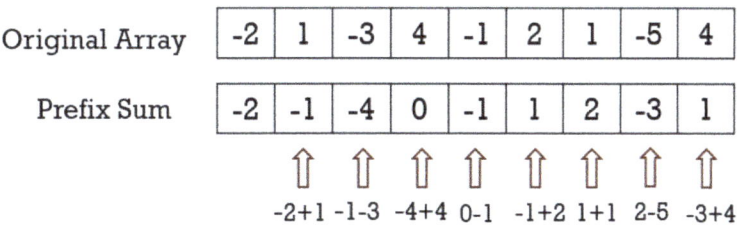

Figure 4-3. *Prefix sum using an array to save previous results*

Listing 4-5. Prefix sum using a naïve approach and Dynamic Programming

```
1.  def prefix_sum_naive(arr):
2.      prefix_sum = []
3.      for i in range(len(arr)):
4.          local_sum = 0
5.          for j in range(i+1):
6.              local_sum += arr[j]
7.          prefix_sum.append(local_sum)
8.      return prefix_sum
9.
10. def prefix_sum_dp(arr):
11.     prefix_sum = [0] * len(arr)
12.     prefix_sum[0] = arr[0]
13.     for i in range(1, len(arr)):
14.         prefix_sum[i] = prefix_sum[i-1] + arr[i]
15.     return prefix_sum
16.
17. if __name__ == "__main__":
18.     arr = [-2, 1, -3, 4, -1, 2, 1, -5, 4]
19.     print (prefix_sum_naive(arr))
20.     print (prefix_sum_dp(arr))
```

```
In [1]: run Listing_4_5_prefix_sum.py
[-2, -1, -4, 0, -1, 1, 2, -3, 1]
[-2, -1, -4, 0, -1, 1, 2, -3, 1]
```

Let us use the same array [-2, 1, -3, 4, -1, 2, 1, -5, 4] for another question. Suppose this time you will need to find the maximum subarray. To be precise, a subarray is a contiguous array of numbers that is part of the original array. For example, [1, -3, 4] or [4, -1, 2, 1] or [4] or the entire array.

CHAPTER 4　DYNAMIC PROGRAMMING

A naïve approach would find all subarrays, calculate their sums, and pick the largest. For an array of size n, we would have $n(n+1)/2$ possible subarrays. And then it takes linear time to calculate the sum for each subarray. Overall, this requires $O(n^3)$ time.

Certainly, we can do better than this. Why don't we try a DP solution using the procedures laid out above? First, let $S(i)$ be the maximum sum of a subarray from $a_0, a_1, ..., a_i$. Then we need to find the recurrence relation of $S(i)$ using $\{S(i-1), S(i-2), ... S(0)\}$, and/or $\{a_0, a_1, ..., a_i\}$.

So far so good. Can we find the recurrence relation? Well ..., it seems difficult since $S(i-1)$ stores the summation of an arbitrary subarray of $a_0, a_1, ..., a_{i-1}$, and for $S(i)$, we do not know if it considers a_i or not. However, we can *strengthen* the definition a bit; let $S(i)$ be the maximum sum of a subarray from $a_0, a_1, ..., a_i$, *ending at a_i*. Based on this definition, $S(i)$ must include a_i as part of sum calculation. Then we only need to check the sign of $S(i-1)$- if it is negative, ignore it as addition of a negative number will bring down the value of total summation, but otherwise include it. In sum, we have found the recurrence relation of $S(i) = a_i + \max(S(i-1), 0)$.

The code is now straightforward to write (Listing 4-6). It takes linear time $O(n)$ to find the answer.

Listing 4-6. The implementation of the maximum subarray

```python
1.  def max_sum_subarray(arr):
2.      sum_arr = [0] * len(arr)
3.      sum_arr[0] = arr[0]
4.      for i in range(1, len(arr)):
5.          sum_arr[i] = arr[i] + max(sum_arr[i-1], 0)
6.      return max(sum_arr)
7.
8.  if __name__ == "__main__":
9.      arr = [-2, 1, -3, 4, -1, 2, 1, -5, 4]
10.     print (max_sum_subarray(arr))
```

```
In [2]: run Listing_4_6_max_subarray.py
6
```

One thing to note is that the answer is not necessarily located at the end of the table. For instance, in the current example, it is in the middle. The subarray [4, -1, 2, 1] yields the largest sum of 6.

Longest Common Subsequence and Substring

When my son's teacher Mrs. Wessels first taught him rhyming words at kindergarten, he often came home excited, chanting "Cat – Rat – Sat – Bat – Mat – Fat – Hat – Flat – Chat rhyme!" These rhyming words really got him interested in learning and remembering English words. Let us now look at two rhyming words, for example, "nature" and "nurture," and try to find the length of the longest subsequence and substring of both words. Before that, let us review what a subsequence and a substring are for an English word. By definition, a substring consists of consecutive letters of a word, whereas a subsequence is not necessarily consecutive. In the current case, the longest substring for both words is "ture" with a length of 4; the longest subsequence is "nture" with a length of 5.

Finding either the longest subsequence or substring seems to be a challenging task. Nonetheless, let us give it a try and do the subsequence first. The naïve approach would be to find all subsequences of both words and then compare and find the longest matching subsequence. Clearly, this is time-consuming. Since this chapter is about Dynamic Programming, maybe we can devise a more efficient solution using DP.

Let us first draw an analogy to the Fibonacci problem. In Fibonacci case, we have the straightforward recurrence relation for the nth number, i.e., $F(n) = F(n-2) + F(n-1)$; we will need to find the recurrence relation for the string case here. Let $L(i,j)$ correspond to the maximum length of the longest subsequence of the first i characters of string 1 and first j characters of string 2. The goal is to find the relation of $L(i,j)$ with $L(i-1, j-1)/L(i, j-1)/L(i-1, j)$. That is to say, the maximum length of longest subsequence for both strings can be deduced based on that of the shorter strings.

Before we move on, let us create a two-dimensional table where the y axis is for "nature", the x axis is for "nurture", and the value at each cell records the maximum length of a subsequence so far (Table 4-2). Maybe we can find the hidden relation by doing this exercise.

CHAPTER 4 DYNAMIC PROGRAMMING

Table 4-2. *Finger exercise to find the maximum common subsequence of "nature" and "nurture"*

	n	u	r	t	u	r	e
n	1	1	1	1	1	1	1
a	1	1	1	1	1	1	1
t	1	1	1	2	2	2	2
u	1	2	2	2	3	3	3
r	1	2	3	3	3	4	4
e	1	2	3	3	3	4	5

As shown in Table 4-2, each cell is the answer to a subproblem of the original problem. For example, the top left cell asks: What is the longest common subsequence of "n" and "n"? And the answer is 1. Take another example: the cell where 2 appears first records the longest common subsequence of "nat" and "nurt", which is "nt" with a length of 2. In addition, the first row and first column are special cases where it compares the first character of one word against the other word. Both can be populated first in the table.

For the second character onward, it follows:

$$L(i, j) = \begin{cases} L(i-1, j-1) + 1, & \text{if } s[i] == s[j] \\ \max(L(i-1, j), L(i, j-1)), & \text{if } s[i] != s[j] \end{cases}$$

Here, we compare the last characters of both strings first. If they are equal, we have one common character there already. To find the total length of common characters, we add the value of both strings, one character smaller. Alternatively, if the last characters are different in both words, we consider both cases where one string is one character shorter than the other. The code for implementing the longest common subsequence is in Listing 4-7.

CHAPTER 4 DYNAMIC PROGRAMMING

Listing 4-7. Implementation of the longest common subsequence of two strings

```
1.  def longest_common_subsequence(A, B):
2.      dp = [[0 for i in range(len(B))] for i in range(len(A))]
3.
4.      # fill in the first row
5.      if A[0] == B[0]:
6.          dp[0][0] = 1
7.      else:
8.          dp[0][0] = 0
9.
10.     for i in range(1, len(B)):
11.         if B[i] == A[0]:
12.             dp[0][i] = dp[0][i-1] + 1
13.         else:
14.             dp[0][i] = dp[0][i-1]
15.
16.     # fill in the first col
17.     for i in range(1, len(A)):
18.         if A[i] == B[0]:
19.             dp[i][0] = dp[i-1][0] + 1
20.         else:
21.             dp[i][0] = dp[i-1][0]
22.
23.     # fill in the rest of the matrix
24.     for i in range(1, len(A)):
25.         for j in range(1, len(B)):
26.             if A[i] == B[j]:
27.                 dp[i][j] = dp[i-1][j-1] + 1
28.             else:
29.                 dp[i][j] = max(dp[i-1][j], dp[i][j-1])
30.     return dp[-1][-1]
31.
32. if __name__ == '__main__':
33.     print (longest_common_subsequence('nature', 'nurture'))

In [3]: run Listing_4_7_longest_common_subsequence.py
5
```

To find the max length of a common subsequence, we go to the last cell of the DP table since it compares the full length of strings 1 and 2, which gives the longest sequence of common characters. The time complexity is O(m×n) where m and n are the lengths of strings 1 and 2, respectively, and the same for space complexity.

CHAPTER 4　DYNAMIC PROGRAMMING

Next, let us apply the same technique to find the longest common substring of "nature" and "nurture". Similarly we will need an $L(i,j)$ that corresponds to the max length of the longest substring of the first i characters of string 1 and first j characters of string 2. The goal is to find the relation of $L(i,j)$ based on $L(i-1,j-1)/L(i,j-1)/L(i-1,j)$.

Let us give it a try. Analogous to the longest common subsequence case, we compare the last character of string 1 and string 2. If they are the same, we will simply add 1. But, wait, we cannot simply find the relation based on $L(i-1,j-1)$ or $L(i,j-1)$ or $L(i-1,j)$. We do not know whether the longest common substring contains this last common character or not. It does not need to. Here is one counterexample. Suppose s1 = "aacb", s2 = "aaab". The last character is the same character "b". We cannot simply add 1, because the longest common substring for s1 and s2 is "aa" which does not contain the last character of "b".

To mitigate this issue, as in the case of finding the max sum of a subarray in the previous Section, we can **strengthen** our definition of $L(i,j)$ a bit: we will need one additional constraint on top of current definition. The new definition of $L(i,j)$ is that it records the length of the longest common substring of the first i characters of string 1 and first j characters of string 2, **with both the ith character of string 1 and jth character of string 2 in the common substring**.

With this extra constraint, it is now possible to find a recurrence relation as below.

$$L(i,j) = \begin{cases} L(i-1,j-1)+1, \text{if } s[i] == s[j] \\ 0, \text{if } s[i] != s[j] \end{cases}$$

Let us now construct a table for "nature" and "nurture" using this relation; see Table 4-3.

Table 4-3. *The Dynamic Programming table for the maximum common substring of "nature" and "nurture"*

	n	u	r	t	u	r	e
n	1	0	0	0	0	0	0
a	0	0	0	0	0	0	0
t	0	0	0	1	0	0	0
u	0	1	0	0	2	0	0
r	0	0	2	0	0	3	0
e	0	0	0	0	0	0	4

CHAPTER 4 DYNAMIC PROGRAMMING

We see a lot of 0s where the ending characters of both substrings are different.

In this example, the max length appears at the last element of the table, but it does not need to. It could appear at any place in the table. For the "aacb" and "aaab" example, it is in the middle of the table.

Table 4-4. *The Dynamic Programming table for the maximum common substring of "aacb" and "aaab"*

	a	a	a	b
a	1	1	1	0
a	1	2	2	0
c	0	0	0	0
b	0	0	0	1

The code implementation is in Listing 4-8. The time and space are the same O(m×n) where m and n are the lengths of strings 1 and 2, respectively.

101

Listing 4-8. Implementation of the longest common substring of two strings

```python
1.  def longest_common_substring(A, B):
2.      dp = [[0 for i in range(len(B))] for j in range(len(A))]
3.      # fill in the first row
4.      for i in range(len(B)):
5.          if A[0] == B[i]:
6.              dp[0][i] = 1
7.          else:
8.              dp[0][i] = 0
9.
10.     # fill in the first col
11.     for i in range(len(A)):
12.         if B[0] == A[i]:
13.             dp[i][0] = 1
14.         else:
15.             dp[i][0] = 0
16.
17.     # fill in the rest of the matrix
18.     max_len = 0
19.     for i in range(1, len(A)):
20.         for j in range(1, len(B)):
21.             if A[i] == B[j]:
22.                 dp[i][j] = dp[i-1][j-1] + 1
23.             else:
24.                 dp[i][j] = 0
25.
26.             max_len = max(max_len, dp[i][j])
27.     return max_len
28.
29. if __name__ == '__main__':
30.     print (longest_common_substring('nature', 'nurture'))
```

In [4]: run Listing_4_8_longest_common_substring.py

4

Knapsack

Let us continue practicing Dynamic Programming by looking at a problem of a different flavor. Say you have a backpack with a total capacity of 24 pounds. There are also four items in the room, each with a weight of 16, 14, 10, and 5 pounds, and a value of 16, 12, 8, and 1 dollars, respectively. The goal is to collect items that can fit into your backpack and have the most total value.

Let us summarize the conditions in Table 4-5.

Table 4-5. *The value and weight of all items*

	Item 1	Item 2	Item 3	Item 4
Value ($)	16	12	8	1
Weight (lb)	16	14	10	5

As an initial attempt, we are tempted to grab item 1 since it has the largest value of 16 dollars, but it takes up much of the allowed capacity. If we do pick item 1, we can only fit item 4 into the bag. Then the total value is $17. Here we just exercised a **Greedy Algorithm**, though we should not rely on value alone to determine the item to choose; use the per-pound dollar amount as a criterion instead. Let us add an additional row to Table 4-5. It turns out the items are already sorted based on value/weight ratio (Table 4-6). Using the ratio as a guide, we still arrive at item 1 and item 4 with a combined value of $17.

Table 4-6. *Add an extra row of value/weight ratio to the previous table*

	Item 1	Item 2	Item 3	Item 4
Value ($)	16	12	8	1
Weight (lb)	16	14	10	5
Value/Weight ($/lb)	1	0.857	0.8	0.2

But it is a suboptimal solution since a combination of items 2 and 3 gives $20. It is not surprising that the Greedy Algorithm fails to find the optimal solution. The requirement here is to maximize the dollar amount subject to the capacity constraint of the backpack. The complexity here is that the weights are discrete – it is very likely we do not use up the full capacity of the bag. For example, in our suboptimal solution, we used only 21 of the 24 allowed capacity. To make the Greedy Algorithm work in this scenario, we will need to *relax* the constraints on weight – allowing us to put part of the item in the backpack. As a concrete example, let us say items 1, 2, 3, and 4 are, respectively, dusts of gold, silver, bronze, and iron. Then we will collect all 16 pounds of gold and 8 pounds of silver, reaching a total value of 16 + (8/14) × 12 = $22.86 (obviously, gold/silver is way more expensive in real life).

Let us now go back to the original problem with an integer weight value. We will need to devise a Dynamic Programming solution. Let us follow the procedures outlined in Section "The Generic Way of Designing a Dynamic Programming Solution" and give it a try.

Let us formalize the problem in mathematical notation. Given a number of items, $i = 0, 1, \ldots, n$, we want to maximize total value of V, subject to the constraint that the total weights are no greater than C. As a first attempt, we will see if we can calculate $V(i)$, i.e., the maximum achievable value of first i items, based on $V(i-1)$, $V(i-2)$, …, $V(1)$, etc. Use the example above, $V(1) = 16$, and then the second item comes in, and due to capacity constraint, we cannot include it to the bag, so $V(2)$ is still 16. Then arrives the third item; we know the best value for $V(3)$ is 20, but we cannot simply derive it based on $V(1)$ and/or $V(2)$, which are both 16.

It seems a one-dimensional array is oversimplified for the current problem. Maybe we need to add a second dimension, capacity, to our process. We now maximize the maximum retainable value $V(i, c)$, given a subset of items $1, 2, \ldots, i$, and a bag of the capacity constraint of c. To find the recursion relation, we ask if we *can* fit the last item i into the bag. If not, $V(i, c) = V(i-1, c)$, i.e., the maximum attainable value is the same with or without the last item. But if we can, we continue to ask if we *want* to include the item i into the bag. See the flow diagram in Figure 4-4.

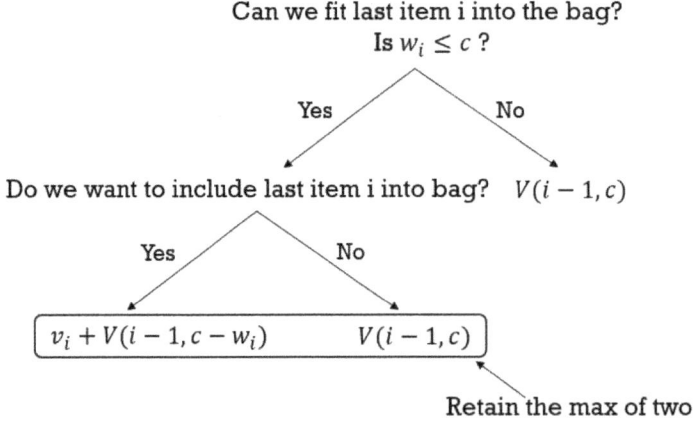

Figure 4-4. A flow diagram to devise a DP solution for the knapsack problem without repeats

We can construct the DP table for the current problem, based on this diagram. The two-dimensional table is shown below.

CHAPTER 4 DYNAMIC PROGRAMMING

Table 4-7. *The DP table for the knapsack problem without repeats*

	0	1	2	3	4	5	6	7	8	9	10	11	12	13	14	15	16	17	18	19	20	21	22	23	24
0	0	0	0	0	0	0	0	0	0	0	0	0	0	0	0	0	0	0	0	0	0	0	0	0	0
1	0	0	0	0	0	0	0	0	0	0	0	0	0	0	0	0	16	16	16	16	16	16	16	16	16
2	0	0	0	0	0	0	0	0	0	0	0	0	0	0	12	12	16	16	16	16	16	16	16	16	16
3	0	0	0	0	0	0	0	0	0	0	8	8	8	8	12	12	16	16	16	16	16	16	16	16	20
4	0	0	0	0	0	1	1	1	1	1	8	8	8	8	12	12	16	16	16	16	16	17	17	17	20

The x axis is the capacity, increasing from 0 to 24, whereas the y axis is for the number of items, from 0 to 4. As usual, we introduce the 0th row and 0th column with 0s values for convenience. The maximum attainable value is at the bottom right of the table. The implementation of it is in Listing 4-9.

Listing 4-9. The DP solution for the knapsack problem without repeats

```
1.  def knapsack_no_repeat(weights, values, capacity):
2.      n = len(weights)
3.      V = [[0 for i in range(capacity + 1)] for j in range(n + 1)]
4.
5.      for i in range(1, n + 1):
6.          for c in range(1, capacity + 1):
7.              if weights[i - 1] > c:
8.                  V[i][c] = V[i-1][c]
9.              else:
10.                 V[i][c] = max(V[i-1][c], V[i-1][c - weights[i-1]] + values[i-1])
11.
12.     return V[n][capacity]
13.
14. if __name__ == "__main__":
15.     weights = [16, 14, 10, 5]
16.     values = [16, 12, 8, 1]
17.     C = 24
18.     print (knapsack_no_repeat(weights, values, C))
```

```
In [5]: run Listing_4_9_knapsack_no_repeat.py
20
```

The time and space complexity of the current program are both O(n×C) where n denotes the number of items and C is the capacity of the bag. But is it an efficient algorithm? It does not seem so. We see lots of 0s in the DP table (Table 4-7). As a contrived example, say, we have the same four items, but have a bag of a capacity of 1 billion pounds. Well, we

CHAPTER 4   DYNAMIC PROGRAMMING

humans can tell the answer in a few seconds (i.e., grab all items), but the computer still must loop through billions of scenarios to arrive at the correct answer. As a matter of fact, the knapsack problem is NP-complete and has no known polynomial solution so far.

Let us now look at a variant of the original knapsack problem. This time, suppose there are infinite supplies of each item – you can take however many copies of the same items you want. Then what is the maximum attainable value? I guess we can follow the same logic as the non-repeat case and construct a similar flow diagram in Figure 4-5. We first check if we *can* fit the last item into the bag. If so, do we *want* to include it? We see only one slight difference here after we decide to include the item into the bag (highlighted in red in Figure 4-5). The total value is $v_i + V(i, c - w_i)$ instead of $v_i + V(i - 1, c - w_i)$ in the non-repeat case. This is because we can now pick up any items we want, including the ith item.

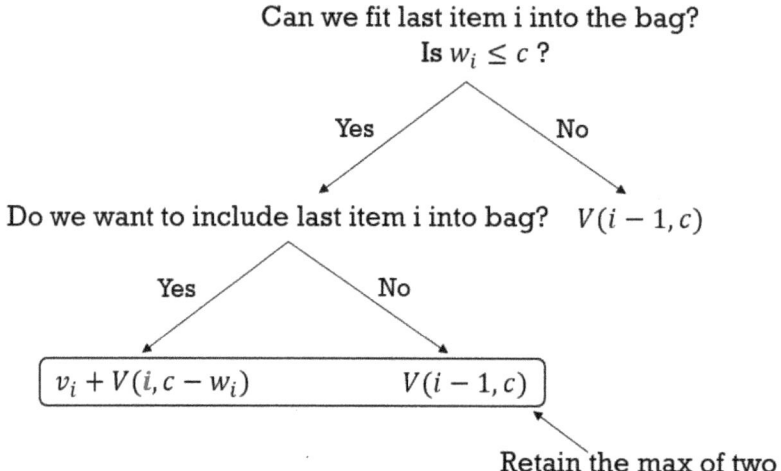

Figure 4-5. *A flow diagram to devise a DP solution using a two-dimensional table for the knapsack problem with repeats*

This works, and the modification to the previous code is minimal, just change the index at line 10 in Listing 4-9. But do we really need to construct a two-dimensional DP table? If we do a one-dimensional table instead, we aim to find the maximum value of $V(i)$ given a multiset of items 1, 2, 3, ..., i. We aim to find the recursion relation based on $V(i-1)$, $V(i-2)$, ..., and $V(1)$. But as in the non-repeat case, we will need additional information of capacity to construct a two-dimensional table. Instead of $V(i)$, how about $V(c)$? The problem is then reduced to find the maximum attainable value of V given a capacity c.

106

Since all items are available, we can iterate through them all and find the max value of V (make sure the item can fit into the bag, i. e., $w_i \leq c$). If none of them can fit into the bag, $V(c) = 0$. See the flow diagram in Figure 4-6.

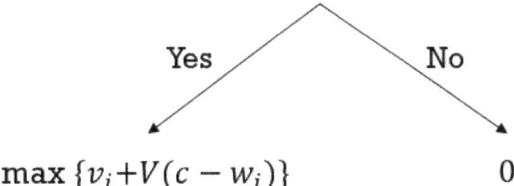

Figure 4-6. *A flow diagram to devise a DP solution using a one-dimensional table for the knapsack problem with repeats*

The one-dimensional DP table and code are shown below (Table 4-8 and Listing 4-10). Same as the non-repeat scenario, the max value is at the last entry of the table. The time and space complexity are the same $O(n \times C)$.

Table 4-8. *The DP table for the knapsack problem with repeats. The x axis is the capacity of the knapsack*

0	1	2	3	4	5	6	7	8	9	10	11	12	13	14	15	16	17	18	19	20	21	22	23	24
0	0	0	0	0	1	1	1	1	1	8	8	8	8	12	12	16	16	16	16	16	17	17	17	20

Listing 4-10. The DP solutions for the knapsack problem with repeats

```
1.  def knapsack_with_repeat(weights, values, capacity):
2.      n = len(weights)
3.      dp = [0 for i in range(capacity + 1)]
4.      for b in range(1, capacity + 1):
5.          for i in range(n):
6.              if weights[i] <= b:
7.                  dp[b] = max(dp[b], values[i] + dp[b -weights[i]])
8.      return dp[capacity]
9.
10. def knapsack_repeat_2D(weights, values, capacity):
11.     n = len(weights)
12.     dp = [[0 for i in range(capacity + 1)] for j in range(n + 1)]
13.
14.     for i in range(1, n + 1):
15.         for b in range(1, capacity + 1):
16.             if weights[i - 1] > b:
17.                 dp[i][b] = dp[i-1][b]
18.             else:
19.                 dp[i][b] = max(dp[i-1][b], dp[i][b - weights[i-1]] + values[i-1])
20.     return dp[n][capacity]
21.
22. if __name__ == "__main__":
23.     weights = [16, 14, 10, 5]
24.     values = [16, 12, 8, 1]
25.     B = 24
26.     print (knapsack_with_repeat(weights, values, B))
27.     print (knapsack_repeat_2D(weights, values, B))
```

In [6]: run Listing_4_10_knapsack_with_repeat.py

20

20

Application

When you browse a website on a computer, a cell phone, or a tablet, have you ever wondered why the images do not get squashed or stretched upon resizing the browser window? When resizing the windows, it uses an algorithm named Seam Carving to preserve the content. The algorithm was originally developed by Shai Avidan and Ariel Shamir [7]. A seam is a path of the pixels of an image that contains the least energy. A seam can be removed to decrease the size of an image or added to expand an image. Let us look at a concrete example to elaborate on these points.

The overall flow for an image resizing using seam carving is shown in Figure 4-7.

CHAPTER 4 DYNAMIC PROGRAMMING

Start with an image   Calculate energy of each pixel   Calculate seams, ranked by energy   Remove low energy seams   Final image

Figure 4-7. *The flow of a seam carving using an image as an example [8]*

We start with an image and calculate its energy pixel-wise. Connect the pixels with low energy to form seams across the image. Remove the low-energy seams to decrease the size of the image.

In terms of the implementation, we follow these steps:

(1) Calculate gradients of each pixel in the image based on its gray scale value, along the x axis and y axis. The energy will be the sum of the absolute values of the partial derivatives.

$$e(I) = \left|\frac{\partial}{\partial x}I\right| + \left|\frac{\partial}{\partial y}I\right|$$

(2) Calculate the cumulative energy for each pixel using Dynamic Programming. Figure 4-8 provides a visual example.

5	1	2	4	3
1	8	3	2	5
1	3	4	2	8

Initial energy

5	1	2	4	3
1+1	8+1	3+1	2+2	5+3
1	3	4	2	8

Cumulative energy – fill second row

5	1	2	4	3
2	9	4	4	8
1+2	3+2	4+4	2+4	8+4

Cumulative energy – fill last row

5	1	2	4	3
2	9	4	4	8
3	5	8	6	12

Back track lowest energy pixel to find seams

Figure 4-8. *The process to find seams via DP and backtracking*

CHAPTER 4   DYNAMIC PROGRAMMING

Start with an initial energy 2D matrix. To calculate the cumulative energy, the first row remains the same. Each pixel in the second row will choose its three neighboring pixels in the previous row, and pick the lowest value to add. Notice, the pixels at both edges only have two neighboring pixels. Repeat the same process for the third row and onward. Finally, a map of cumulative energy for each pixel is generated.

(3) Based on the cumulative energy map, we backtrack the minimums bottom-up to recover the seam with minimal energy. In this case, the seam is highlighted in red.

(4) Depending on the number of seams specified, you remove the seam iteratively.

Let us do it step-by-step. We will implement the first step, i.e., calculate the gradient of the pixel in Listing 4-11.

Listing 4-11. Calculate the gradient of a 2D matrix

```
1.  import numpy as np
2.  def calculate_gradient(I):
3.      R, C = len(I), len(I[0])
4.      Ix = [[0 for _ in range(C)] for _ in range(R)]
5.      Iy = [[0 for _ in range(C)] for _ in range(R)]
6.      # calculate Ix
7.      for c in range(C):
8.          Ix[0][c] = I[1][c] - I[0][c]
9.          Ix[R-1][c] = I[R-1][c] - I[R-2][c]
10.     for r in range(1, R-1):
11.         for c in range(C):
12.             Ix[r][c] = (I[r+1][c] - I[r-1][c]) / 2
13.     # calculate Iy
14.     for r in range(R):
15.         Iy[r][0] = I[r][1] - I[r][0]
16.         Iy[r][C-1] = I[r][C-1] - I[r][C-2]
17.     for r in range(R):
18.         for c in range(1, C-1):
19.             Iy[r][c] = (I[r][c+1] - I[r][c-1]) /2
20.     return Ix, Iy
21.
22. def calculate_energy(Ix, Iy):
23.     R, C = len(Ix), len(Ix[0])
24.     E = [[0 for _ in range(C)] for _ in range(R)]
25.     for r in range(R):
```

```
26.         for c in range(C):
27.             E[r][c] = abs(Ix[r][c]) + abs(Iy[r][c])
28.     return E
29.
30. if __name__ == "__main__":
31.     """
32.     Given a 2D image matrix calculate its gradient along x, y axes
33.         I = [1 2 1]
34.             [0 0 1]
35.             [3 2 1]
36.         Ix = [-1 -2 0]
37.              [1 0 0]
38.              [3 2 0]
39.         Iy = [1 0 -1]
40.              [0 0.5 1]
41.              [-1 -1 -1]
42.     The result should be equivalent to np.gradient(I)
43.     x|
44.      |
45.      |
46.      |
47.     y ------------
48.     """
49.     I = [[1, 2, 1],
50.          [0, 0, 1],
51.          [3, 2, 1]]
52.     print (np.gradient(I)[0])
53.     print (np.gradient(I)[1])
54.     print (calculate_gradient(I)[0])
55.     print (calculate_gradient(I)[1])
```

In [7]: run Listing_4_11_seam_carving_calculate_gradient.py

[[-1. -2. 0.]
 [1. 0. 0.]
 [3. 2. 0.]]
[[1. 0. -1.]
 [0. 0.5 1.]
 [-1. -1. -1.]]
[[-1, -2, 0], [1.0, 0.0, 0.0], [3, 2, 0]]
[[1, 0.0, -1], [0, 0.5, 1], [-1, -1.0, -1]]

Numpy has a built-in function np.gradient for calculating the gradient of a matrix. Let us cross-validate our code with that. Given an input matrix I = [[1, 2, 1], [0, 0, 1], [3, 2, 1]]. Both yield the same result for I_x = [[-1, -2, 0], [1, 0, 0], [3, 2, 0]] and I_y = [[1, 0, -1], [0, 0.5, 1], [-1, -1, -1]].

One thing to keep in mind is that in image processing, the x direction is vertical, while the y direction is horizontal, which might be contrary to our intuition. Another important point is that the image that is loaded into the program may likely be in the data type of np.uint8 format,

CHAPTER 4 DYNAMIC PROGRAMMING

which covers a data range from 0 to 255. It will always convert the result into this range. See the example below. Therefore, when using the gradient function, be sure to convert the data type to allow the result to be of a wider data range. A simple way is to convert it to a Python list.

```
In [8]: arr = np.array([1,2,3], dtype=np.uint8)
In [9]: arr
Out[9]: array([1, 2, 3], dtype=uint8)
In [10]: arr * 100
Out[10]: array([100, 200,  44], dtype=uint8)
In [11]: arr - 4
Out[11]: array([253, 254, 255], dtype=uint8)
```

Move on to Step (2); Listing 4-12 calculates the cumulative energy based on Dynamic Programming. We verify it against our handwritten example in Figure 4-8, and they do agree.

Listing 4-12. Calculate the cumulative energy given an original energy matrix

```
1.  def calculate_cumulative_energy(E):
2.      R, C = len(E), len(E[0])
3.      cumu_E = [[0 for _ in range(C)] for _ in range(R)]
4.      cumu_E[0] = E[0]
5.      for r in range(1, R):
6.          for c in range(C):
7.              if c == 0:
8.                  cumu_E[r][c] = E[r][c] + min(cumu_E[r-1][c], cumu_E[r-1][c+1])
9.              elif c == C-1:
10.                 cumu_E[r][c] = E[r][c] + min(cumu_E[r-1][c-1], cumu_E[r-1][c])
11.             else:
12.                 cumu_E[r][c] = E[r][c] + min(cumu_E[r-1][c-1], cumu_E[r-1][c],
                                    cumu_E[r-1][c+1])
13.     return cumu_E
14.
15. if __name__ == "__main__":
16.     E = [[5, 1, 2, 4, 3], [1, 8, 3, 2, 5], [1, 3, 4, 2, 8]]
17.     print (calculate_cumulative_energy(E)
```

```
In [12]: run Listing_4_12_seam_carving_calculate_cumulative_energy.py

[[5, 1, 2, 4, 3], [2, 9, 4, 4, 8], [3, 5, 8, 6, 12]]
```

Next is to find a single seam based on the cumulative energy (Listing 4-13). The program returns the indexes of the pixels with the lowest energies.

Listing 4-13. *Find a single seam from the cumulative energy matrix*

```python
1.  def find_single_seam_from_cumu_energy(cumu_E):
2.      R, C = len(cumu_E), len(cumu_E[0])
3.      col_indexes_to_be_removed = []
4.      # index to be removed at last row
5.      last_col_index = cumu_E[-1].index(min(cumu_E[-1]))
6.      col_indexes_to_be_removed.append(last_col_index)
7.      for r in range(R-1, 0, -1):
8.          if last_col_index == 0:
9.              if cumu_E[r-1][0] <= cumu_E[r-1][1]:
10.                 second_last_index = 0
11.             else:
12.                 second_last_index = 1
13.         elif last_col_index == C - 1:
14.             if cumu_E[r-1][C-2] <= cumu_E[r-1][C-1]:
15.                 second_last_index = C-2
16.             else:
17.                 second_last_index = C-1
18.         else:
19.             cumu_energy_second_last = [(cumu_E[r-1][last_col_index -1],
                                             last_col_index -1),
20.                                        (cumu_E[r-1][last_col_index],
                                             last_col_index),
21.                                        (cumu_E[r-1][last_col_index + 1
                                            ],last_col_index + 1)]
22.             cumu_energy_second_last.sort()
23.             second_last_index = cumu_energy_second_last[0][1]
24.         last_col_index = second_last_index
25.         col_indexes_to_be_removed.append(last_col_index)
26.     seam_pixels_indexes = [(r, c) for r, c in zip(range(R),
        col_indexes_to_be_removed[::-1])]
27.     return seam_pixels_indexes
28.
29. if __name__ =="__main__":
30.     cumu_E =[[5, 1, 2, 4, 3], [2, 9, 4, 4, 8], [3, 5, 8, 6, 12]]
31.     print (find_single_seam_from_cumu_energy(cumu_E))
```

In [13]: run Listing_4_13_find_single_seam.py

[(0, 1), (1, 0), (2, 0)]

After running the program, it returns (0,1), (1,0), and (2,0), which correspond to the second pixel in the first row, the first pixel in the second row, and the first pixel in the third row. This agrees with our hand calculation in Figure 4-8.

Finally, as displayed in Listing 4-14 we can write a seam_carving function to remove the desired number of seams and create a GIF image to show the seam carving in process. Make sure we have created a directory "tower_images" which will be used to save all intermediate images before generating a GIF image.

CHAPTER 4   DYNAMIC PROGRAMMING

Listing 4-14. The code to remove a desired number of seams for a given image

```
1.  import cv2
2.  import glob
3.  import numpy as np
4.  from PIL import Image
5.  from Listing_4_11_seam_carving_calculate_gradient import calculate_energy, calculate_gradient
6.  from Listing_4_12_seam_carving_calculate_cumulative_energy import calculate_cumulative_energy
7.  from Listing_4_13_find_single_seam import find_single_seam_from_cumu_energy
8.
9.  def seam_carving(color_image, gray_scale_image, num_seams = 10):
10.     I = gray_scale_image
11.     for i in range(num_seams):
12.         R = len(I)
13.         C = len(I[0])
14.         Ix, Iy = calculate_gradient(I.tolist())
15.         E = calculate_energy(Ix, Iy)
16.         cumu_E = calculate_cumulative_energy(E)
17.         seam_pixels_indexes = find_single_seam_from_cumu_energy(cumu_E)
18.         # draw seams as red
19.         for r, c in seam_pixels_indexes:
20.             color_image[:, :, 0][r,c] = 0    # this is blue channel
21.             color_image[:, :, 1][r,c] = 0    # this is green channel
22.             color_image[:, :, 2][r,c] = 255  # this is red channel
23.         cv2.imshow("current_seam", color_image)
24.         cv2.imwrite(f"tower_images/seam_#{i + 1}.jpg", color_image)
25.         # remove seam
26.         mask = np.ones((R, C), dtype = bool)
27.         for r, c in seam_pixels_indexes:
28.             mask[r][c] = False
29.
30.         blue_channel = color_image[:, :, 0][mask].reshape(R, C-1)
31.         green_channel = color_image[:, :, 1][mask].reshape(R, C-1)
32.         red_channel = color_image[:, :, 2][mask].reshape(R, C-1)
33.         gray_channel = I[mask].reshape(R, C-1)
34.         color_image = np.dstack((blue_channel,green_channel,red_channel))
35.         I = gray_channel
36.     cv2.imwrite(f"final_image_after_seam_carving.jpg", color_image)
37.
38. def create_a_gif(fp_in = "tower_images/*.jpg", fp_out = "seam_carving_in_action.gif"):
39.     imgs = (Image.open(f) for f in sorted(glob.glob(fp_in),
40.                             key = lambda image_name:
                                    int(image_name.split(".")[0].split("#")[1])))
41.     img = next(imgs)
42.     img.save(fp = fp_out,
43.             format = "GIF",
44.             append_images = imgs,
45.             save_all = True,
46.             duration=10,
47.             loop=0)
48.
49. if __name__ == "__main__":
50.     gray_scale_image = cv2.imread('Broadway_Tower.jpg', cv2.IMREAD_GRAYSCALE)
51.     color_image = cv2.imread('Broadway_Tower.jpg', cv2.IMREAD_COLOR)
52.     seam_carving(color_image, gray_scale_image, num_seams = 5)
53.     create_a_gif()
```

A comparison between the original image [8] and the current implementation after removing 500 seams is shown in Figure 4-9. Despite the downscaling of the image, the feature of the castle is largely preserved. Instead, many of the pixels from the sky and grass are removed.

Figure 4-9. *The castle image before and after removing 500 seams*

Summary

In this chapter, we introduce Dynamic Programming via the example of the Fibonacci sequence. We solve it by storing the previous Fibonacci numbers in a one-dimensional table. We then lay out the general approach to design a Dynamic Programming solution, where sometimes we need to *strengthen* the definition to find the recurrence relation. We further look at the long common substring/subsequence and knapsack problems before we wrap up the chapter with a real-world application of the Seam Carving algorithm. Dynamic Programming can be difficult to grasp at the beginning, but with plenty of practice, it will become natural for you to spot the pattern (i.e., identifying overlapping subproblems) and design a solution with it.

CHAPTER 5

RSA Cryptosystem

When you enter a password at a website or make online purchases, have you ever wondered how the data is securely transmitted over the Internet? Yes, you guessed it right – the modern browsers use security protocols such as HTTPS to protect our data in transit. In this chapter, we will review one of the well-known public key cryptography methods called the RSA Cryptosystem, named after its inventors, Ron **R**ivest, Adi **S**hamir, and Leonard **A**dleman. In RSA, both sender and receiver (even the attacker) know the public key beforehand. The sender uses the public key to encrypt the message, and the receiver uses the private key known only to himself/herself to decrypt the message. The RSA involves a bit of math, including finding the greatest common divisor of two integers and a primality test using Fermat's Little Theorem. Fret not, let us unpack it slowly.

Caesar Cipher

Before we discuss the modern algorithm to encrypt data, let us see how the ancient greats protected their data. The Roman general Julio Cesar once developed an encryption method, named the Caesar cipher, and used it in his correspondence. The idea is simple (Figure 5-1): for any letter in the original text, replace it with a new letter that is shifted by a fixed number of places down the alphabet. For example, if the word is "ABC" and the right shift is three places, the encrypted message would become "DEF". Note that the alphabetic order is cyclic, that is, if the word is "XYZ", the new message will be "ABC".

Chapter 5 RSA Cryptosystem

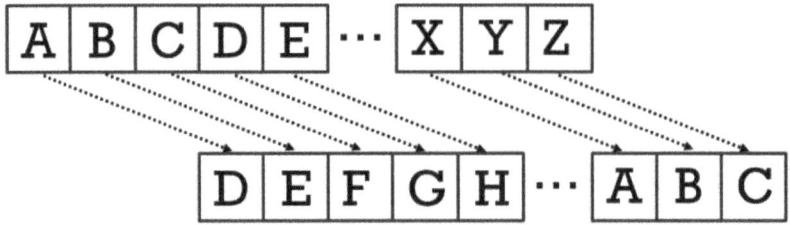

Figure 5-1. *An example of a Caesar cipher where each letter is shifted by three positions*

The implementation of the Caesar cipher is in Listing 5-1. We leverage the built-in package string for quick access to all 26 lowercase letters and uppercase letters. In the encryption function caesar_cipher_encrypt, we loop through the characters one by one: if the character is either a lowercase or uppercase letter, we find its index and shift it by the desired places as specified in the input parameter shift. The modulo operation at lines 8 and 12 fulfills the cyclic requirement of the alphabet. If the character is not in the alphabet, such as a white space or a punctuation mark, we record it as is. Note that the decryption function is just the reverse operation of the encryption: we only need to pass -shift as an input parameter to the caesar_cipher_encrypt function.

Listing 5-1. The Caesar cipher

```python
1.  from string import ascii_lowercase, ascii_uppercase
2.
3.  def caesar_cipher_encrypt(message, shift):
4.      encrypted_msg = ""
5.      for char in message:
6.          if char in ascii_lowercase:
7.              char_index = ascii_lowercase.index(char)
8.              new_char_index = (char_index + shift) % 26
9.              encrypted_msg += ascii_lowercase[new_char_index]
10.         elif char in ascii_uppercase:
11.             char_index = ascii_uppercase.index(char)
12.             new_char_index = (char_index + shift) % 26
13.             encrypted_msg += ascii_uppercase[new_char_index]
14.         else:
15.             encrypted_msg += char
16.     return encrypted_msg
17.
18. def caesar_cipher_decrypt(message, shift):
19.     return caesar_cipher_encrypt(message, -shift)
20.
21. if __name__ == "__main__":
22.     message = "Stay hungry. Stay foolish."
23.     shift = 3
24.     encrypted_msg = caesar_cipher_encrypt(message, shift)
25.     decrypted_msg = caesar_cipher_decrypt(encrypted_msg, shift)
26.     print ("encrypted msg:", encrypted_msg)
27.     print ("decrypted msg:", decrypted_msg)
28.     assert message == decrypted_msg
```

As an example, if we provide a quote "Stay hungry. Stay foolish." as input to our cipher, it outputs a secret message: "Vwdb kxqjub. Vwdb irrolvk."

```
In [1]: run Listing_5_1_caesar_cipher.py
encrypted msg: Vwdb kxqjub. Vwdb irrolvk.
decrypted msg: Stay hungry. Stay foolish.
```

The Caesar cipher is not secure. The only secret parameter in the cipher is the `shift` which can be easily figured out by brute force. In this chapter, we will learn how modern encryption algorithm, i.e., the RSA Cryptosystem, works. Using RSA, when we encrypt a message, we can use a public key and make it known to others. The receiver will decrypt the message with a private key.

CHAPTER 5   RSA CRYPTOSYSTEM

RSA Initial Encounter

Let us delve a little bit into the well-known and widely used RSA public key Cryptosystem. Believe it or not, we can implement an initial version of RSA following the below instructions.

Here are the steps:

(1) Find two prime numbers p and q ($p \neq q$).

(2) Calculate n which is $p \times q$.

(3) Calculate t which is $(p - 1) \times (q - 1)$.

(4) Find e such that $e < t$ and e, t are coprime or relatively prime.

(5) Find d such that $d \times e \% t = 1$.
(for a message, $m < n$)

(6) With public key pair (e, n), you encrypt the message by $m^e \% n$.

(7) With private key pair (d, n), you decrypt the encrypted message, m' by $(m')^d \% n$.

In Step (4), the coprime or relatively prime means the Greatest Common Divisor (GCD) of those two numbers is 1. In the Python `math` module, there is a function called `gcd`, and we can use it here. The code implementation is shown in Listing 5-2.

Listing 5-2. An initial version of RSA

```python
1.  import math
2.
3.  def rsa_encrypt(p, q, message):
4.      N = p * q
5.      t = (p -1) * (q - 1)
6.      e = 2
7.      while e < t:
8.          if math.gcd(e, t) == 1:
9.              break
10.         e += 1
11.     d = 0
12.     while True:
13.         if d * e % t == 1:
14.             break
15.         d += 1
16.     # encryption
17.     encrypted_text = pow(message, e, N)
18.     return encrypted_text, d, e, N
19.
20. def rsa_decrypt(message, d, N):
21.     # decryption
22.     decrypted_text = pow(message, d, N)
23.     return decrypted_text
24.
25. if __name__ == "__main__":
26.     p, q, message = 53, 59, 89
27.     print (f"Original message is {message}")
28.     encrypted_msg, d, e, N = rsa_encrypt(p, q, message)
29.     print (f"Encrypted message is {encrypted_msg}")
30.     decrypted_msg = rsa_decrypt(encrypted_msg, d, N)
31.     print (f"Decrypted message is {decrypted_msg}")
```

Let us try with an original message of 89. The encrypted message becomes 1394, which is decrypted to its original value.

```
In [2]: run Listing_5_2_rsa_encryption_initial.py
Original message is 89
Encrypted message is 1394
Decrypted message is 89
```

Greatest Common Divisor

Let us take a deeper look at some of the methods used in the previous code. First, we will examine the Greatest Common Divisor. In ~300 BC, the great Greek mathematician Euclid described a method to find the GCD of two integers in his *Elements*. Here is a concrete example using the Euclidean algorithm. Suppose we have two integer numbers (57, 24), we first calculate their remainder, as 57%24 = 9. We replace the first number with the second and the second with the remainder. After this, the number pair becomes (24, 9). Moving on to calculate the remainder of the new numbers, as 24 % 9 = 6, and the pair becomes (9, 6). Then the new remainder = 9 % 6 = 3, and the new number pair is (6, 3). Finally, 6%3 = 0, the number pair becomes (3,0). Since the second number equals 0. The algorithm stops, and the GCD of (57, 24) is 3, which is the first number in the final pair (3,0).

Euclid finds the GCD of two integers in an iterative manner. We can implement it either in an iterative way or in a recursive way (Listing 5-3).

Listing 5-3. Find the GCD of two integers iteratively and recursively

```python
import math
def find_greatest_common_divisor_iterative(num_1, num_2):
    # make sure num_1 >= num_2
    if num_1 < num_2:
        num_1, num_2 = num_2, num_1

    while num_2 != 0:
        num_1, num_2 = num_2, num_1 % num_2
    return num_1

def find_greatest_common_divisor_recursive(num_1, num_2):
    # make sure num_1 >= num_2
    if num_1 < num_2:
        num_1, num_2 = num_2, num_1

    if num_2 == 0:
        return num_1
    else:
        return find_greatest_common_divisor_recursive(num_2, num_1 % num_2)

if __name__ == "__main__":
    num_1, num_2 = 153, 123
    print (math.gcd(num_1, num_2))
    print (find_greatest_common_divisor_iterative(num_1, num_2))
    print (find_greatest_common_divisor_recursive(num_1, num_2))
```

In [3]: run Listing_5_3_find_greatest_common_denominator.py

3

3

3

Find Prime Numbers

The prime numbers play a critical role in the security of the RSA algorithm, thanks to the fact that there is no efficient algorithm for prime factorization. Let us think about how to decide if a number is prime or not. By definition, a number is a prime number if its factors are only 1 and itself. So, any even number (except for 2) cannot be a prime number. For an odd number, say, 9, we check from 2 to 8, if any of the numbers from 2 to 8 is divisible by 9. The fact that 9%3=0 means that 3 is another factor of 9, making it a composite number. Naïvely, we can implement it by looping through all numbers less than the current number and checking the remainder of the current number % number. If any of the remainder is 0, it is not a prime number. As an improvement, we can check with a smaller range, that is, up until the *square root* of the odd number in interest, and round down to the nearest integer.

Let us now write a function to find all prime numbers with a given number of digits in Listing 5-4.

Listing 5-4. Find prime numbers for an N-digit number

```
import math
def is_an_odd_number_prime_number(odd_num):
    upper_bound = math.floor(math.sqrt(odd_num))
    for divisor in range(3, upper_bound + 1):
        if divisor % 2 == 1 and odd_num % divisor == 0:
            return False
    return True

def find_prime_numbers_modulo_method(num_digits):
    if num_digits == 1:
        return [2,3,5,7]

    prime_numbers = []
    for num in range(10 ** (num_digits - 1), 10 ** num_digits):
        if  num % 2 == 1 and is_an_odd_number_prime_number(num): # num must be an odd number to be a prime number:
            prime_numbers.append(num)
    print (f"There are in total {len(prime_numbers)} prime numbers for a number of {num_digits} digits")
    return prime_numbers

if __name__ == '__main__':
    print (find_prime_numbers_modulo_method(2))
```

```
In [4]: run Listing_5_4_find_prime_numbers.py
There are in total 21 prime numbers for a number of 2 digits
[11, 13, 17, 19, 23, 29, 31, 37, 41, 43, 47, 53, 59, 61, 67, 71, 73, 79, 83, 89, 97]
```

CHAPTER 5 RSA CRYPTOSYSTEM

We can find 21 prime numbers with 2 digits. They are 11, 13, 17, 19, 23, 29, 31, 37, 41, 43, 47, 53, 59, 61, 67, 71, 73, 79, 83, 89, and 97.

This method above finds prime numbers correctly. But there is a more efficient way of finding prime numbers, called "The Sieve of Eratosthenes," which is named after the Greek polymath Eratosthenes. Here is a story of him measuring the circumference of the earth.

Eratosthenes observed that on the Summer Solstice, the sunlight shined to the bottom of a well in his hometown, Syene (modern Aswan), which indicates that the sun was directly above the well on the day of the Summer Solstice. However, a pole standing on the ground in Alexandria, Egypt's second largest city, far to the north, cast a brief shadow on the same day. Eratosthenes believed that this shadow was created by the angle of the pole and the sunlight in Alexandria. He measured the length of the pole and the shadow and found that the angle was about 7.2°. This angle was created by the fact that the earth is a sphere. Since 360° equals 50 times 7.2°, it means that the circumference of the Earth is 50 times the distance between Alexandria and Syene. At that time, it took 50 days to travel by camel from Alexandria to Syene. The camels walk approximately 18.5 kilometers throughout the day. Based on this estimation, the distance between the two cities is approximately 925 km, and the circumference of the earth is 50 times that distance, or approximately 46,250 km. Compared to the established circumference of the Earth's equator, which is approximately 40,076 km, this is a marvelous achievement!

Back to our discussion of finding primes. Here is how "The Sieve of Eratosthenes" works:

For a positive integer n, find all prime numbers that are not greater than $\sqrt{n}$. In the range 1, 2, ...n, cross out all the multiples of all prime numbers (e.g., 2×, 3×, etc.); what is left are the prime numbers less than n.

Let us try with an example. Find all prime numbers up to 20.

(1) Find all odd primes that are less than the $\sqrt{20}$. That is, 3 only.

(2) Find all odd numbers from 1 to 20, that is, [3, 5, 7, 9, 11, 13, 15, 17, 19].

(3) Cross out the multiples of 3.

(4) The rest are all prime numbers up to 20, [3, 5, 7, 11, 13, 17, 19].

Below is the code (Listing 5-5) to find all prime numbers given the number of digits using "The Sieve of Eratosthenes."

CHAPTER 5 RSA CRYPTOSYSTEM

Listing 5-5. The Sieve of Eratosthenes

```python
import math
def find_prime_numbers_eratosthenes_method(num_digits):
    if num_digits == 1:
        return [2,3,5,7]
    min_num = 10 ** (num_digits - 1)
    max_num = 10 ** num_digits - 1
    # all odd numbers within the range can be the candidates for prime numbers
    prime_numbers_candidates = set([num for num in range(min_num, max_num) if num % 2 == 1])
    pseudo_prime_numbers = [num for num in range(3, math.floor(math.sqrt(max_num)) + 1) if num % 2 == 1]
    for pseudo_prime_number in pseudo_prime_numbers:
        multiplier = 2
        while pseudo_prime_number * multiplier <= max_num:
            if pseudo_prime_number * multiplier in prime_numbers_candidates:
                prime_numbers_candidates.remove(pseudo_prime_number * multiplier)
            multiplier += 1
    print(f"There are in total {len(prime_numbers_candidates)} prime numbers for a number of {num_digits} digits")
    return prime_numbers_candidates

if __name__ == '__main__':
    find_prime_numbers_eratosthenes_method(5)
```

```
In [5]: run Listing_5_5_find_prime_numbers_eratosthenes.py
There are in total 8363 prime numbers for a number of 5 digits
```

At line 9, we do not use the prime numbers but use the odd numbers instead, since it is easier this way to implement, though it has incurred some extra calculations. After running the program, we now know there are 8363 prime numbers with 5 digits.

An Improved Version of RSA

Let us recap how RSA works. Say we have two friends, Alice and Bob. Alice wants to send a message to Bob and does not want it to be intercepted by others. So, Alice decides to encrypt her message. Since RSA is a public key cryptosystem, no communication between Alice and Bob is needed.

CHAPTER 5   RSA CRYPTOSYSTEM

Here are the detailed steps:

(1) Bob finds two large prime numbers p and q and calculates $N = p \times q$ and a totient $(p - 1) \times (q - 1)$.

(2) Bob finds e such that $gcd(e, (p - 1) \times (q - 1)) = 1$. In other words, e and totient are relatively prime.

(3) Bob calculates also a private key d such that $d \times e \;\%\; (p - 1) \times (q - 1) = 1$.

(4) Bob publishes the public key pair (N, e).

(5) Alice uses public key pair (N, e) to encrypt her message, m. The encrypted message $m' = m^e \;\%\; N$.

(6) Bob receives the encrypted message m' and decrypts it using the private key pair (N, d) to retrieve the original message $m = (m')^d \;\%\; N$.

Bob knows both public and private key pairs, while Alice only knows the former. There is no need to have private communication between Alice and Bob, as Bob makes the public key pair known to both.

Let us revisit our initial version of RSA in Section "RSA Initial Encounter". In Step (1), for the prime numbers p and q, we have chosen 53 and 59. But both are so small that they can be easily figured out, making our encrypted message insecure. In real applications, the prime numbers used are at least a couple of thousand bits.

To generate a prime number with a thousand bits, we can generate a random number with, say, 1000 bits. After all, it is just a concatenation of 0s and 1s. Python's built-in `random` package has a method `getrandbits` for an easy generation of such a large number. For example, `random.getrandbits(1000)` generates one such a number with ~300 digits:

60642203054214841193506902603297307095709119977667267793332225248586381562125249544855290822706983932902380365031855395235518485145337243124132406704845409828374511371770743704961052586674098277290821892272362626355371716444050596491471073244743467538907913766469445960731150163529181128910365595621161.

After we have a random number, the next task is to test if it is a prime number. If we do a series of modulo operations up to the square root of the number, as we did in the previous section, it would be impossible to complete it in a reasonable time since we would need ~10^{150} checks. Instead, we will do a primality test leveraging Fermat's Little Theorem. Suppose we have a prime number p, according to Fermat's Little Theorem, for any integer z, $1 \leq z < p$, $z^{p-1} \% p = 1$.

Let us test it with an example, say $p = 7$, then for any $1 \leq z < 7$, $z^6 \% 7 = 1$. That is, all $1^6 \% 7$, $2^6 \% 7$, $3^6 \% 7$, $4^6 \% 7$, $5^6 \% 7$, $6^6 \% 7$ should evaluate to 1. A quick check confirms that this is indeed correct.

For the primality test, we will pick up one number randomly, say, z, that is smaller than the large number generated, p. To test if p is a prime number or not. We will test if condition $z^{p-1} \% p = 1$ is satisfied or not. If it does not, then p is a composite number. But if it does, we are not 100 % sure it is a prime. In practice, we sample k such random numbers that are smaller than p, and test the condition repeatedly. If all k such cases pass the check, we are very confident that the randomly generated number is a prime.

But wait, we will need to calculate $z^{p-1} \% p$ but p and $p - 1$ are such large numbers with ~300 digits. Python's built-in function pow will fail miserably. We will need to find an efficient algorithm to do this.

Let us look at one example. Suppose we need to calculate $2^7 \% 3$. One way is bottom – up (left part of Figure 5-2), that is, calculate $2^1 \% 3$ first, and then plug in the result of $2^1 \% 3$ to $2^2 \% 3$, and then calculate $2^3 \% 3$ using the result in the previous step. Repeat this seven times to get the final answer.

We still need to perform ~10^{300} rounds of modulo operations. This is no good. Instead, we can do a repeated squaring (right part of Figure 5-2). To calculate $2^7 \% 3$, we need to find $2^6 \% 3$. Since 6 is an even number, we just need to calculate $2^3 \% 3$, then $2^1 \% 3$. Even for a large number such as ~10^{300}, we only need to do eight or nine modulo arithmetic calculations ($2^8=256 < 300 < 2^9=512$). Note to implement the repeated squaring, we will need to discuss if the exponent is odd or even.

$2^1 \% 3 = 2$

$2^2 \% 3 = 2 \times 2 \% 3 = 1$

$2^3 \% 3 = 1 \times 2 \% 3 = 2$

$2^4 \% 3 = 2 \times 2 \% 3 = 1$

$2^5 \% 3 = 1 \times 2 \% 3 = 2$

$2^6 \% 3 = 2 \times 2 \% 3 = 1$

$2^7 \% 3 = 1 \times 2 \% 3 = 2$

$2^7 \% 3 = 2 \times 2^6 \% 3 = 2 \times 1 \% 3 = 2$

$2^6 \% 3 = (2^3)^2 \% 3 = 2^2 \% 3 = 1$

$2^3 \% 3 = 2 \times (2^1)^2 \% 3 = 2 \times (2)^2 \% 3 = 2$

$2^1 \% 3 = 2 \% 3 = 2$

Figure 5-2. *Run the modulo operation efficiently using a repeated squaring method*

Let us continue to review the RSA steps. In Step (2), we will find e. We can use Euclid's algorithm to find the greatest common divisor of e and $(p-1) \times (q-1)$. Typically, we choose a small prime number for e, such as 3, 5, 7, 11, 13, 17, or 19. If any of these numbers is not relatively prime to $(p-1) \times (q-1)$, we will go back to Step (1) and regenerate a new pair of large prime numbers p and q.

In Step (3) we will need to find the private key d such that $d \times e \% (p-1) \times (q-1) = 1$. In our initial version, we start from 1 and increase it by one each time. This is obviously not efficient for a huge totient number, $(p-1) \times (q-1)$. Instead, we can use the more efficient *extended Euclid's algorithm* to find d. It takes two positive integer numbers x and y as inputs (suppose $x > y$) and returns (1) GCD of x and y (2) α (3) β, such that $d = x \times \alpha + y \times \beta$.

In Step (3), we will pass $(p-1) \times (q-1)$ as x and e as y to the *extended Euclid's algorithm* and obtain GCD of $(p-1) \times (q-1)$ and e, α, and β. The GCD of $(p-1) \times (q-1)$ and e will be 1 as we have already checked in Step (2) – both numbers are co – prime. Then β from extended Euclid algorithm is what we need for d.

Now let us shift our focus to the *extended Euclid's algorithm*. Let us build some intuition by looking at one example in Figure 5-3. Say we have two integers 30 and 20, we will find gcd(30, 20), α, and β. Using Euclid's GCD algorithm, we reduce gcd(30, 20) to gcd(20, 10) in the next step. In the final step, we stop at gcd(10, 0) that tells us the GCD is 10. Once we know GCD, we can calculate $\alpha = 10 / 10 = 1$. Going up one step, we can calculate $\beta = $ (gcd - $\alpha \times 20) / 10 = (10 - 20) / 10 = -1$. We have (10, 1, -1) as our result.

CHAPTER 5 RSA CRYPTOSYSTEM

$$\gcd(x, y) = \alpha \times x + \beta \times y$$

$$\gcd(30, 20) = \alpha \times 30 + \beta \times 20$$

$$\gcd(20, 30\%20) = \gcd(20, 10) = \alpha \times 20 + \beta \times 10 \quad \gcd = 10, \beta = -1$$

$$\gcd(10, 20\%10) = \gcd(10, 0) = \alpha \times 10 + \beta \times 0 \implies \gcd = 10, \alpha = 1$$

Figure 5-3. *An example of extended Euclid's algorithm*

Formally, we can write the following pseudocode for the extended Euclid algorithm in Figure 5-4. For the base case, the algorithm stops at $y = 0$ and returns x, 1, 0. For a general case, the values returned are explained in the red box below.

```
Extended-Euclid(x, y)
    Input: integers x, y where x≥ y>0
    Output: integers d, α, β where d = gcd(x, y) and d = α x + β y
If y =0, return x, 1, 0
d, α', β' = Extended-Euclid(y, x % y)
Return d, β', α' -⌊x/y⌋ β'
```

$$d, \alpha', \beta' = \text{Extended-Euclid}(y, x \% y)$$
$$d = \alpha' y + \beta' (x \% y)$$
$$= \alpha' y + \beta' (x - \lfloor x/y \rfloor y)$$
$$= \beta' x + (\alpha' - \lfloor x/y \rfloor \beta') y$$

Figure 5-4. *The pseudocode for extended Euclid's algorithm*

Let us finish our review of the RSA steps. After Step (4), where the public key pair is published, finally, in Steps (5) and (6), we will use repeated squaring for fast modular arithmetic calculation.

Combining all the above discussions, we can now implement the RSA algorithm as a Python class, RSA, as displayed in Listing 5-6. At line 2, we use a seed of 1234 (or any other integer number as a seed) to generate reproducible results.

CHAPTER 5   RSA CRYPTOSYSTEM

Listing 5-6. A complete implementation of RSA with prime numbers of a thousand bits

```
1.  import random
2.  random.seed(1234)
3.  class RSA:
4.      def __init__(self):
5.          self.num_bits = 1000 # number of bits for p and q
6.
7.      def fast_modular_arithmetic(self, base, exponent, N):
8.          # calculate modular operations using repeated squaring
9.          # base ** exponent % N
10.         if exponent == 0:
11.             return 1
12.
13.         z = self.fast_modular_arithmetic(base, exponent // 2, N)
14.         if exponent % 2 == 0:
15.             return z**2 % N
16.         else:
17.             return base * z**2 % N
18.
19.     def greatest_common_divisor(self, num_1, num_2):
20.         # make sure num_1 >= num_2
21.         if num_1 < num_2:
22.             num_1, num_2 = num_2, num_1
23.
24.         if num_2 == 0:
25.             return num_1
26.         else:
27.             return self.greatest_common_divisor(num_2, num_1 % num_2)
28.
29.     def extended_euclid(self, num_1, num_2):
30.         # make sure num_1 >= num_2
31.         if num_1 < num_2:
32.             num_1, num_2 = num_2, num_1
33.
34.         if num_2 == 0:
35.             return num_1, 1, 0
36.
37.         d, alpha, beta = self.extended_euclid(num_2, num_1 % num_2)
38.         return d, beta, alpha - num_1 // num_2 * beta
39.
40.     def generate_random_prime(self):
41.         large_num = random.getrandbits(self.num_bits)
42.         while not self.primality_test(large_num):
43.             large_num = random.getrandbits(self.num_bits)
44.         return large_num
45.
46.     def primality_test(self, large_num, k = 200):
```

130

```python
47.            k_random_nums = [random.randint(0, large_num) for _ in range(k)]
48.            for num in k_random_nums:
49.                if self.fast_modular_arithmetic(num, large_num - 1, large_num) != 1:
50.                    return False # not a prime
51.            return True
52.
53.       def find_p_q_e(self):
54.            possible_e_vals = [3, 5, 7, 11, 13, 17, 19]
55.            while True:
56.                p, q = self.generate_random_prime(), self.generate_random_prime()
57.                totient = (p-1) * (q-1)
58.
59.                for e in possible_e_vals:
60.                    if self.greatest_common_divisor(totient, e) == 1:
61.                        return p, q, e
62.
63.       def rsa_encrypt(self, message):
64.            p, q, e = self.find_p_q_e()
65.            N = p * q
66.            totient = (p - 1) * (q - 1)
67.            _, _, d = self.extended_euclid(e, totient) # keep d secret
68.            d = d % totient
69.            if d < 0:
70.                d += totient
71.            # publish public key (N, e)
72.            print (f"p --> {p}")
73.            print (f"q --> {q}")
74.            print (f"e --> {e}")
75.            print (f"N --> {N}")
76.            print (f"d --> {d}")
77.            print (f"totient --> {totient}")
78.            print (f"message --> {message}")
79.            # encrypt
80.            encrypted_msg = self.fast_modular_arithmetic(message, e, N)
81.            return encrypted_msg, d, e, N
82.
83.       def rsa_decrypt(self, message, d, N):
84.            decrypted_msg = self.fast_modular_arithmetic(message, d, N)
85.            return decrypted_msg
86.
87. if __name__ == "__main__":
88.     rsa = RSA()
89.     message = 83116971213210411711010311412146328311697121321021111111108105115110433
90.     print (f"Original message is {message}")
91.     encrypted_msg, d, e, N  = rsa.rsa_encrypt(message)
92.     print (f"Encrypted message is {encrypted_msg}")
93.     decrypted_msg = rsa.rsa_decrypt(encrypted_msg, d, N)
94.     print (f"Decrypted message is {decrypted_msg}")
```

CHAPTER 5   RSA CRYPTOSYSTEM

While implementing and testing the program above, we may encounter several issues. First, we may have got the "maximum recursion depth is exceeded" message. It turned out the d value returned from extended Euclid algorithm (line 67) was negative and during the decryption step (line 84), the recursive fast modular method fails to hit the base condition (i. e., the exponent becomes 0) as the exponent is always negative. This is because the β value from the extended Euclid algorithm can take a negative value. For example, in our previous example, gcd (30, 20), we have − 1 for β. If β is negative, we can force it to be positive by adding the totient value (see line 70 in Listing 5-6).

In addition, when generating k random numbers less than a large number, we first tried the handy random.sample(range(N), k) function. But since N is huge, it caused an overflow error: Python int too large to convert to C ssize_t. Instead, we resorted to random.randint(N) (line 47).

Furthermore, the fast_modular_arithmetic method may fail at larger prime numbers p and q with 1500 bits or above where the same stack overflow message showed up. For the current program, we stick to 1000 bits for p and q, on the safe side. This is expected as more bits are introduced, more work needs to be done for modular operations. It is fine to choose a thousand − bit prime number for p and q.

Let us encrypt a message: "Stay hungry. Stay foolish!" For converting the Unicode characters to integers, we can use the built-in ord function. For example, ord ("S") returns 83, ord(" ")→ 32 and ord(".")→ 46 and ord("!") → 33. Then the message is represented in integer form as 8311697121321041171101031141214632831169712132102111111110810511510433. The reverse function is chr that takes in an integer as input and returns the corresponding character.

After running RSA algorithm, the encrypted message becomes 274048837315349413830944253740649285089457986612143670943949246041337497333326621671636664544673503901886956027512693481064463522857392406448045385284711854480373805114213416136025422356787298483876054560762246062028678969863054767591534292852824031965577576244823083938800050182839301216888975866207363618659815270863900435578417196988540540036307828014357275226706493672678632378315741764630176947128510306525156177968411928884123061802795151675933795090101454209722961391375566177.

We can get the original message back by calling the rsa_decrypt method. The intermediate parameters including p, q, e, N, d, and totient are also printed out; see below.

132

CHAPTER 5   RSA CRYPTOSYSTEM

```
In [6]: run Listing_5_6_rsa_all_in_one.py
```

Original message is 8311697121321041171101031141214632831169712132102111111108105115110433

p -->
7937135350224987544523768059148611489821522810049229164771015606954550216386093246527934649428926561297637887709994011595804412685303289331513597978096129982074745324133403124252693663156713057149239637016846331359166761510670397322306103653440183330864958373687493661786756290039288271759471989197771

q -->
8794792245718326640843345977958918180896487739834895483719520757544063375952667363884485704683047673200755298656600874613818525694681830061350798362276375991530415238099563629023087519400475291081936897750795064303425385155592458854743748638388267564201627574440041078796163654968240610163469221799111

e --> 7

N -->
6980545643137553523584531710576964171363143237807623854155949146895428900582241475223615897100760201438497641513625441973474219953186930272567680332953111100574361111357207338382571621150146806967349134999079584331308893076332795915886220393715858292505168162967837596500838414122625370328776254189631282805889540362512346454647286086741229016417070905510531039112165060946287158923852691416532802845041208683809615899088195041360963769435140137333511252355716021855196954726374975984348374265462808023565316161685398561006154234325235408996707547768643102994207132017081522262500399715017015942217838

d -->
39888832246500305849054466917582652407789389930329279166605423696545308003327094144134947983432915436791415094363573954134138399732496744414672459045446349146139206350612613362186123549429410325527709342851883339036050817579044548090778402249804904528600960931244786265719076652129287830450150023940740626360742548749107484247117666493773930852906672192224095670536538087376508702431777446254531884069596784811726002795328436656202780698293572968869022146271961389545157821586625575673363989753354655376492134730893986462877321542882613492257026552913797662177679898514942199982553077038511051720457543

totient -->
6980545643137553523584531710576964171363143237807623854155949146895428900582241475223615897100760201438497641513625441973474219953186930272567680332953111100574361111357207338382571621150146806967349134999079584331308893076332795915886220393715858292505168162967837596500838414122625370328776254189629609613129946031093809743245591636410437899258667633639216742343894165290889022925561053094543079712179437342052050489182476414835486622201375269552078875597593243170402618777659475742838698206837064690886123577906447631003531270004457361144979646759914590881093982240114884996946788481739434051080070

message --> 8311697121321041171101031141214632831169712132102111111108105115110433

Encrypted message is
2740488373153494138309442537406492850894579866121436709439492460413374973332662167163666454467350390188695602751269348106446352285739240644804538528471185448037805114213416136025422356787298483876054560762246062028678969863054767591534292852824031965577576244823083938800050182839301216888975866207363618659815270863900435578417196988540540036307828014357275226706493672678632378315741764630176947128510306525156177968411928884123061802795151675933795090101454209722961391375566177

Decrypted message is
8311697121321041171101031141214632831169712132102111111108105115110433

133

CHAPTER 5   RSA CRYPTOSYSTEM

Application

RSA is a cornerstone of modern cryptography and plays a critical role in securing communications over the Internet. RSA is central to Secure Sockets Layer (SSL)/Transport Layer Security (TLS), the cryptographic protocols that encrypt data sent over networks (such as HTTPS for websites). RSA helps encrypt the session key during the initial handshake, ensuring a private and secure communication between the client and server. As another example, RSA is used for creating digital signatures where it can verify a message or document has not been altered and it was indeed sent by the purported sender. RSA also finds applications in email encryption protocols such as Pretty Good Privacy (PGP) and Secure/Multipurpose Internet Mail Extensions (S/MIME).

Summary

In this chapter, we review the RSA Cryptosystem. It is a public key cryptosystem where both sender and receiver know the public key, whereas only the receiver has the private key to decrypt the message. The security of RSA lies in the fact that it is difficult to factor a large integer number (e.g., in Section "An Improved Version of RSA", the N is of ~600 digits). As a reference to the state of the art, the mathematicians are excited at being able to factor the ninth Fermat number $2^{512}-1$ by using a nationwide network of computers, which has "only" 155 decimal digits. Barred from any breakthrough, the RSA will remain secure.

We start the chapter by implementing a naïve version of RSA where the prime number chosen is so small that it can be guessed by brute force. In the enhanced version of RSA, we have chosen prime numbers with a thousand bits. To handle mathematical operations on large numbers, we have introduced several techniques including (1) the Euclidean algorithm to find the Greatest Common Divisor of two integers, (2) repeated squaring to do fast modular arithmetic, (3) Fermat's Little Theorem for primality test, and (4) the Extended Euclidean Algorithm to find the private key. We close the chapter by encrypting and decrypting a real message using the RSA algorithm.

CHAPTER 6

Monte Carlo

The movie *Oppenheimer*, directed by Christopher Nolan, is a great hit, bagging a whopping seven Academy Awards including Best Picture, Best Director, Best Actor, and Best Supporting Actor. The movie unfolds against the backdrop of the Manhattan Project. During the famous Manhattan Project, computer simulations were used to simulate nuclear chain reactions. The Monte Carlo method was invented at the same time by Stanislaw Ulam and John von Neumann. In this chapter, we will learn how to generate random numbers and test their uniformity and independence statistically. We will also see Monte Carlo in action: from finding the value of π to solving integrals. We will further introduce the Markov Chain Monte Carlo and one of its applications: drawing samples from a probability density function using the Metropolis–Hastings algorithm. We will conclude the chapter by presenting an application of Monte Carlo in simulating the endemic.

Generate a Random Number

Monte Carlo is a simple but beautiful technique. You give a series of instructions to a computing machine, let it run the experiment many times, and each time feed it with random inputs. The result from this type of experiment can then be utilized to approximate the outcome of a real event. It is a simulation technique that leverages random numbers to gain insights into problems that would have otherwise been mathematically intractable. It is more like an engineering way of finding an approximate result rather than giving a robust mathematical proof.

The key to the success of the Monte Carlo method is the generation of random numbers. In the early days, people generated random numbers by casting lots, throwing dices, dealing out cards, or drawing numbered balls from a well-stirred urn. Some publishers also published a big book of 1 million random numbers. Of course, as long as it was published, it is not random anymore.

CHAPTER 6 MONTE CARLO

Back then at Los Alamos, two great minds, John von Neumann and Nicholas Metropolis, devised the famous *mid-square method*. Here is how it works: You start with a four-digit integer, square it, pick up the middle four digits, and repeat. You would end up with a sequence of random numbers. For example, you start with $X_0 = 6632$, square it to get 43983424, and take the middle part for $X_1 = 9834$. Do it again to get $X_2 = 7075$.

This seems to be a smart way to generate random numbers, and it is easy to code it up (Listing 6-1). And using a seed number of 6632, we get 20 random numbers, [0.9834, 0.7075, 0.0556, 0.3091, 0.5542, 0.7137, 0.9367, 0.7406, 0.8488, 0.0461, 0.2125, 0.5156, 0.5843, 0.1406, 0.9768, 0.4138, 0.123, 0.5129, 0.3066, 0.4003].

Listing 6-1. Generate a random number using the mid-square method

```
1.  def random_number_mid_square_method(seed_num, N):
2.      random_numbers = []
3.      fractional_numbers = []
4.      cur_num = seed_num
5.      random_numbers.append((0, None, seed_num))
6.      fractional_numbers.append(seed_num / 10000.)
7.      for i in range(N):
8.          prev_num = cur_num
9.          squared_num = str(prev_num ** 2).zfill(8)
10.         middle_part = int(squared_num[2:6])
11.         random_numbers.append((i + 1, int(squared_num), int(middle_part)))
12.         fractional_numbers.append(int(middle_part) / 10000.)
13.         cur_num = int(middle_part)
14.     return random_numbers, fractional_numbers
15.
16. if __name__ == "__main__":
17.     print (random_number_mid_square_method(6632, 20)[1])
18.     print (random_number_mid_square_method(1009, 20)[1])
```

In [1]: run Listing_6_1_middle_square.py

[0.6632, 0.9834, 0.7075, 0.0556, 0.3091, 0.5542, 0.7137, 0.9367, 0.7406, 0.8488, 0.0461, 0.2125, 0.5156, 0.5843, 0.1406, 0.9768, 0.4138, 0.123, 0.5129, 0.3066, 0.4003]

[0.1009, 0.018, 0.0324, 0.1049, 0.1004, 0.008, 0.0064, 0.004, 0.0016, 0.0002, 0.0, 0.0, 0.0, 0.0, 0.0, 0.0, 0.0, 0.0, 0.0, 0.0, 0.0]

Let us try with different seeds, for example, 0003 or 1009? With a seed of 3, we get [0.0003, 0.0, 0.0, 0.0, 0.0, 0.0, 0.0, 0.0, 0.0, 0.0, 0.0, 0.0, 0.0, 0.0, 0.0, 0.0, 0.0, 0.0, 0.0, 0.0, 0.0]; with 1009, it is [0.1009, 0.018, 0.0324, 0.1049, 0.1004, 0.008, 0.0064, 0.004, 0.0016, 0.0002, 0.0, 0.0, 0.0, 0.0, 0.0, 0.0, 0.0, 0.0, 0.0, 0.0, 0.0]. Alas, the numbers degenerate!

The *mid-square method* certainly has limitations. Inspired by the Fibonacci sequence, some proposed the following to get random numbers:

$$X_i = (X_{i-1} + X_{i-2}) \% m, i = 1, 2 \ldots$$

where X_{-1} and X_0 are seeds, then the random number $R_i = X_i/m$.

Unfortunately, this is a horrible method as the numbers generated are monotonously increasing, not random at all. Before we talk about good random number generators, let us ponder: Can a deterministic computer generate truly random numbers? No, it cannot. The computer can at best generate a long sequence of non-repeating numbers. However, if the sequence is long enough, for example, in the order of a billion numbers, then this sequence of numbers, usually called pseudorandom numbers (PRNs), can be used for practical applications such as in gambling, engineering, and stock market prediction. On the other hand, to get truly random numbers, one needs to rely on the truly random events occurring in nature such as atmospheric noise, thermal noise, and other external electromagnetic/quantum phenomena. Oh, yes, you can also turn to lava lamps for help! As shown in the video [9], one can leverage the stochastic nature of the lava lamp to generate random numbers. If you take a snapshot of the array of the lava lamps at the interval of even a split second, pixel by pixel, none of these snapshots will be the same. Believe it or not, the security of the Internet can be protected by lava lamps!

Let us now look at the Linear Congruential Generator (LCG). The computer uses LCG to generate random numbers. A typical procedure is as follows:

(1) Choose an integer "seed", $X(0)$.

(2) Set $X(i) = a\, X(i - 1) \% m$, where a and m are carefully chosen constants.

(3) Set the ith pseudorandom number as $U(i) = X(i)/m$.

As an example, let set seed $X(0) = 4$, and set $X(i) = 5\, X(i-1) \% 7$. Then $X(1) = 20 \% 7 = 6$, $X(2) = 2$, $X(3) = 3$, $X(4) = 1$, $X(5) = 5$, etc. Then $U(1) = X(1)/m = 6/7$, $U(2) = 2/7$, $U(3) = 3/7$.

Obviously, since the cycle is just 7, the PRNs are not random enough. Here is a better LCG, also called *Desert Island Generator*, which is used in several simulation languages and has nice properties, including long cycle times. Below is its formula. Can we find the first 20 random numbers from it? Let us set the seed as 12345678 and implement it in Listing 6-2.

CHAPTER 6   MONTE CARLO

$$X_i = 16807 X_{i-1} \% (2^{31}-1), i=1,2,3\ldots$$

$$R_i = X_i / (2^{31}-1), i=1,2,3\ldots$$

Listing 6-2. Implement a Desert Island Generator

```
1.  def linear_congruent_generator_16807(seed, N):
2.      random_nums = [seed]
3.      cycle = 2**31 - 1
4.      prev_num = seed
5.      for _ in range(N):
6.          cur_num = 16807 * prev_num % cycle
7.          random_nums.append(cur_num)
8.          prev_num = cur_num
9.      return [round(rand_num / cycle, 4) for rand_num in random_nums]
10.
11. if __name__ == "__main__":
12.     print (linear_congruent_generator_16807(12345678, 20))
```

In [2]: run Listing_6_2_linear_congruent_generator_16807.py

[0.0057, 0.6218, 0.1772, 0.0029, 0.8434, 0.762, 0.6095, 0.6834, 0.2, 0.693, 0.5222, 0.161, 0.2775, 0.5923, 0.1444, 0.1316, 0.0235, 0.1857, 0.3281, 0.1644]

The first 20 random numbers from LCG-16807 are 0.0057, 0.6218, 0.1772, 0.0029, 0.8434, 0.762, 0.6095, 0.6834, 0.2, 0.693, 0.5222, 0.161, 0.2775, 0.5923, 0.1444, 0.1316, 0.0235, 0.1857, 0.3281, 0.1644.

It is easy to note that the seed plays an important role. Once the formula and seed are set, the sequence of PRN is determined. In simulation, you can set a seed for consistent results and debugging. But in general, you need different sequences of PRNs to do the Monte Carlo simulation. In such a case, we can resort to the Python random package. It will generate a distinct random seed each time based on your system time. By the way, Python uses the Mersenne Twister developed by Makoto Matsumoto and Takuji Nishimura [10], which has a period of $2^{19937} - 1$.

Test Uniformity and Independence of Random Numbers

We have just explored various ways to generate pseudorandom numbers using a computer. We need ways to test how good these numbers are. To be specific, we are going to test the uniformity and the independence of the generated number sequence.

CHAPTER 6   MONTE CARLO

To test the quality of the random numbers, we will do a statistical test. Our null hypothesis H_0 would be *the generated sequence is uniform (or independent)* and the alternative hypothesis H_1 would be the opposite – *the sequence is not uniform (or independent)*. We will calculate some test statistic z_0 and compare it with the value derived from the probability density distribution. This comparison will help us accept or reject the null hypothesis H_0. One real – life example of the statistical test comes from the pharmaceutical field. In the United States, the pharmaceutical companies must conduct clinical trials before submitting drugs to the Food and Drug Administration (FDA) for approval. The null hypothesis H_0 in a clinical trial would be that the drug is not effective in curing the disease. The alternative hypothesis H_1 is that the drug is effective. In such scenarios, a *p* value is often calculated and is compared against α, the significance level, which is usually chosen as 0.05. If *p* value is less than α, we reject the null hypothesis, and the study is considered statistically significant.

We will do four tests on random numbers. The first is to test if the numbers are **uniform** within [0,1]. Here, the null hypothesis is that *the observations are uniform*. We will do a χ^2 goodness-of-fit test. Let us look at one example in Figure 6-1.

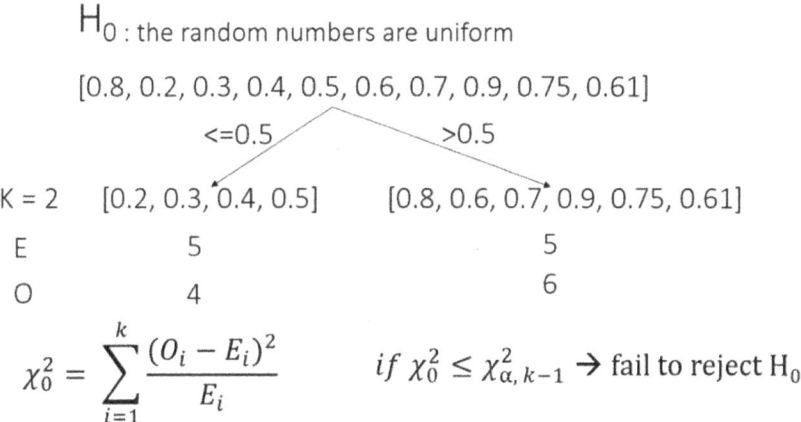

Figure 6-1. Uniformity test on an array of numbers

Suppose we have generated a sequence of 10 random numbers [0.8, 0.2, 0.3, 0.4, 0.5, 0.6, 0.7, 0.9, 0.75, 0.61]. We decide to divide the numbers into *k* groups (in the example *k*=2). We then count how many observations fall into *k* buckets. In our example, bucket 1 holds numbers in the range [0, 0.5], and bucket 2 holds numbers (0.5, 1.0]. If the numbers are uniform, we would expect each bucket to have 5 (i.e., E_i) numbers, but the count numbers O_i may deviate from the expectation. A test statistic χ_0^2 is calculated and compared with the $\chi_{\alpha,k-1}^2$ to decide if we keep or reject the null hypothesis.

CHAPTER 6   MONTE CARLO

We can find the $\chi^2_{\alpha,k-1}$ programmatically by using `scipy.stats.chi2.ppf(1-α, k-1)` where α is the significance level and $k-1$ is the degree of freedom. In this dummy example, $\chi^2_0 = 0.4$ and $\chi^2_{0.05,1} = 3.84$. Since $\chi^2_0 < \chi^2_{0.05,1}$, we fail to reject the null hypothesis. We can now claim that the numbers are uniform.

Moving on, we will do tests to check if the numbers are independent. Here, the null hypothesis is that *the observations are independent*. In the **Up and down** test, we convert the numbers into either a "+" or "-" sign. Start from the second number and look at its left neighbor; if it is bigger than the neighbor, then we record a "+" sign, otherwise a "-" sign. In contrast, for the **Above and below the mean** test, if the number is bigger than or equal to 0.5, we place a "+" sign, otherwise a "-" sign. Then we count how many consecutive "+" or "-" signs. In both cases, both counts are 3; see Figure 6-2.

[0.8, 0.2, 0.3, 0.4, 0.5, 0.6, 0.7, 0.9, 0.75, 0.61]
[0.8, -, +, +, +, +, +, +, -, -]   Up and down test   A = 3
[+, -, -, -, +, +, +, +, +, +]   Above and below the mean test   B = 3

Figure 6-2. *Test the independence of random numbers*

Let A denote the total number of runs "up and down" out of n observations. If n is large (≥ 20) and numbers are independent, then

$$A \approx Nor\left(\frac{2n-1}{3}, \frac{16n-29}{90}\right)$$

$$Z_0 = \frac{A - E[A]}{\sqrt{Var(A)}}$$

where $Nor(\mu, \sigma)$ denotes the normal distribution with a mean of μ and a standard deviation of σ. Likewise, let B denote the total number of runs "above and below the mean test" out of n observations, of which n_1 observations ≥ 0.5 and n_2 observations < 0.5. If n is large (≥ 20) and numbers are independent, then

$$B \approx Nor\left(\frac{2n_1 n_2}{n} + \frac{1}{2}, \frac{2n_1 n_2(2n_1 n_2 - n)}{n^2(n-1)}\right)$$

$$Z_0 = \frac{B - E[B]}{\sqrt{Var(B)}}$$

A third test on independence is the **autocorrelation test**. We define the lag-1 correlation of random numbers R_is by $\rho = Corr(R_i, R_{i+1})$. Ideally ρ should equal 0. An estimator for ρ is

$$\hat{\rho} = \left(\frac{12}{n-1} \sum_{k=1}^{n-1} R_k R_{k+1} \right) - 3$$

$$\hat{\rho} \approx Nor\left(0, \frac{13n-19}{(n-1)^2} \right)$$

The test statistic $Z_0 = \hat{\rho} / \sqrt{Var(\hat{\rho})}$.

In all three tests, we reject H_0 if $|Z_0| > z_{\alpha/2}$. If $\alpha = 0.05$. then $z_{\alpha/2} = 1.96$.

We can now incorporate all these four statistical tests into a Python class StatisticalTestRandomNumbers (in Listing 6-3) that takes a sequence of random numbers as an input and has four methods to test uniformity and independence of the random numbers specified by the users. Let us generate, say, 10000 random numbers using Python's built-in random package and test its uniformity and independence. Sure enough, it passes all four tests.

CHAPTER 6   MONTE CARLO

Listing 6-3. Statistical tests on uniformity and independence of randomly generated numbers

```
1.   import scipy.stats as stats
2.   import random
3.   random.seed(1234)
4.
5.   class StatisticalTestRandomNumbers:
6.       def __init__(self, nums):
7.           self.nums = nums
8.           self.N = len(self.nums)
9.
10.      def count_num_plus_minus(self, plus_and_minus):
11.          if not plus_and_minus:
12.              return
13.
14.          count = 1
15.          last_seen = plus_and_minus[0]
16.          for i in range(1, len(plus_and_minus)):
17.              cur_sign = plus_and_minus[i]
18.              if cur_sign == last_seen:
19.                  continue
20.              else:
21.                  count += 1
22.                  last_seen = cur_sign
23.          return count
24.
25.      def uniformity_chi_square_test(self, k):
26.          E, remainder = divmod(self.N, k)
27.          if remainder != 0:
28.              raise Exception(f"The random numbers cannot be equally divided into {k} parts")
29.
30.          interval_size = 1. / k
31.          chi_square = 0
32.          for i in range(k):
33.              O = 0
34.              lower_bound = i * interval_size
35.              upper_bound = (i + 1) * interval_size
36.              for num in self.nums:
37.                  if lower_bound <num <= upper_bound:
38.                      O += 1
39.              chi_square += (O - E)**2 / E
40.          chi_square_table_value = stats.chi2.ppf(0.95, k- 1)
41.          print (f"chisquare = {chi_square}")
42.          if chi_square > chi_square_table_value:
43.              return False
44.          return True
45.
46.      def independence_up_and_down_test(self):
47.          plus_and_minus = []
48.          for i in range(1, self.N):
49.              if self.nums[i] >= self.nums[i-1]:
50.                  plus_and_minus.append("+")
51.              else:
52.                  plus_and_minus.append("-")
53.          A = self.count_num_plus_minus(plus_and_minus)
54.          n = self.N
```

```python
55.            u = (2*n - 1) / 3
56.            sigma = ((16 * n - 29) / 90)**0.5
57.            z0 = abs((A - u) / sigma)
58.            # alpha = 0.05
59.            print(f"z0 = {z0}")
60.            if z0 > 1.96:
61.                return False
62.            return True
63.
64.        def independence_above_and_below_mean_test(self):
65.            plus_and_minus = []
66.            n1 = 0 # number of observations >=0.5
67.            n2 = 0 # number of observations <0.5
68.            n = self.N
69.            for num in self.nums:
70.                if num >= 0.5:
71.                    plus_and_minus.append("+")
72.                    n1 += 1
73.                else:
74.                    plus_and_minus.append("-")
75.                    n2 += 1
76.            B = self.count_num_plus_minus(plus_and_minus)
77.            u = 2 * n1 * n2 / n + 0.5
78.            sigma = (2 * n1 * n2 *(2 * n1 * n2 - n) / (n**2 * (n-1)))**0.5
79.            z0 = abs((B - u) / sigma)
80.            print(f"z0 = {z0}")
81.            if z0 > 1.96:
82.                return False
83.            return True
84.
85.        def independence_correlation_test(self):
86.            n = self.N
87.            corr_sum = 0
88.            for i in range(n - 1):
89.                corr_sum += self.nums[i] * self.nums[i+1]
90.            rou = (12. / (n-1)) * corr_sum - 3.
91.            sigma = ((13 * n - 19) / (n -1)**2)**0.5
92.            z0 = rou / sigma
93.            print(f"z0 = {z0}")
94.            if z0 > 1.96:
95.                return False
96.            return True
97.
98.    if __name__ == "__main__":
99.        rand_nums_from_python = [random.random() for _ in range(10000)]
100.       test_random_nums = StatisticalTestRandomNumbers(nums = rand_nums_from_python)
101.       # chi square test
102.       print(test_random_nums.uniformity_chi_square_test(5))
103.       # up and down test
104.       print(test_random_nums.independence_up_and_down_test())
105.       # above and below mean test
106.       print(test_random_nums.independence_above_and_below_mean_test())
107.       # correlation test
108.       print(test_random_nums.independence_correlation_test())
```

CHAPTER 6 MONTE CARLO

```
In [3]: run Listing_6_3_statistical_test_random_numbers.py
chisquare = 2.726
True
z0 = 0.5850743919007171
True
z0 = 0.9077623096792725
True
z0 = 1.070576252162124
True
```

Examples of Simple Monte Carlo Simulations

When introducing Monte Carlo simulations, the numerical estimation of π is often used as an example. The way to approach it is intuitive. Consider a circle of radius r inscribed in a square in the Cartesian system. We know the area ratio of the circle to the unit square is

$$\frac{S_{circle}}{S_{square}} = \frac{\pi r^2}{(2r)^2} = \frac{\pi}{4}$$

$$\pi = 4 \times \frac{S_{circle}}{S_{square}}$$

The rest of the task is to find the area ratio of the circle to the square.

To calculate the ratio, we can generate a random point (x, y) with $-1 \leq x, y \leq 1$ and see if it falls inside the circle or outside of it. Then π can be calculated based on the following formula:

$$\pi = 4 \times \frac{Count\ Points\ Inside\ Circle}{Total\ Count\ Random\ Points}$$

This is illustrated in Figure 6-3 where random points fall either within the square (blue) or outside of it (red).

CHAPTER 6 MONTE CARLO

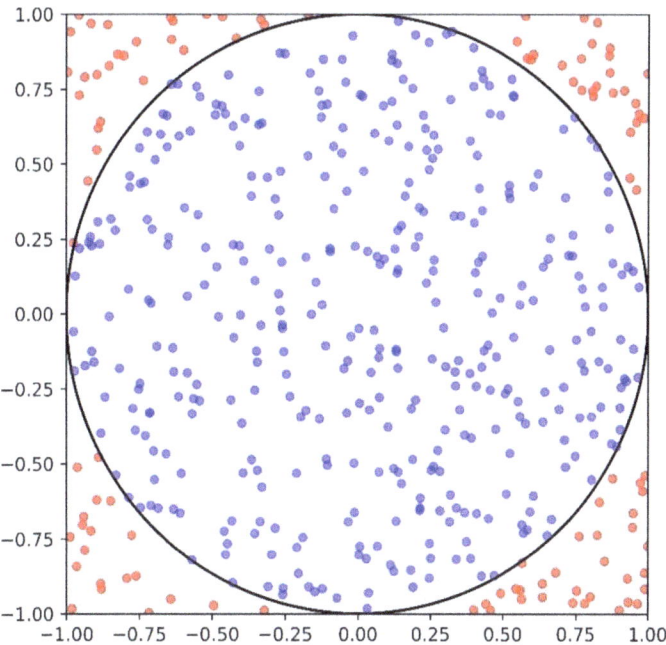

Figure 6-3. *Estimation of π by tracking points falling within the inscribed circle and the square*

The code to generate Figure 6-3 is in Listing 6-4.

Listing 6-4. Illustration of estimating the value of π using Monte Carlo

```
1.  import numpy as np
2.  import matplotlib.pyplot as plt
3.  np.random.seed(1234)
4.
5.  num_trials = 500
6.  x = np.random.uniform(low=-1.0, high=1.0, size=num_trials)
7.  y = np.random.uniform(low=-1.0, high=1.0, size=num_trials)
8.
9.  radius = 1.0
10. theta = np.linspace(0, 2 * np.pi, 1000)
11. x_circle = radius * np.cos(theta)
12. y_circle = radius * np.sin(theta)
13.
14. inside_circle = x ** 2 + y ** 2 <= 1
15. x_inside, x_outside = x[inside_circle], x[~inside_circle]
16. y_inside, y_outside = y[inside_circle], y[~inside_circle]
17. plt.scatter(x_inside, y_inside, s=20, c='b', alpha=0.5)
18. plt.scatter(x_outside, y_outside, s=20, c='r', alpha=0.5)
19. plt.plot(x_circle, y_circle, 'k')
20. plt.xlim(-1, 1)
21. plt.ylim(-1, 1)
22. plt.gca().set_aspect('equal')
23. plt.tight_layout()
24. plt.show()
```

145

CHAPTER 6   MONTE CARLO

To implement it programmatically, we can use random.uniform(-1,1) to generate random points and count how many of those are within the square; see Listing 6-5 and Figure 6-4.

Listing 6-5. Find π using the Monte Carlo method

```
1.  import numpy as np
2.  import matplotlib.pyplot as plt
3.  np.random.seed(1234)
4.
5.  def compute_pi(N_trials):
6.      x = np.random.uniform(low=-1.0, high=1.0, size=N_trials)
7.      y = np.random.uniform(low=-1.0, high=1.0, size=N_trials)
8.      inside_circle = x ** 2 + y ** 2 <= 1
9.      pi = 4.0 * np.sum(inside_circle) / N_trials
10.     return pi
11.
12. x = [10**i for i in range(8)]
13. y = [compute_pi(i) for i in x]
14. x_log = [np.log10(i) for i in x]
15. plt.plot(x_log, y, 'bo-', markersize = 12)
16. plt.xlabel('Number of trials, log10', fontsize = 12)
17. plt.ylabel('Computed Pi', fontsize = 12)
18. plt.title('Compute Pi with Monte Carlo')
19. plt.hlines(np.pi, min(x_log), max(x_log), 'r', 'dotted', lw=2)
20. plt.tight_layout()
21. plt.show()
```

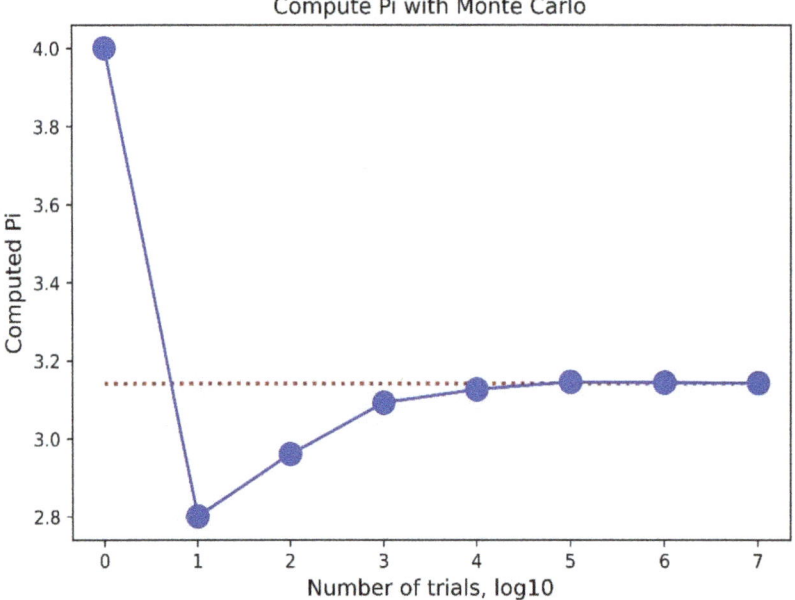

Figure 6-4. *The accuracy of numerical estimation of π increases with increasing number of simulations. The red dotted line denotes the true value of π*

CHAPTER 6   MONTE CARLO

As shown in Figure 6-4, the simulated value of π stabilizes after ~10000 trials. The Monte Carlo simulation result is close to the true value.

Here is another fun problem. Say you have a rod of unit length, and you accidentally break it into three pieces. What is the probability that the three pieces can form a triangle? Suppose, the lengths of three broken pieces are a, b, c. In order to form a triangle, and according to the Triangle Inequality Theorem, these conditions must be satisfied, i.e., $a + b > c$, $a + c > b$, and $b + c > a$. We can run many trials using the Monte Carlo technique. Now the key task is to generate three random numbers such that their sum is equal to 1. Here we are looking for a *Dirichlet distribution*, and we can use numpy.random.dirichlet to generate random values for a, b, c with a constraint that $a + b + c = 1$.

The implementation now becomes straightforward (Listing 6-6). After 100,000 trials, the probability of forming a triangle is estimated to be ~0.25.

Listing 6-6. The probability of forming a triangle with a broken rod

```
import numpy as np

def can_form_valid_triangle(a, b, c):
    if a + b > c  and a + c > b and b + c > a:
        return True
    return False

def probability_form_a_triangle(num_trials = 100000):
    success = 0
    for i in range(num_trials):
        a, b, c = np.random.dirichlet(np.ones(3), size = 1)[0]
        if can_form_valid_triangle(a, b, c):
            success += 1
    return success / num_trials

if __name__ == "__main__":
    print (probability_form_a_triangle())
```

```
In [4]: run Listing_6_6_broken_rod.py

0.25137
```

We can also draw random numbers from different probability distributions and feed them to a Monte Carlo simulation. In the following example (Figure 6-5), suppose we have three metal parts of rectangular shapes. The length of the first part follows a triangular distribution with min, mode, and max of 3.5, 4, and 5, respectively. The second follows a Gaussian of mean and standard deviation of 6 and 1, respectively. The last piece follows a uniform distribution with min and max of 4.5 and 5.5, respectively. The question is, when joining them together head-to-head, can they fit in a mold of 15 in length?

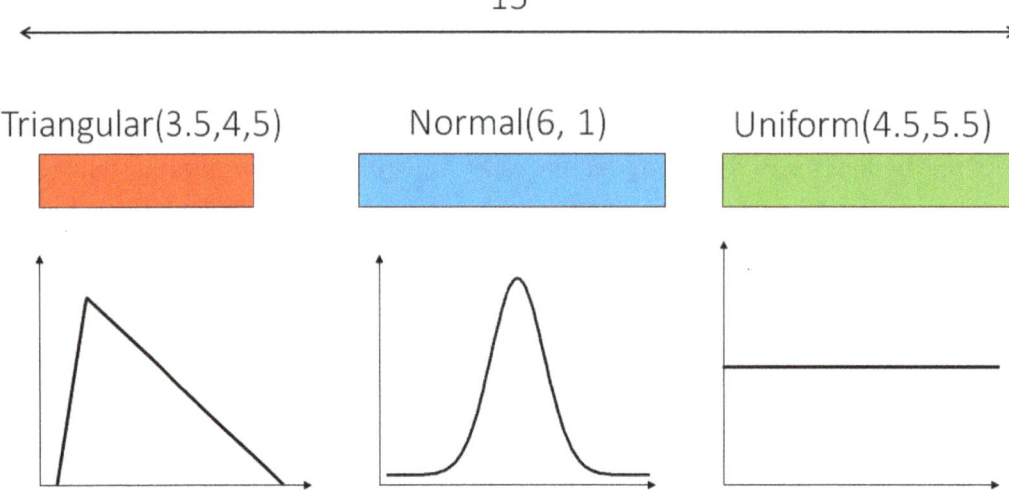

Figure 6-5. *The lengths of the three method parts follow different distributions*

The numpy.random module has implementations of probability distributions of various sorts, including the triangular, normal, and uniform distributions we are interested in. The code is shown in Listing 6-7. After 1 million trials, the probability of fitting pieces into the mold is estimated to be ~0.44.

Listing 6-7. *The probability of fitting metal parts to a mold*

```
1.  import numpy as np
2.  np.random.seed(1234)
3.  def prob_fitting_parts_in_a_mold(num_trials=1000000):
4.      length_mold = 15
5.      part_1_length = np.random.triangular(3.5,4,5, num_trials)
6.      part_2_length = np.random.normal(6,1, num_trials)
7.      part_3_length = np.random.uniform(4.5, 5.5, num_trials)
8.      total_part_length = part_1_length + part_2_length + part_3_length
9.      num_success_trials = sum(total_part_length <=length_mold)
10.     return num_success_trials / num_trials
11.
12. if __name__ == "__main__":
13.     print (prob_fitting_parts_in_a_mold())
```

```
In [5]: run Listing_6_7_fitting_parts_in_a_mold.py
0.440198
```

Just want to add a few words about the triangular distribution. A closely related distribution, the PERT distribution [11], is often used in Commercial Forecasting. It takes the same min, mode, and max values as inputs, but it has a much smoother probability density curve than the triangular counterpart. The Commercial Forecasting is complicated with various linear and nonlinear steps. Nonetheless, we can still resort to Monte Carlo to perform uncertainty estimation, i.e., putting error bars on the output parameters. The procedure is essentially similar to the simple examples discussed above: we repeatedly draw samples from input distributions and go through various calculation steps before arriving at the outputs. Since outputs are also distributions, we can do typical statistical analysis on them, such as estimation of a confidence interval. Throughout the entire procedure, we can also perform a sensitivity analysis to check how sensitive it is that the outputs respond to the perturbation of the inputs.

Monte Carlo Integration

Another application of Monte Carlo simulation is to calculate the integral numerically. Suppose we have a finite integral and we want to find its result.

$$I = \int_0^5 \sqrt[5]{10x^4 + 15x^3 + 25x^2 + 35x + 50} \times e^{-x} dx$$

It is certainly challenging to solve it by hand. But as a numerical estimation, we can plot it first and see what it looks like (Figure 6-6).

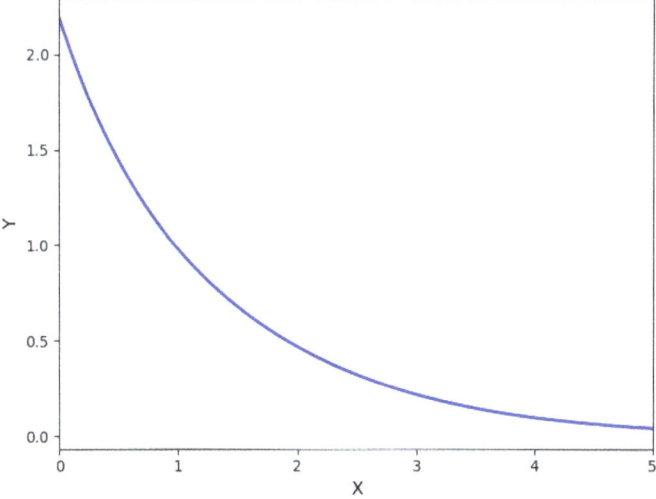

Figure 6-6. *A plot of the integrand*

CHAPTER 6   MONTE CARLO

Despite its seemingly complicated mathematical formula, its plot is easy to interpret – the curve has a max value of $\sqrt[5]{50} \approx 2.1867$ at $x = 0$ and smoothly decreases to ~ 0.0416 at $x = 5$. To estimate the value of the integral, we can compute the area under the curve.

In numerical computation, several popular methods are used to estimate a finite integral. The first is the Riemann sum. It approximates the area under the curve from a to b by adding up the areas of n adjacent rectangles of width $\Delta x = (b - a)/n$ and height $f(x_i)$ where $x_i = a + i \times \Delta x$ is the right-hand endpoint of the ith rectangle.

$$\int_a^b f(x)dx \approx \sum_{i=1}^{n} f(x_i)\Delta x = \frac{b-a}{n}\sum_{i=1}^{n} f\left(a + \frac{i(b-a)}{n}\right)$$

Next is the numerical integration via the Trapezoid Rule. Instead of dividing the area under the curve into rectangles, one can divide it into trapezoids. The formula to estimate the integral is listed below. The Trapezoid Rule works a little better than Riemann since approximation as a trapezoid is slightly more accurate than as a rectangle.

$$\int_a^b f(x)dx \approx \left[\frac{f(x_0)}{2} + \sum_{i=1}^{n-1} f(x_i) + \frac{f(x_n)}{2}\right]\Delta x = \frac{b-a}{n}\left[\frac{f(a)}{2} + \sum_{i=1}^{n-1} f\left(a + \frac{i(b-a)}{n}\right) + \frac{f(b)}{2}\right]$$

Lastly, we can do a Monte Carlo integration. There are in general two flavors. The first one resembles the example of the estimation of π. We bound the curve with a rectangle box whose area, call it S, can be easily calculated. Then we draw N uniform random points within the rectangle and count the points falling below the curve (C). Then the integral can be estimated as $S \times C/N$. The second method is *mean value method*. It works as follows. Let $U_1, U_2, \ldots U_n$ denote a sequence of uniform (0, 1) random numbers; one can estimate the integral using below formula.

$$\int_a^b f(x)dx \approx \frac{b-a}{n}\sum_{i=1}^{n} f\left(a + (b-a)U_i\right)$$

As in Listing 6-8, we have incorporated all these integration methods into a class MonteCarloIntegration. At line 7, we initialize seven parameters, with n being number of trials for Monte Carlo simulation, a and b being the limits of integral, whereas the last four specify the size of the rectangle used in the first Monte Carlo integration method discussed above. Whenever possible, we leverage the vectorization power of the numpy package to speed up things. The estimations of the current integral using various methods are printed to the console. We ran 1 million Monte Carlo trials.

Listing 6-8. Code for Monte Carlo integration

```
1.   import matplotlib.pyplot as plt
2.   import numpy as np
3.   from scipy import integrate
4.   np.random.seed(1234)
5.
6.   class MonteCarloIntegration:
7.       def __init__(self, n, a, b, xmin, xmax, ymin, ymax):
8.           self.n = n # 1000000
9.           self.a = a # 0
10.          self.b = b # 5
11.          self.xmin = xmin
12.          self.xmax = xmax
13.          self.ymin = ymin
14.          self.ymax = ymax
15.
16.      # define function
17.      def func(self, x):
18.          return (10 * x**4 + 15 * x**3 + 25 * x**2 + 35 * x + 50)**0.2 * np.exp(-x)
19.
20.      # plot curve
21.      def plot_func(self):
22.          x_arr = np.linspace(self.a, self.b, self.n)
23.          y_arr= self.func(x_arr)
24.          plt.plot(x_arr, y_arr, "b-", lw=2)
25.          plt.xlim([self.a,self.b])
26.          plt.xlabel("X", fontsize = 12)
27.          plt.ylabel("Y", fontsize = 12)
28.          plt.tight_layout()
29.          plt.show()
30.
31.      def area_under_curve_rectangle(self):
32.          # Riemann sum
33.          dx = (self.b-self.a) / self.n
34.          sigma_sum = np.sum(self.func(self.a + np.arange(1, self.n + 1) * dx))
35.          auc = dx * (sigma_sum)
36.          return auc
37.
38.      def area_under_curve_trapezoid(self):
39.          dx = (self.b - self.a)/self.n
40.          sigma_sum = np.sum(self.func(self.a + np.arange(1, self.n)*dx))
41.          auc = dx * (self.func(self.a) * 0.5 + self.func(self.b) * 0.5 + sigma_sum)
42.          return auc
43.
44.      def monte_carlo_mean_value_method(self):
45.          dx = (self.b - self.a) / self.n
46.          Us = np.random.uniform(size = self.n)
47.          I = dx * np.sum(self.func(self.a + (self.b-self.a) * Us))
48.          return I
49.
50.      def monte_carlo_area_ratio_method(self):
51.          rectangle_area = (self.xmax - self.xmin) * (self.ymax - self.ymin)
52.          random_pts_x = np.random.uniform(self.xmin,self.xmax,self.n)
53.          random_pts_y = np.random.uniform(self.ymin,self.ymax,self.n)
54.          pts_below_curve = np.sum(self.func(random_pts_x) > random_pts_y)
55.          I = rectangle_area * pts_below_curve / self.n
56.          return I
57.
```

```
58.     # Scipy Integration
59.     def scipy_quad_integration(self):
60.         I, error = integrate.quad(self.func, self.a, self.b)
61.         return I
62.
63.     def run_with_different_methods(self):
64.         try:
65.             I_rectangle = self.area_under_curve_rectangle()
66.             print (f"The integral is estimated to be {I_rectangle} via Riemann sum")
67.         except Exception as e:
68.             print (e)
69.
70.         try:
71.             I_trapezoid = self.area_under_curve_trapezoid()
72.             print (f"The integral is estimated to be {I_trapezoid} via Trapezoid
                    method")
73.         except Exception as e:
74.             print (e)
75.
76.         try:
77.             I_MC_mean_value = self.monte_carlo_mean_value_method()
78.             print (f"The integral is estimated to be {I_MC_mean_value} via Monte Carlo
                    mean value method")
79.         except Exception as e:
80.             print (e)
81.
82.         try:
83.             I_MC_area_ratio = self.monte_carlo_area_ratio_method()
84.             print (f"The integral is estimated to be {I_MC_area_ratio} via Monte Carlo
                    area ratio method")
85.         except Exception as e:
86.             print (e)
87.
88.         try:
89.             I_scipy_quad = self.scipy_quad_integration()
90.             print (f"The integral is estimated to be {I_scipy_quad} via SciPy quad
                    integration")
91.         except Exception as e:
92.             print (e)
93.
94. if __name__ == "__main__":
95.     smooth_integral = MonteCarloIntegration(1000000, 0, 5, 0, 5, 0, 2.2)
96.     smooth_integral.run_with_different_methods()
97.     rapid_varying_integral = MonteCarloIntegration(1000000, 0, 2, 0, 2, 0, 1)
98.     rapid_varying_integral.func = lambda x: (np.sin(1/(x * (2-x))))**2
99.     rapid_varying_integral.run_with_different_methods()
```

If we trust SciPy's quad method as a golden standard, then the integral should be evaluated to a value ~2.72728151947. Indeed, the trapezoidal method returns the same value up to the 11th decimal point. Riemann sum agrees up to the fourth decimal point. Both Monte Carlo methods are accurate to the second decimal point.

CHAPTER 6   MONTE CARLO

```
In [6]: run Listing_6_8_monte_carlo_integration.py
The integral is estimated to be 2.7272761566677823 via Riemann sum
The integral is estimated to be 2.7272815194783377 via Trapezoid method
The integral is estimated to be 2.7289312613125887 via Monte Carlo mean value method
The integral is estimated to be 2.728506 via Monte Carlo area ratio method
The integral is estimated to be 2.7272815194744933 via SciPy quad integration
```

The integration of a smooth curve does not showcase the strength of Monte Carlo integration. Let us now look at another integral [12].

$$I = \int_0^2 \sin^2\left[\frac{1}{x(2-x)}\right] dx$$

This is a tricky integral because if we plug in the lower bound and upper bound values into the integral, we would encounter a `ZeroDivisionError`. Anyway, let us plot it first using the `plot_func` method of `MonteCarloIntegration`. We see wild oscillations at both ends (Figure 6-7).

```
1. rapid_varying_integral = MonteCarloIntegration(1000000, 0, 2, 0, 2, 0, 1)
2. rapid_varying_integral.func = lambda x: (np.sin(1/(x * (2-x))))**2
3. rapid_varying_integral.plot_func()
```

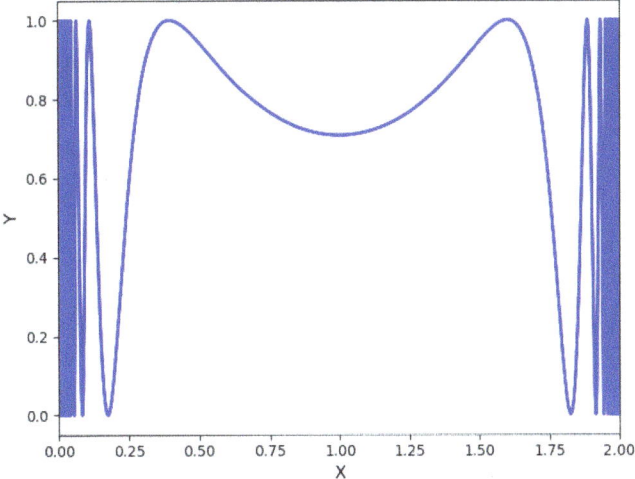

Figure 6-7. *A plot of a rapidly varying integrand at both limits*

CHAPTER 6   MONTE CARLO

Why don't we try estimating the integral value using different methods in the MonteCarloIntegration class, which would be straightforward by calling run_with_different_methods(). As a result, both the Riemann sum and trapezoidal methods broke. In contrast, both Monte Carlo methods survived. The integral is estimated to be ~1.45.

```
In [7]: run Listing_6_8_monte_carlo_integration.py
~\CODE\LISTING\Listing_6_8_monte_carlo_integration.py:99: RuntimeWarning: divide by zero encountered in true_divide
  rapid_varying_integral.func = lambda x: (np.sin(1/(x * (2-x))))**2
~\CODE\LISTING\Listing_6_8_monte_carlo_integration.py:99: RuntimeWarning: invalid value encountered in sin
  rapid_varying_integral.func = lambda x: (np.sin(1/(x * (2-x))))**2
The integral is estimated to be nan via Riemann sum
division by zero
The integral is estimated to be 1.4512644165779052 via Monte Carlo mean value method
The integral is estimated to be 1.451394 via Monte Carlo area ratio method
~\CODE\LISTING\Listing_6_8_monte_carlo_integration.py:61: IntegrationWarning: The maximum number of subdivisions (50) has been achieved.
  If increasing the limit yields no improvement it is advised to analyze
  the integrand in order to determine the difficulties.  If the position of a
  local difficulty can be determined (singularity, discontinuity) one will
  probably gain from splitting up the interval and calling the integrator
  on the subranges.  Perhaps a special-purpose integrator should be used.
    I, error = integrate.quad(self.func, self.a, self.b)
The integral is estimated to be 1.4516877509810684 via SciPy quad integration
```

As we can see, Monte Carlo is good at solving integrals with non-smooth curves. Additionally, it is known for better solving multiple integrals than traditional methods.

How Likely Will It Rain Tomorrow?

Here is a fun problem. Suppose we know that if today is sunny, then it is 90% likely that tomorrow is also sunny; conversely, if today is rainy, then there is a half/half chance that tomorrow is sunny or rainy. For a random day in the future, what is the probability of sunny and/or rainy for that day?

We can think of it as a full binary tree, as in Figure 6-8. Starting from the root node, initially, we can assume there is a 50% chance of rain or sunny. Then, according to the conditions given, we can iteratively construct the tree as below, with the transition probability between the states shown on the edge. Under the current setting, the probability that the day after tomorrow is sunny can be evaluated to be 0.78.

$$P(\text{Sunny the day after tomorrow}) = 0.5 \times 0.9 \times 0.9 + 0.5 \times 0.1 \times 0.5 + \\ 0.5 \times 0.5 \times 0.9 + 0.5 \times 0.5 \times 0.5 = 0.78$$

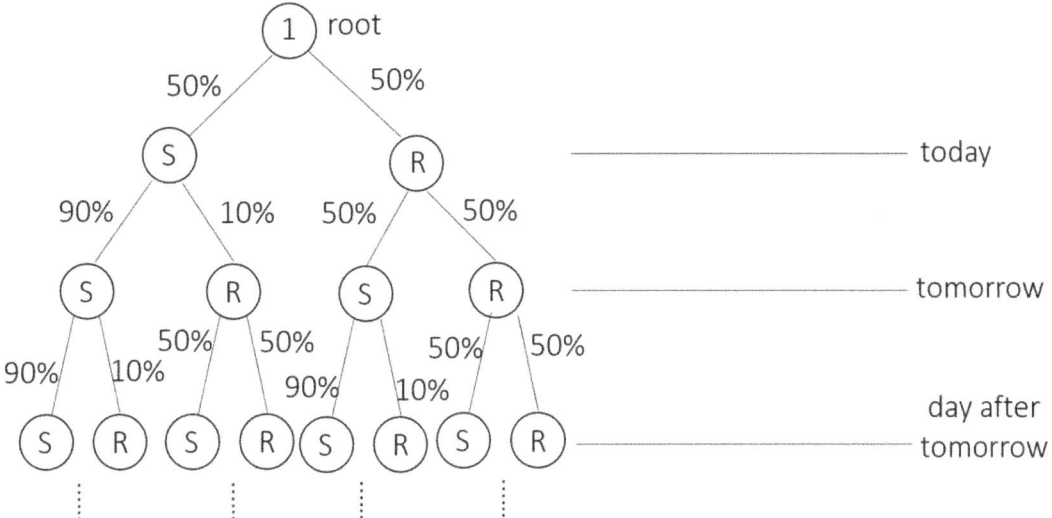

Figure 6-8. *Construct a binary tree to answer the question*

We can further go to the next day and calculate P(Sunny) for that day to be 0.78 × 0.9 + (1 − 0.78) × 0.5 = 0.812, then the next day 0.825, 0.83, etc. We can see that after a few iterations, the P(Sunny) stabilizes at ~0.83, which is the probability that is asked for.

We can also ask the computer to simulate a sequence of states. The first state could be rain or sunny with equal probability. To simulate this, we generate a random uniform (0,1) number, and if the number is less than 0.5, we stick with R (rain), otherwise S (sunny). We can continue to build this chain of states based on the transition probabilities given. At the end of the day, the sequence could be

'S', 'S', 'S', 'S', 'S', 'S', 'S', 'S', 'S', 'R', 'S', 'S', 'S', 'S', 'S', 'S', 'S', 'S', 'S', 'S', 'S', 'R',...

Or 'R', 'R', 'S', 'S', 'S', 'S', 'S', 'S', 'S', 'S', 'S', 'S', 'S', 'S', 'S', 'S', 'S', 'S', 'R', 'S', 'S', 'S', 'R', 'R'...

CHAPTER 6   MONTE CARLO

We then can count the number of "S" and "R" and find the probability for P(sunny), which is # "S" / (# "S" + # "R"). If the sequence is long enough, the answer will be the same regardless of the initial state chosen.

The code implementation (Listing 6-9) is straightforward, and indeed, the probability for a sunny day is ~0.833. In Figure 6-9, we also explored the impact of the length of the sequence – the probability stabilizes after 1000 states.

Listing 6-9. Find the probability of rain with Markov Chain Monte Carlo

```
"""
Given
P(R-tomorrow|R-today) = 0.5
P(S-tomorrow|R-today) = 0.5
P(R-tomorrow|S-today) = 0.1
P(S-tomorrow|S-today) = 0.9
What is probability it rains on a random day?
Answer: P(S) = 0.833 and P(R) = 0.167
"""
import random
from collections import Counter
import matplotlib.pyplot as plt
import numpy as np
random.seed(1234)

def generate_mcmc_chain(chain_length):
    chain = ["R" if random.random() <= 0.5 else "S"]
    for i in range(chain_length - 1):
        if chain[-1] == "R":
            if random.random() <= 0.5:
                chain.append("R")
            else:
                chain.append("S")
        else:
            if random.random() <= 0.1:
                chain.append("R")
            else:
                chain.append("S")
    count_dict = Counter(chain)
    num_sunny_days = count_dict["S"]
    num_rainy_days = count_dict["R"]
    percent_rainy = num_rainy_days / chain_length
    print (f"chain_length: {chain_length}")
    print (f"number sunny days: {num_sunny_days}")
    print (f"number rainy days: {num_rainy_days}")
    return percent_rainy

length_chain_arr = [100, 1_000, 10_000, 100_000, 1_000_000, 10_000_000]
percent_rainy_arr = [generate_mcmc_chain(length) for length in length_chain_arr]
percent_sunny_arr = [1 - percent_rain for percent_rain in percent_rainy_arr]
plt.figure(figsize=(10,7))
```

CHAPTER 6   MONTE CARLO

```
42. plt.plot(range(2, len(length_chain_arr) + 2), percent_rainy_arr, "bD-", markersize =
    14,lw = 2, label = "probability of rainy on a random day")
43. plt.plot(range(2, len(length_chain_arr) + 2), percent_sunny_arr, "rD-", markersize =
    14,lw = 2, label = "probability of sunny on a random day")
44. plt.xlabel("Length of Markov Chain in 10 base exponential", fontsize = 16)
45. plt.ylabel("Probability of Rain", fontsize = 16)
46. plt.legend(loc= 0)
47. plt.title("Probability of rainy on a random day with Markov Chain length",
    fontsize = 18)
48. plt.grid()
49. plt.tight_layout()
50. plt.show()
```

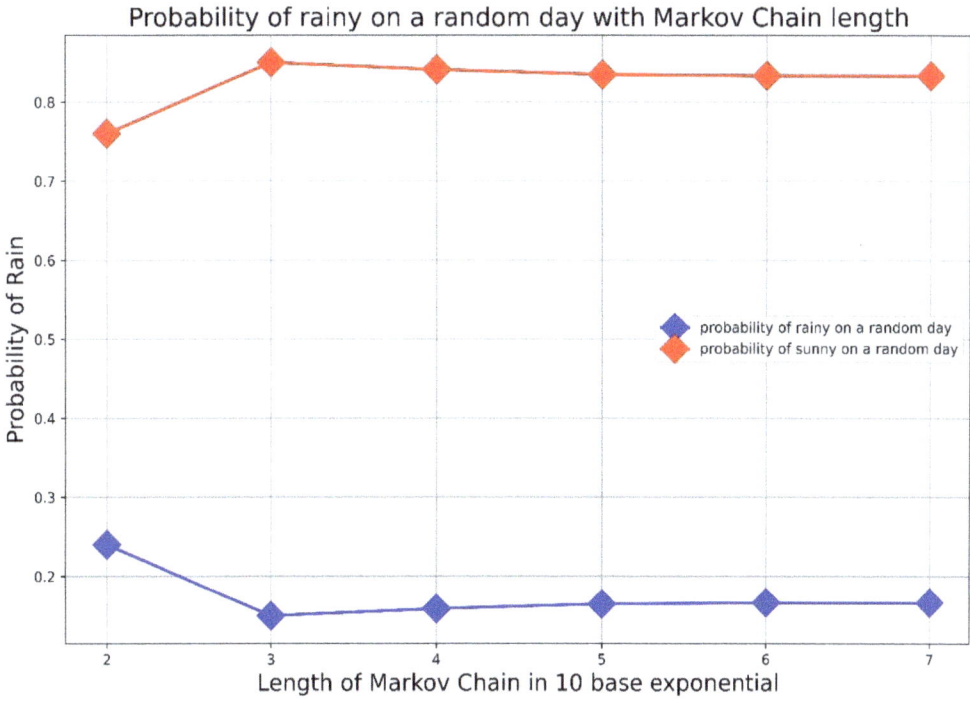

Figure 6-9. *Probability of rain with the length of the Markov chain*

CHAPTER 6   MONTE CARLO

```
In [8]: run Listing_6_9_weather_prediction_mcmc.py
chain_length: 100
number sunny days: 76
number rainy days: 24
chain_length: 1000
number sunny days: 850
number rainy days: 150
chain_length: 10000
number sunny days: 8410
number rainy days: 1590
chain_length: 100000
number sunny days: 83485
number rainy days: 16515
chain_length: 1000000
number sunny days: 833392
number rainy days: 166608
chain_length: 10000000
number sunny days: 8333083
number rainy days: 1666917
```

This simple weather prediction problem is an example of Markov Chain Monte Carlo (MCMC). The Monte Carlo part is that you decide based on conditional probability (e.g., roll a dice) which state to transition to from the current state, and you end up with a sequence of states, called a Markov Chain. MCMC satisfies several properties:

- Markov Property: Future state only depends on the current state.
- Irreducible: Transition probability from one state to another must be positive.
- Aperiodic: It cannot get trapped in cycles.

In real applications, we will discard certain numbers of initial states as the equilibrium has not been achieved. This initial period is called a "burn-in" period. We then rely on the rest of the states which are believed to have reached equilibrium. Also, it is common to build several Markov Chains and aggregate them later.

The problem statement can be encoded into the following diagram (Figure 6-10). Note that the arrow describes the transition probabilities.

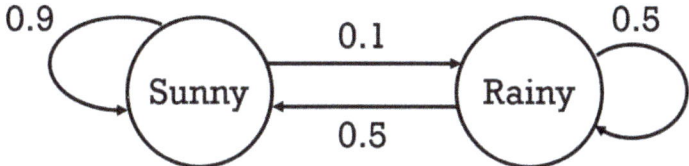

Figure 6-10. A Markov chain state transition diagram

Also in matrix form, the transition probabilities can be represented as

$$P = \begin{bmatrix} 0.9 & 0.1 \\ 0.5 & 0.5 \end{bmatrix}$$

The initial state can be stored as a vector $x^0 = [1,0]$. Here we assume the first day is sunny. Then the probability for sunny / rainy for the next day $x^1 = x^0 P = [0.9, 0.1]$; we can repeat it many times until the x^n stabilizes. The code in Listing 6-10 finds the equilibrium state of $[0.833, 0.167]$.

Listing 6-10. Find the probability of rain via the matrix operation

```
1.  import numpy as np
2.  # calculate the stationary distribution programmatically
3.  Q = np.array([[0.9, 0.1],[0.5, 0.5]])
4.  init_s = np.array([[1.0, 0]])
5.  epsilon =1
6.  while epsilon>10e-9:
7.      next_s = np.dot(init_s,Q)
8.      epsilon = np.sqrt(np.sum(np.square(next_s - init_s)))
9.      init_s = next_s
10. print(init_s)
```

In [9]: run Listing_6_10_weather_prediction_mcmc_matrix.py

[[0.83333334 0.16666666]]

Alternatively, we can find the equilibrium state by solving the following equation, i.e.:

$$xP = x$$

where $x = [q_1, q_2]$ and $q_1 + q_2 = 1$. We arrive at the same answer of $[0.833, 0.167]$.

CHAPTER 6   MONTE CARLO

Metropolis–Hastings

Suppose we know some probability density function $P(x)$. How can we draw samples from it?

We can think of some special cases. For example, if the $P(x)$ is a normal distribution, say $Nor(0, 1)$, according to the empirical 68-95-99.7 rule, 99.7% of data fall within +/- 3 σ range (Figure 6-11).

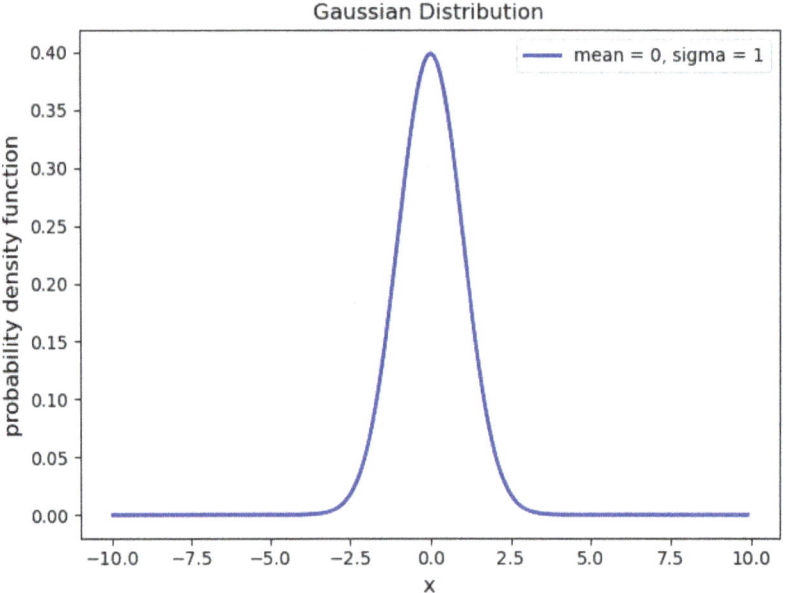

Figure 6-11. *A Gaussian distribution with mean 0 and standard deviation of 1*

We will probably choose data within [-3,3] since they have a higher probability. Say we pick up three samples, i.e., $x = -1$, $x = 0$, and $x = 2$; their corresponding probabilities are calculated to be 0.242, 0.399, and 0.05, respectively, by typing the following codes at an IPython console.

```
In [10]: from scipy.stats import norm
In [11]: probs = [norm(0,1).pdf(x) for x in [-1,0,2]]
In [12]: probs
Out[12]: [0.24197072451914337, 0.3989422804014327, 0.05399096651318806]
```

CHAPTER 6   MONTE CARLO

To make the sampling correctly reflect the probability distribution, we will perhaps need to sample x=-1, 242 times, x=0, 399 times, and x=2, 54 times, a total of 695 samples! These samples contain many duplicates. Also, as more samples are drawn, the number of samples will have to be recalculated. Overall, it is not scalable.

Instead, we will look at a more efficient sampling technique, namely, the Metropolis-Hastings (M-H) algorithm, which is regarded as one of the top ten most influential algorithms in the 20th century by the *Computing in Science & Engineering* magazine [13].

Suppose we have some target distribution P(x), such as the one below.

$$P(x) = \frac{2e^{\frac{-(x+4)^2}{2}} + 3e^{\frac{-x^2}{2}} + e^{\frac{-(x-3)^2}{2}}}{\int_{-\infty}^{\infty} 2e^{\frac{-(x+4)^2}{2}} + 3e^{\frac{-x^2}{2}} + e^{\frac{-(x-3)^2}{2}} dx}$$

In fact, we do not even need to know the denominator, which is just a normalizing constant, and, in most cases, its integral is intractable. All we need is

$$P(x) \sim 2e^{\frac{-(x+4)^2}{2}} + 3e^{\frac{-x^2}{2}} + e^{\frac{-(x-3)^2}{2}}.$$

Let us plot unnormalized P(x) first. As indicated by Figure 6-12, all nonzero data fall within a [-10,10] region.

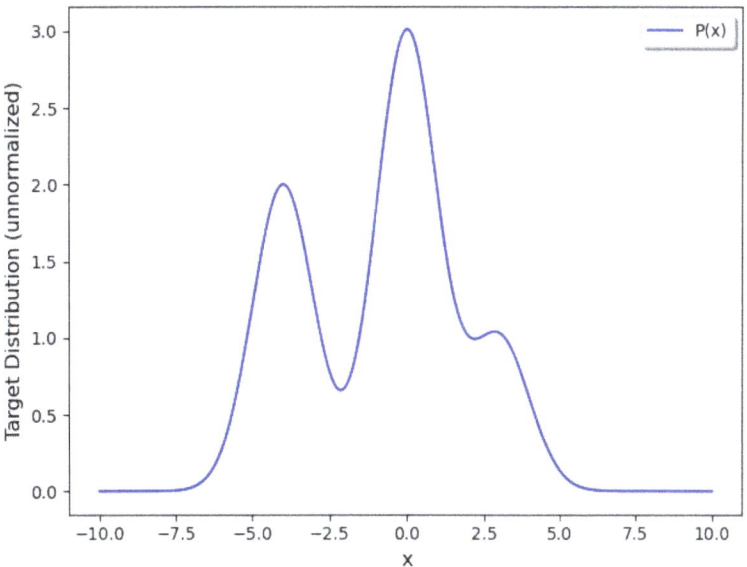

Figure 6-12. *A visualization of P(x)*

CHAPTER 6 MONTE CARLO

Also, we can see three peaks at $x = -4$, $x = 0$, and $x = 3$, respectively. By the way, the denominator is evaluated to be ~15.04.

```
1. from scipy import integrate
2. def P(x):
3.     return 2*np.exp(-(x + 4)**2/2) + 3*np.exp(-x**2/2) + np.exp(-(x-3)**2/2)
4. Z, error = integrate.quad(P, -10, 10)
```

In [13]: Z

Out[13]: 15.039769642836779

Here is the Metropolis–Hastings algorithm for drawing random samples from $P(x)$:

1. We start with a proposal distribution $Q(x)$, a random start point x_t at time t.

2. We draw a proposal sample x^* from $Q(x)$ based on x_t.

3. We calculate the acceptance probability A, to decide whether we accept x^*.

$$A = \min\left(1, \frac{P(x^*)}{P(x_t)} \times \frac{Q(x_t|x^*)}{Q(x^*|x_t)}\right)$$

4. We generate a random uniform number from [0,1], u.

$$x_{t+1} = \begin{cases} x^* & \text{if } A \geq u \\ x_t & \text{otherwise} \end{cases}$$

5. The sequence of values x_t are the samples from $P(x)$.

In Step 4, the algorithm accepts the proposed data point with a probability of A calculated in Step 3. On the other hand, it rejects the proposed data point and retains the previous data point one time unit earlier. As for the proposal distribution here, it can be of any distribution, but in practice, the normal distribution is often used. The advantage of using a normal distribution is that the Q term in Step 3 will be evaluated to 1.

$$\frac{Q(x_t|x^*)}{Q(x^*|x_t)} = \frac{\frac{1}{\sqrt{2\pi}\sigma} e^{-\frac{(x^*-x_t)^2}{2\sigma^2}}}{\frac{1}{\sqrt{2\pi}\sigma} e^{-\frac{(x_t-x^*)^2}{2\sigma^2}}}$$

CHAPTER 6 MONTE CARLO

This is not always true for other distributions. If the Q terms get cancelled out, the algorithm is also called the **Metropolis algorithm**. If choosing a normal distribution as the proposal distribution, in Step (3), we are just left with the P term. Since it is the ratio of $P(x)$, we will not bother with the denominator terms in the probability density function $P(x)$. The mean for the normal distribution will be x_t but what value should be used for σ? In essence, the sampling process is equivalent to a random walk (along x – axis in current case). The σ in the proposal function decides the step size. Obviously the σ value will be case – dependent. But by looking at the plot of target distribution $P(x)$ in Figure 6-12, we can start with $\sigma = 1$ for our case.

Another factor to consider is the "burn-in" period; since the sequence of proposed values forms an MCMC chain, we typically do not trust the initial points which are not at an equilibrium state and discard data in the "burn-in" period. For that, we can define a burn_in_ratio parameter and select the most recent data based on it. We can also keep track of the acceptance rate while implementing the M-H algorithm. Displayed in Listing 6-11 is an implementation of the Metropolis–Hastings algorithm based on the discussion so far. As shown in Figure 6-13, the samples in green color match the true probability density function well. Note here we have normalized both so that we can compare apples with apples.

CHAPTER 6 MONTE CARLO

Listing 6-11. The sampling of an arbitrary probability density function, *P(x)* using Metropolis–Hastings

```
1.  import numpy as np
2.  import matplotlib.pyplot as plt
3.  import random
4.  from scipy import integrate
5.  random.seed(1234)
6.
7.  def P(x):
8.      return 2*np.exp(-(x + 4)**2/2) + 3*np.exp(-x**2/2) + np.exp(-(x-3)**2/2)
9.
10. def plot_target_distribution(x_arr, y_arr):
11.     plt.xlabel("x", fontsize = 12)
12.     plt.ylabel("Target Distribution", fontsize = 12)
13.     plt.plot(x_arr, y_arr, 'b-', label='P(x)')
14.     plt.legend(loc='upper right', shadow=True)
15.     plt.tight_layout()
16.     plt.show()
17.
18. def metropolis_hasting(num_iter=100000, burn_in_ratio = 0.5, start_x = 0, sigma = 1):
19.     samples = []
20.     prev_x = start_x
21.     num_accept = 0
22.     num_reject = 0
23.     for _ in range(num_iter):
24.         proposal_x = random.normalvariate(prev_x, sigma)
25.         accept_prob = min(P(proposal_x) / P(prev_x), 1)
26.         U = random.uniform(0,1)
27.         if accept_prob > U:
28.             new_x = proposal_x
29.             num_accept += 1
30.         else:
31.             new_x = prev_x
32.             num_reject += 1
33.         samples.append(new_x)
34.         prev_x = new_x
35.     acceptance_rate = num_accept / num_iter
36.     print (acceptance_rate)
37.     return samples[int(num_iter * burn_in_ratio):]
38.
39. def plot_samples_from_metropolis_hasting(x_arr, y_arr, Z, samples):
40.     plt.hist(samples, bins=50, histtype='bar', facecolor='g', alpha=0.75, density=1, label='bins')
41.     plt.xlabel("x", fontsize = 12)
42.     plt.ylabel("Distribution", fontsize = 12)
43.     plt.plot(x_arr, y_arr/Z, 'r', label='P(x)')
44.     plt.title('Metropolis Hastings')
45.     plt.legend(loc='upper right', shadow=True)
46.     plt.show()
47.
48. if __name__ == "__main__":
49.     x_arr = np.linspace(-10, 10, 1000)
50.     y_arr = P(x_arr)
51.     Z, error = integrate.quad(P, -10, 10)
52.     samples= metropolis_hasting(num_iter
53.     plot_target_distribution(x_arr, y_arr)=100000, burn_in_ratio = 0.5, 
        start_x = 0, sigma = 1)
54.     plot_samples_from_metropolis_hasting(x_arr, y_arr, Z, samples)
```

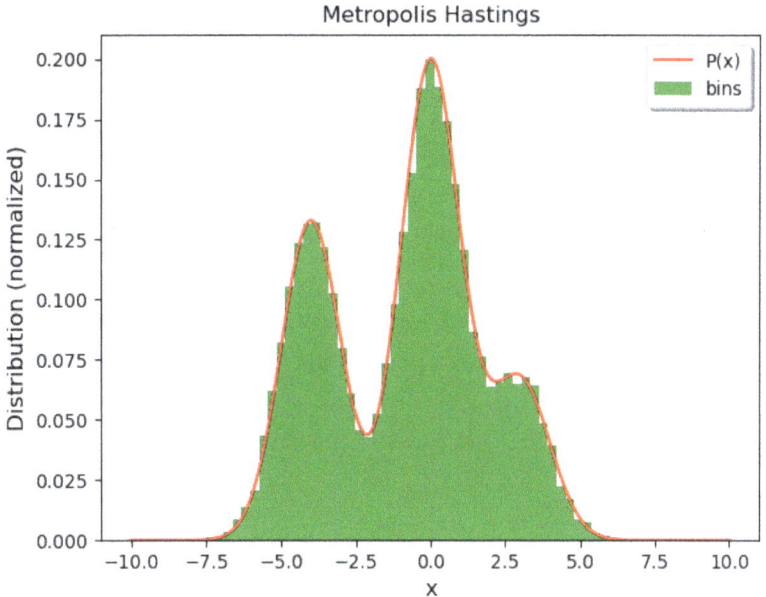

Figure 6-13. *A comparison of the true probability density and the sampling in bins*

Let us examine the acceptance rate for the simulation. It is ~0.793 for σ=1. If increasing σ, for σ=2, 5, 10, and 20, the acceptance rate monotonously decreases to ~0.678, ~0.478, ~0.288, and ~0.150, respectively. The step size of the random walk does impact the performance of M-H sampling.

Application

Monte Carlo methods leverage random sampling to obtain numerical results. They are widely used in many fields, particularly in situations where it is challenging to model systems analytically. Some of the key applications of Monte Carlo methods include risk analysis in finance, statistical mechanics in physics, Bayesian inference (leveraging Markov Chain Monte Carlo) in machine learning and AI, and solutions to optimization problems. In this section, we will apply Monte Carlo to study the endemic.

CHAPTER 6   MONTE CARLO

One of the well-known compartment models to mathematically model the spread of infectious diseases is the SIR model where S, I, and R stand for, respectively, Susceptible, Infectious, and Recovered. The entire population is assigned to different compartments and may progress between them. The susceptible becomes the infectious after being in contact with the latter. The infectious group is the group that has been infected and can infect the susceptible. The recovered are those who are either immune or deceased and can no longer be infected.

Suppose no birth and death, the laws governing the movements of people between compartments are a system of ordinary differential equations (ODEs) as listed below.

$$\frac{dS}{dt} = -\frac{\beta}{N}IS$$

$$\frac{dI}{dt} = \frac{\beta}{N}IS - \gamma I$$

$$\frac{dR}{dt} = \gamma I$$

Here, β is the infection rate constant in the unit number of people infected per day per infected person, and γ is the recovery rate constant in the unit fraction of a person recovered per day per infected person, when time is in unit day. N is the total population. If adding three ODEs, we have:

$$\frac{dS}{dt} + \frac{dI}{dt} + \frac{dR}{dt} = 0$$

This suggests the total population is conserved at any point in time. The ratio of β and γ gives R_0, which is the basic reproduction number, indicating the expected number of new infections from a single infection in a population where all subjects are susceptible.

Consider a population of 1000 where 900 are susceptible and 100 are infectious. The infection rate and recovery rate are set as 0.4 and 0.1, respectively. Our goal is to find the numbers of S, I, and R in a time horizon of 50 days. In Listing 6-12, as a first method, we can leverage the mature scientific package from scipy to solve a system of ODEs. At line 4, we import the solve_ivp module that numerically integrates a system of ordinary differential equations given an initial value. From lines 7–13, we define the ODEs, and from lines 15–22, we solve the ODEs given the initial state of S, I, and R.

Alternatively, we can also do a Monte Carlo simulation to find out the evolution of S, I, and R with time. At lines 24–54, a single Monte Carlo simulation trial is defined. First, we generate a population with an initial distribution of S, I, and R values. We use a list of length 1000 to store the population where the susceptible, the infectious, and the recovered are denoted, respectively, as 0, 1, and 2 (lines 25–31). Next, from lines 33-52, we update the values for S, I, and R each day by simulating the interaction between people at various compartments. Specifically, for the infected group:

(1) We pick a random number from [0,1]; if the number is less than the infection rate (β), we randomly draw X number of people from the population where X equals the number of the currently infected, and convert them to the inflected if applicable. (i.e., if the people drawn are from susceptible group, they will be converted to the infected; if people drawn are from the infected or recovered groups, do nothing).

(2) We pick another random number from [0,1]; if the number is less than the recovery rate (γ), we move all currently infected people to the recovered compartment. Note the use of a while loop at line 48.

We can certainly run the simulation multiple times to obtain a better aggregated result (lines 56–69). Finally, we can visualize the results from both methods (lines 71–82).

Listing 6-12. Numerical simulation of the SIR model by solving ODE and using Monte Carlo

```python
import random
import numpy as np
import matplotlib.pyplot as plt
from scipy.integrate import solve_ivp
random.seed(1234)

def sir_model_func(t, z, beta, gamma):
    S, I, R = z
    N = S + I + R
    dS_dt = -beta * I * S / N
    dI_dt = beta * I * S / N - gamma * I
    dR_dt = gamma * I
    return [dS_dt, dI_dt, dR_dt]

def solve_using_scipy_ode_solver(beta, gamma, S_0, I_0, R_0, num_days):
    t_span = [0, num_days]
    initial_state = [S_0, I_0, R_0]
    ode_solution = solve_ivp(sir_model_func, t_span, initial_state, args=(beta, gamma), dense_output=True)
    t = [i for i in range(num_days)]
    z = ode_solution.sol(t)
    S, I, R = z
    return S, I, R, t

def sir_model_monte_carlo(beta, gamma, S_0, I_0, R_0, num_days):
    N = S_0 + I_0 + R_0
    # denote 0: susceptibles; 1: infected; 2: recovered
    S = [0 for _ in range(num_days)]
    I = [0 for _ in range(num_days)]
    R = [0 for _ in range(num_days)]
    population = [0 for _ in range(S_0)] + [1 for _ in range(I_0)] + [2 for _ in range(R_0)]
    random.shuffle(population)

    for n in range(num_days):
        num_susceptibles = population.count(0)
        num_infected = population.count(1)
        num_recovered = population.count(2)
        S[n] = num_susceptibles
        I[n] = num_infected
        R[n] = num_recovered
        for i in range(int(num_infected)):
            if random.random() < beta:
                rand_index = random.randint(0, N-1)
                if population[rand_index] == 0:
                    population[rand_index] = 1

        for i in range(int(num_infected)):
            if random.random() < gamma:
                while True:
                    rand_index = random.randint(0, N-1)
                    if population[rand_index] == 1:
                        population[rand_index] = 2
                        break
    t = [i for i in range(num_days)]
    return S, I, R, t
```

```python
56. def run_monte_carlo_multiple_times(num_trials, beta, gamma, S_0, I_0, R_0, num_days):
57.     S = np.zeros(num_days)
58.     I = np.zeros(num_days)
59.     R = np.zeros(num_days)
60.
61.     for _ in range(num_trials):
62.         cur_S, cur_I, cur_R, t = sir_model_monte_carlo(beta, gamma, S_0, I_0, R_0, num_days)
63.         S += np.array(cur_S)
64.         I += np.array(cur_I)
65.         R += np.array(cur_R)
66.     S /= num_trials
67.     I /= num_trials
68.     R /= num_trials
69.     return S, I, R, t
70.
71. def plot_results(S1, I1, R1, S2, I2, R2, t):
72.     y_data = [S1, I1, R1, S2, I2, R2]
73.     labels = ["S1", "I1", "R1", "S2", "I2", "R2"]
74.     symbols = ["b-", "r-", "g-", "b--", "r--", "g--"]
75.     for y, label, symbol in zip(y_data, labels, symbols):
76.         plt.plot(t, y, symbol, lw=2, label = label)
77.     plt.xlabel('Time (days)', fontsize = 12)
78.     plt.ylabel('Population', fontsize = 12)
79.     plt.legend(loc=0)
80.     plt.title('SIR Model')
81.     plt.tight_layout()
82.     plt.show()
83.
84. if __name__ == "__main__":
85.     conditions = dict(beta=0.4, gamma=0.1, S_0 = 900, I_0=100, R_0=0, num_days=50)
86.     S1, I1, R1, t = solve_using_scipy_ode_solver(**conditions)
87.     S2, I2, R2, t = run_monte_carlo_multiple_times(num_trials=1000, **conditions)
88.     plot_results(S1, I1, R1, S2, I2, R2, t)
```

We can compare the results from both methods (we run Monte Carlo simulations 1000 times). In Figure 6-14, the solid lines are from numerical integration of the ODEs, whereas the dashed lines are from Monte Carlo simulations. We see an overall good agreement between the two methods. Also, we see an outbreak of the infectious disease (red curve). Can we prevent the outbreak?

CHAPTER 6   MONTE CARLO

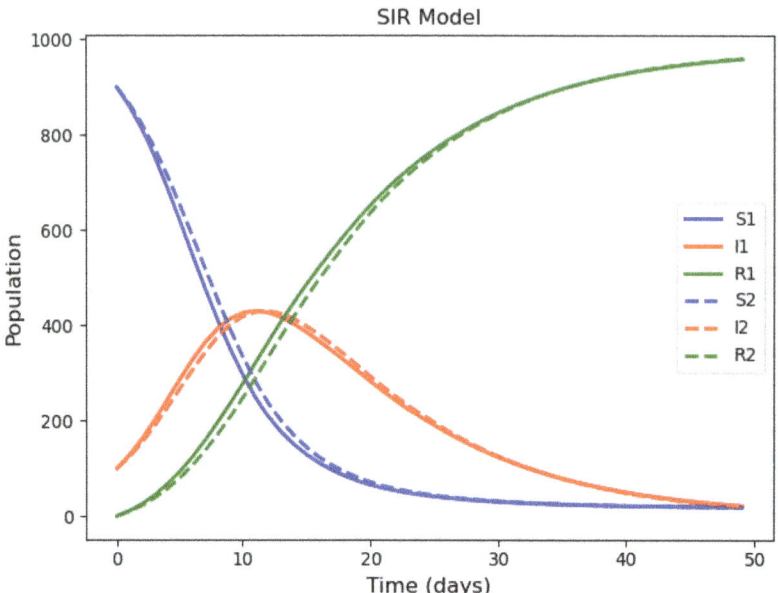

Figure 6-14. *The change of Susceptible, Infectious, and Recovered with time from solving ODE (solid lines) and Monte Carlo simulation (dashed lines)*

Recall the ODE for the infectious:

$$\frac{dI}{dt} = \frac{\beta}{N} IS - \gamma I$$

To prevent an outbreak, the right-hand side of the equation must be nonpositive, and plugging in the initial numbers, we have

$$\frac{\beta}{N} I(0)S(0) - \gamma I(0) \leq 0$$

Rearrange it to arrive at

$$\frac{S(0)}{N} \frac{\beta}{\gamma} \leq 1$$

For the current condition, the left-hand side (LHS) is evaluated to be (900/1000) × (0.4 / 0.1) = 3.6, which is greater than 1. If, however, we reduce the infection rate by a factor of 10, through a "wear your mask" campaign, the LHS number will be reduced to 0.36, and an outbreak of the endemic should be prevented. Let us test this with a reduced β value of 0.04 in the run. As expected, no outbreak is seen in Figure 6-15.

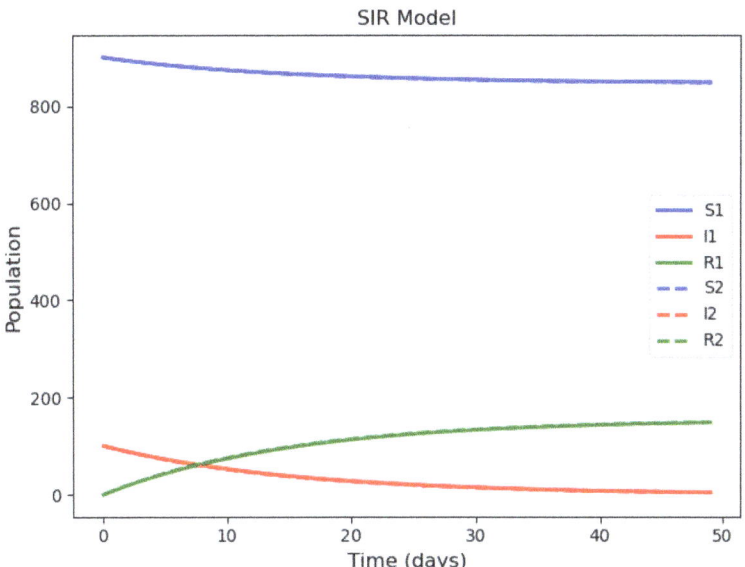

Figure 6-15. *After reducing the infection rate by 10, there is no outbreak of the endemic*

Summary

In this chapter, we learned about Monte Carlo methods. We know that, except for leveraging the naturally occurring events, the computer-generated numbers are not truly random. However, these numbers that are usually generated using a linear congruent generator with a huge cycle are good enough for practical simulation needs. We can statistically test the uniformity (e.g., using χ^2 goodness-of-fit test) and independence of the random numbers (e.g., Up and down/Above and below the mean tests). Once the random numbers pass the tests, we can leverage them to do a variety of simulations, from finding π to solving challenging integrals. Lastly, we learned Markov Chain Monte Carlo (MCMC) via an introductory example of weather prediction. A more sophisticated application of MCMC, i.e., the Metropolis–Hastings algorithm, is explained with an example of drawing sample points from an arbitrary probability density function. Finally, we used Monte Carlo to successfully simulate the endemic using a compartment model.

CHAPTER 7

A Tale of Ten Cities

In this chapter, we will introduce and learn five important algorithms via fictitious examples of a consultant and the ten most populous cities in the United States. The algorithms we are going to review are Simulated Annealing, Genetic Algorithm, Dijkstra's Algorithm, Gradient Descent, and K-means Clustering. Buckle up, and let us begin.

A Traveling Consultant: Part 1

As a consultant, an integral part of this book author's job is to connect with clients. In a planned business trip, he is ambitious enough to visit the ten largest cities in the United States, in terms of population. To save time and mileage, he has decided to devise a route that starts from the home city of New York, goes to other cities in a sequential order, and finally returns to New York, with the constraint of the shortest combined distance. According to Wikipedia [14], the ten most populous US cities based on the 2020 census are New York, Los Angeles, Chicago, Houston, Phoenix, Philadelphia, San Antonio, San Diego, Dallas, and San Jose (Figure 7-1).

The author wonders: What is the best route to connect all cities and make the total distance shortest? The starting city is confirmed, for the second city we have nine choices, for the third city eight, ... and for the penultimate city we have two options, and the last city we have one option. Then we return to NYC. If we consider all permutations, we shall get 9×8×7×6×5×4×3×2×1 = 9! = 362880 different routes. This is not a big number for a computer. We can let it compute all distances and find the shortest.

Sounds like a plan, but how do we calculate the distance between two cities? We can calculate the great-circle distance between two points on a sphere given longitudes and latitudes using the Haversine formula [15].

CHAPTER 7   A TALE OF TEN CITIES

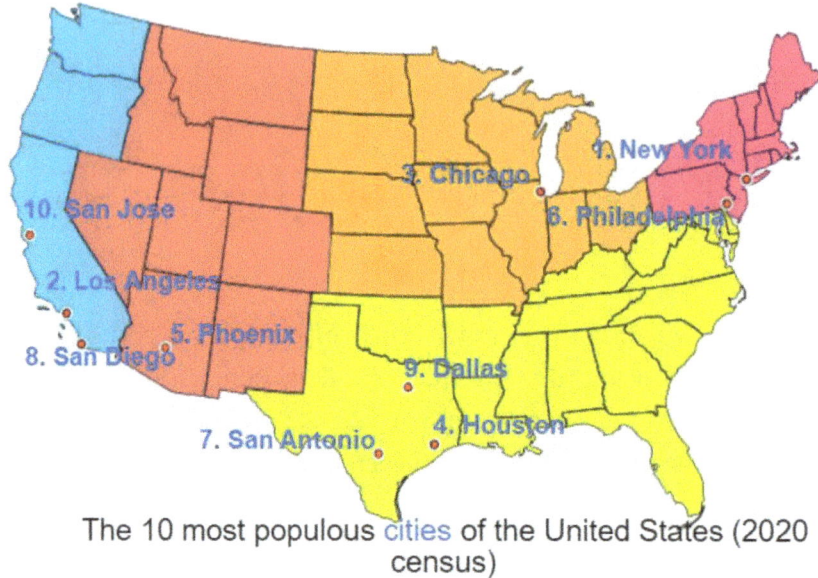

Figure 7-1. *The ten most populous cities in the United States in 2020*

The altitude and longitude of the ten cities are compiled in Table 7-1.

Table 7-1. *The longitude and latitude of the ten most populous US cities in 2020*

Rank	City Name	Longitude	Latitude
1	New York City	-73.940	40.670
2	Los Angeles	-118.410	34.110
3	Chicago	-87.680	41.840
4	Houston	-95.464	29.741
5	Phoenix	-112.070	33.540
6	Philadelphia	-75.130	40.010
7	San Antonio	-98.510	29.460
8	San Diego	-117.140	32.810
9	Dallas	-96.770	32.790
10	San Jose	-121.850	37.300

The author then moved on to write the following code snippet in Listing 7-1 and ran it.

CHAPTER 7   A TALE OF TEN CITIES

Listing 7-1. Find the best route via brute force

```
1.  from itertools import permutations
2.  from math import sin, cos, radians, atan2, sqrt
3.  def haversine_distance(lon1, lat1, lon2, lat2):
4.      R = 3958.8 # Approximate radius of earth in miles
5.      lon1 = radians(lon1)
6.      lat1 = radians(lat1)
7.      lon2 = radians(lon2)
8.      lat2 = radians(lat2)
9.      dlon = lon2 - lon1
10.     dlat = lat2 - lat1
11.     a = sin(dlat / 2)**2 + cos(lat1) * cos(lat2) * sin(dlon / 2)**2
12.     c = 2 * atan2(sqrt(a), sqrt(1 - a))
13.     distance = R * c
14.     return distance
15.
16. def calculate_total_distance(coords):
17.     s = 0.0
18.     for i in range(NUM_CITIES):
19.         s += haversine_distance(coords[i][0], coords[i][1], coords[(i + 1) % NUM_CITIES][0], coords[(i + 1) % NUM_CITIES][1])
20.     return s
21.
22. def brute_force_search(coords):
23.     first_coord = coords[0]
24.     next_coords = coords[1:]
25.     optimal_next_coords = min(permutations(next_coords), key = lambda coords: calculate_total_distance([first_coord] + list(coords)))
26.     return [first_coord] + list(optimal_next_coords)
27.
28. def print_best_route_based_on_coords(coords):
29.     path = ""
30.     for coord in coords:
31.         path += coords_cities_dict[tuple(coord)]
32.         path += "-->"
33.     path += coords_cities_dict[tuple(coords[0])]
34.     return path
35.
36. if __name__ == "__main__":
37.     NUM_CITIES = 10
38.     cities = ["NYC", "LA", "Chicago", "Houston", "Phoenix", "Philadelphia", "San Antonio", "San Diego", "Dallas", "San Jose"]
39.     city_coordinates = [[-73.940, 40.670], # NYC
40.         [-118.410, 34.110], # LA
41.         [-87.680, 41.840],  # Chicago
42.         [-95.464, 29.741],  # Houston
43.         [-112.070, 33.540], # Phoenix
44.         [-75.130, 40.010],  # Philadelphia
45.         [-98.510, 29.460],  # San Antonio
46.         [-117.140, 32.810], # San Diego
47.         [-96.770, 32.790],  # Dallas
48.         [-121.850, 37.300]] # San Jose
49.     coords_cities_dict = {tuple(coord): city for city, coord in zip(cities, city_coordinates)}
50.     brute_force_coords = brute_force_search(city_coordinates)
51.     print(f"brute force total distance = {calculate_total_distance(brute_force_coords)}")
52.     print(f"visit sequence from brute force {print_best_route_based_on_coords(brute_force_coords)}")
```

CHAPTER 7   A TALE OF TEN CITIES

He found out that the shortest route is NYC → Chicago → San Jose → LA → San Diego → Phoenix → San Antonio → Houston → Dallas → Philadelphia → NYC, with a total distance of 5888 miles.

```
In [1]: run Listing_7_1_traveling_salesman_brute_force.py
brute force total distance = 5888.7430592253295
visit sequence from brute force NYC-->Chicago-->San Jose-->LA-->San Diego-->Phoenix-->San
Antonio-->Houston-->Dallas-->Philadelphia-->NYC
```

A total distance of ~6000 miles and an average of ~600 miles between the two cities. Not bad. This is a brute force approach, and we asked our computer to do over 300,000 calculations before landing at the optimal solution. What if we have a large number of cities, say, 20, 50, or even 100? How many possible routes to compute? Well, 10 cities have 9! possible outcomes, then 20 cities have 19! = 121645100408832000, 50 cities have 49! = 608281864034267560872252163321295376887552831379210240000000000, and 100 cities have 99! = 933262154439441526816992388562667004907159682643816214685929638952175999932299156089414639761565182862536979208272237582511852109168640000000000000000000000. That is an astronomical number with 156 digits! If we assume our computer can do a million calculations per second (a very fast computer indeed), it will take 3857, 1.93×10^{49}, and 2.96×10^{142} years, respectively, to complete the job.

We now explore a more efficient way to get an optimal solution or the best one we can. We start by guessing a solution. For example, apart from the starting city, for the rest of the cities, we can get a random sequence of order such as NYC → LA → Philly → San Jose → San Diego → Chicago → Houston → San Antonio → Phoenix → Dallas → NYC. For this route, we can calculate the total distance by using the `calculate_total_distance` function in Listing 7-1.

Here is the proposal to attack the problem:

(1) Let us start with a random sequence of ten cities, with the starting city fixed.

(2) Calculate its total distance.

(3) We swap the order of two cities randomly in the sequence (starting city is not for swap), and calculate the new total distance.

(4) If the new total distance is less than the previous value. We accept the swap.

(5) If the new total distance is greater than the previous value. We do not reject it outright. We accept it with a certain probability.

(6) We will repeat the processes from (2) to (5) for the number of predefined rounds iteratively.

(7) We are happy with the final sequence, though not necessarily the optimal one, but it should be close.

In Step (4), we advocate for the swap that leads to a smaller total distance. If we keep doing that, it will become a greedy approach, and the search will likely get stuck in the local minima. An improvement to that is Step (5), where we also consider the swap that increases the total distance.

Let me elaborate a bit on "accept it with a certain probability" in Step (5). For that, we can define a probability of success as $e^{\frac{-distance}{T}}$, where T is the temperature value. Here we borrow a concept from physics, i.e., given the temperature T, and the activate energy ΔE, the term $e^{\frac{-\Delta E}{kT}}$ gives the probability that activation could happen. Since distance is always positive, so is the temperature; the exponential term always falls within a range of 0 to 1, which agrees with the allowed value for the probability. Also, in our case, given a fixed temperature, if the distance is large, which we do not want, the probability of success will be small. On the other hand, given a fixed distance, a lower temperature leads to a smaller probability. That is to say, the probability formula favors a smaller distance and a larger temperature.

To implement "accept it with a certain probability" programmatically, we can generate a random number between 0 and 1 using `random` library, say, $p1$. And then for each sequence of cities after the swap, we calculate a probability based on temperature and the summed total distance, and call it $p2$. If $p1 < p2$, we reject the swap; otherwise, we accept it. This way we accept the swap with a probability of $p1$.

The code implementation is shown in Listing 7-2, and the result is shown in Figure 7-2. We see an agreement with the route from the brute force method.

CHAPTER 7   A TALE OF TEN CITIES

Listing 7-2. Simulated annealing for the Traveling Salesman problem

```python
import random
import numpy as np
from math import exp
import matplotlib.pyplot as plt
from itertools import permutations
import time
from utils import haversine_distance, drawArrow, cities, city_coordinates, print_best_route_based_on_coords
from copy import deepcopy
random.seed(1234)

t_start = time.time()
N = 10
Tmax = 10.0
Tmin = 1e-3
tau = 1e4

def calculate_total_distance(coords):
    s = 0.0
    for i in range(N):
        s += haversine_distance(coords[i][0], coords[i][1], coords[(i + 1) % N][0], coords[(i + 1) % N][1])
    return s

def brute_force_search(coords):
    first_coord = coords[0]
    next_coords = coords[1:]
    optimal_next_coords = min(permutations(next_coords), key = lambda coords: calculate_total_distance([first_coord] + list(list(coords))))
    return [first_coord] + list(optimal_next_coords)

def compare_paths(coords, sa_coords):
    brute_force_coords = brute_force_search(coords)
    print (f"brute force total distance = {calculate_total_distance(brute_force_coords)}")
    print (f"visit sequence from brute force {print_best_route_based_on_coords(brute_force_coords)}")
    # plot cities
    for i in range(N):
        plt.scatter(coords[i][0], coords[i][1], s=150, marker='*', color = "b")
        plt.text(coords[i][0], coords[i][1], cities[i], fontsize = 14)

    for i in range(1, N + 1):
        drawArrow(sa_coords[i-1], sa_coords[i % N], color = "b", label = "Path from Simulated Annealing" if i == 1 else "")

    for i in range(1, N + 1):
        drawArrow(brute_force_coords[i-1], brute_force_coords[i % N], color = "k", label = "Path from Brute Force Search "if i == 1 else"")

    plt.xlabel("Longitude", fontsize = 14)
    plt.ylabel("Latitude", fontsize = 14)
    plt.legend(loc=0)
    plt.tight_layout()
    plt.savefig("travelling_salesman_path_simulated_annealing.png")
    plt.show()

```

```
51. def swap_array_element(i, j, coords):
52.     coords[i][0], coords[j][0] = coords[j][0], coords[i][0]
53.     coords[i][1], coords[j][1] = coords[j][1], coords[i][1]
54.
55. def run_simulated_annealing(coords):
56.     cur_total_distance = calculate_total_distance(coords)
57.     # Main loop
58.     t = 0
59.     T = Tmax
60.     while T > Tmin:
61.         t += 1
62.         T = Tmax * exp(-t / tau) # cooling
63.         # choose two cities to swap and make sure they are distinct
64.         i, j = random.sample(range(1, N), 2)
65.         # swap them and calculate the change in distance
66.         prev_total_distance = cur_total_distance
67.         swap_array_element(i, j, coords)
68.         cur_total_distance = calculate_total_distance(coords)
69.         diff_distance = cur_total_distance - prev_total_distance
70.         if diff_distance < 0:
71.             continue
72.         else:
73.             if exp(-diff_distance/T) > random.random():
74.                 continue
75.             else:
76.                 swap_array_element(i, j, coords)
77.                 cur_total_distance = prev_total_distance
78.
79.     t_end = time.time()
80.     print (t_end - t_start)
81.     print(f"total distance from simulated annealing = {calculate_total_distance(coords)}")
82.     print (f"sequence from simulated annealing {print_best_route_based_on_coords(coords)}")
83.     return coords
84.
85. if __name__ == "__main__":
86.     city_coordinates_copy_1, city_coordinates_copy_2 = deepcopy(city_coordinates), deepcopy(city_coordinates)
87.     sa_coords = run_simulated_annealing(city_coordinates_copy_1)
88.     compare_paths(city_coordinates_copy_2, sa_coords)
```

In [2]: run Listing_7_2_traveling_salesman_simulated_annealing.py

2.111783027648926

total distance from simulated annealing = 5888.7430592253295
sequence from simulated annealing NYC-->Philadelphia-->Dallas-->Houston-->San Antonio-->Phoenix-->San Diego-->LA-->San Jose-->Chicago-->NYC

brute force total distance = 5888.7430592253295

visit sequence from brute force NYC-->Chicago-->San Jose-->LA-->San Diego-->Phoenix-->San Antonio-->Houston-->Dallas-->Philadelphia-->NYC

CHAPTER 7   A TALE OF TEN CITIES

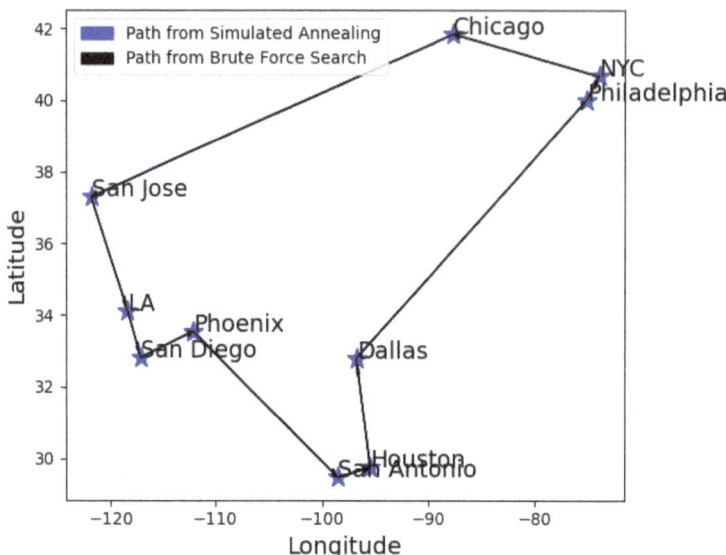

Figure 7-2. *The best route found by Simulated Annealing agrees with that from brute force search*

The approach proposed is called **Simulated Annealing**. It is a term borrowed from metallurgy where a metal is strengthened through *slow* cooling that prevents metal atoms from getting trapped in a random state. In Listing 7-2, the cooling process is mimicked at line 62 using a combination of parameters of Tmax, Tmin, and tau. This is the popular exponential cooling schedule:

$$T = T_0 e^{-t/\tau}$$

where T_0 is the initial temperature and τ is the time constant. The larger τ is, the slower the cooling will be. It can be theoretically proven that if we cool our system slowly enough, it is guaranteed to find the ground state, though the rate of cooling required can be too low to be practical. Note that at line 9 of Listing 7-2, we used a seed of 1234 for reproducible results. If changing it to a different seed number, the result may vary.

A Traveling Consultant: Part 2

We have just explored one way of finding the near-optimal solution for the Traveling Salesman (TSP) problem, using Simulated Annealing. An alternative way to attack the TSP problem is through the Genetic Algorithm (GA), inspired by the Darwinian Evolution Theory. Let us review several terms related to GA. The first term is chromosome. As

CHAPTER 7 A TALE OF TEN CITIES

we know, the chromosome carries the genetic information and passes it on to the next generation. In our TSP case, the chromosome is nothing but a list of unique indexes from 0 to 9 where each index corresponds to a city. The first item in the list is fixed as 0 because the start city is fixed as New York, but the order of the rest indexes is random. Below are the steps to perform a GA algorithm on TSP.

In Step 1 and 2, we will generate a population of N chromosomes. We will rank the chromosomes based on a fitness function, that is, we can calculate the total distance based on a list of indexes. After the chromosomes are ranked. We will pick up the top two as parents and move on to the next steps (Figure 7-3).

Step 1: Generate a population of chromosomes

| 0 | 1 | 2 | 3 | 4 | 5 | 6 | 7 | 8 | 9 | Chromosome 1 |
| 0 | 9 | 3 | 8 | 4 | 6 | 5 | 1 | 2 | 7 | Chromosome 2 |

...

| 0 | 8 | 2 | 1 | 5 | 9 | 7 | 3 | 4 | 6 | Chromosome N |

Step 2: Sort the chromosome and find two chromosomes with the shortest total distances; select them as parents.

| 0 | 1 | 2 | 3 | 4 | 5 | 6 | 7 | 8 | 9 | Chromosome 1 |
| 0 | 9 | 3 | 8 | 4 | 6 | 5 | 1 | 2 | 7 | Chromosome 2 |

Figure 7-3. *Genetic Algorithm in action: generate chromosomes and select parents*

The next step is a crossover step. In this step, we randomly select an index to cross over. To produce better offspring, the genetic code between the best chromosomes will be exchanged. In our case, the indexes 5 and 6 are chosen as crossover points. Then the indexes including and after the crossover points will be first shuffled and swapped between the two chromosomes (Figure 7-4).

CHAPTER 7   A TALE OF TEN CITIES

Step 3: Cross-over

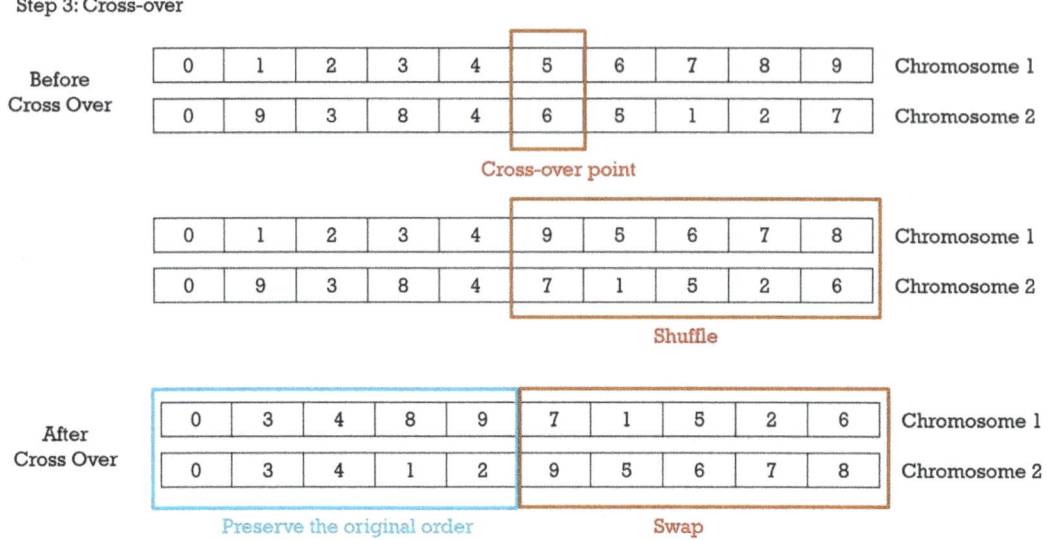

Figure 7-4. *Genetic Algorithm in action: crossover*

So far, so good, except that there is a small problem during the swap. The swapped chromosome likely carries duplicated genetic information. For example, chromosome 1 has a list of indexes of [0, 1, 2, 3, 4, 9, 5, 6, 7, 8] after shuffling. However, after swapping the right part with chromosome 2, it would become [0, 1, 2, 3, 4, 7, 1, 5, 2, 6]. Here, 1, 2 are duplicated, and 8, 9 are missing. To ensure that all ten unique indexes are present in the final chromosome. We can make a copy of the original chromosome 1 and do a linear scan and fill in the left part. Finally, we get [0, 3, 4, 8, 9, 7, 1, 5, 2, 6] for chromosome 1.

Step 4 is mutation (Figure 7-5). You just randomly swap two indexes within either of the chromosomes. After it, we will replace the two chromosomes of the lowest ranks in the population generated in Step 1, since both have the largest total distance and are the least wanted.

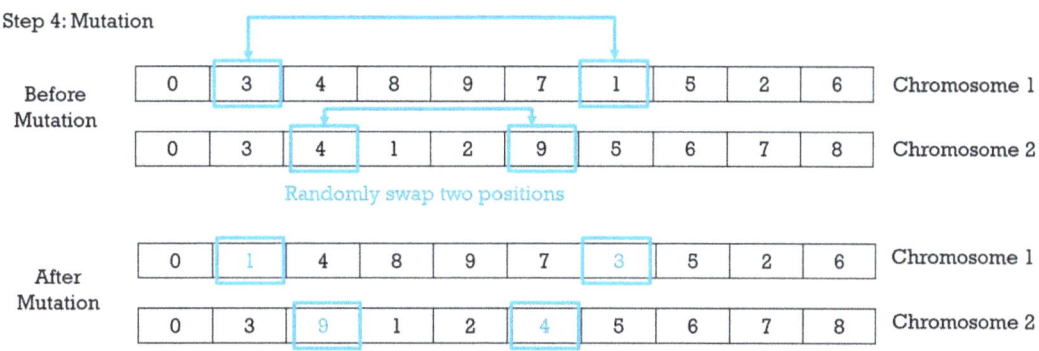

Step 5: Replace the last two chromosomes in the population with the mutated chromosomes in step 4.

Figure 7-5. *Genetic Algorithm in action: mutation*

Similar to Simulated Annealing, we will define a desired round of iterations (i.e., generations), and repeat Steps 2–5. The best chromosome after many generations is supposed to be the best answer.

We can see that both SA and GA include some randomness in the algorithms. In the SA case, we randomly swap indexes inside one array of city indexes (or a "chromosome"), whereas in GA, we perform a series of random operations including crossovers and mutations. Since a brute force solution is practically impossible to solve such a complex global optimization problem, this randomness will gradually guide the algorithm to get closer to the global minimum, step by step. The code of GA is in Listing 7-3, and the result is shown in Figure 7-6.

CHAPTER 7 A TALE OF TEN CITIES

Listing 7-3. Apply the Genetic Algorithm to the Travelling Salesman problem

```python
1.  from utils import city_coordinates, cities, haversine_distance, drawArrow,
    print_best_route_based_on_coords, print_best_route_based_on_indexes
2.  import random
3.  from copy import copy
4.  from itertools import permutations
5.  import matplotlib.pyplot as plt
6.  random.seed(1235)
7.
8.  # These are global params
9.  NUM_CITIES = 10
10. BEST_PATH = None
11. POPULATION = []
12. PARENTS = None
13. NUM_CHROMOSOMES = 100
14. NUM_GENERATIONS = 500
15.
16. # Step 2: Calculate fitness function
17. def calculate_fitness(coord_indexes):
18.     s = 0.0
19.     for i in range(NUM_CITIES):
20.         s += haversine_distance(city_coordinates[coord_indexes[i]][0],
    city_coordinates[coord_indexes[i]][1],
21.                         city_coordinates[coord_indexes[(i + 1) % NUM_CITIES]][0],
    city_coordinates[coord_indexes[(i + 1) % NUM_CITIES]][1])
22.     return s
23.
24. def genetic_algorithm_traveling_salesman():
25.     # Step 1: Generate initial population
26.     other_cities_indexes = [list(range(1, 10)) for _ in range(NUM_CHROMOSOMES)]
27.     for i in range(NUM_CHROMOSOMES):
28.         random.shuffle(other_cities_indexes[i])
29.         POPULATION.append([0] + other_cities_indexes[i])
30.
31.     for _ in range(NUM_GENERATIONS):
32.         # Step 3: Select Parent
33.         POPULATION.sort(key = lambda coordinates: calculate_fitness(coordinates))
34.         BEST = POPULATION[0]
35.         print (f"{print_best_route_based_on_indexes(BEST)}")
36.         print (f"Short distance is {calculate_fitness(BEST)}")
37.         PARENTS = POPULATION[:2]
38.         # Step 4: Cross Over
39.         point_to_cross_over = random.randint(1, NUM_CITIES)
40.         parent_1_copy = copy(PARENTS[0])
41.         parent_2_copy = copy(PARENTS[1])
42.         parent_1_right_part = parent_1_copy[point_to_cross_over:]
43.         parent_2_right_part = parent_2_copy[point_to_cross_over:]
44.         random.shuffle(parent_1_right_part)
45.         random.shuffle(parent_2_right_part)
46.         parent_1 = [item for item in parent_1_copy if item not in parent_2_right_part]
    +parent_2_right_part
47.         parent_2 = [item for item in parent_2_copy if item not in parent_1_right_part]
    +parent_1_right_part
48.         PARENTS = [parent_1, parent_2]
49.         # Step 5: Mutation
50.         for parent in PARENTS:
```

```
51.            i, j = random.sample(range(1, NUM_CITIES), 2)
52.            parent[i], parent[j] = parent[j], parent[i]
53.        # substitute the last two in the POPULATION
54.        POPULATION[-1] = PARENTS[0]
55.        POPULATION[-2] = PARENTS[1]
56.    return BEST
57.
58. def calculate_total_distance(coords):
59.    s = 0.0
60.    for i in range(NUM_CITIES):
61.        s += haversine_distance(coords[i][0], coords[i][1], coords[(i + 1) % NUM_CITIES][0], coords[(i + 1) % NUM_CITIES][1])
62.    return s
63.
64. def brute_force_search(coords):
65.    first_coord = coords[0]
66.    next_coords = coords[1:]
67.    optimal_next_coords = min(permutations(next_coords), key = lambda coords: calculate_total_distance([first_coord] + list(list(coords))))
68.    return [first_coord] + list(optimal_next_coords)
69.
70. def compare_paths(coords, ga_coords):
71.    brute_force_coords = brute_force_search(coords)
72.    print (f"brute force total distance = {calculate_total_distance(brute_force_coords)}")
73.    print (f"visit sequence from brute force {print_best_route_based_on_coords(brute_force_coords)}")
74.    # plot cities
75.    for i in range(NUM_CITIES):
76.        plt.scatter(coords[i][0], coords[i][1], s=150, marker='*', color = "b")
77.        plt.text(coords[i][0], coords[i][1], cities[i], fontsize = 14)
78.
79.    for i in range(1, NUM_CITIES + 1):
80.        drawArrow(ga_coords[i-1], ga_coords[i % NUM_CITIES], color = "g", label = "Path from Genetic Algorithm" if i == 1 else"")
81.
82.    for i in range(1, NUM_CITIES + 1):
83.        drawArrow(brute_force_coords[i-1], brute_force_coords[i % NUM_CITIES], color = "k", label = "Path from Brute Force Search" if i == 1 else"")
84.
85.    plt.xlabel("Longitude", fontsize = 14)
86.    plt.ylabel("Latitude", fontsize = 14)
87.    plt.legend(loc=0)
88.    plt.tight_layout()
89.    plt.savefig("travelling_salesman_path_genetic_algorithm.jpg", dpi = 600)
90.    plt.show()
91.
92. if __name__ == "__main__":
93.    ga_indexes = genetic_algorithm_traveling_salesman()
94.    ga_coords = [city_coordinates[ga_index] for ga_index in ga_indexes]
95.    compare_paths(city_coordinates, ga_coords)
```

CHAPTER 7   A TALE OF TEN CITIES

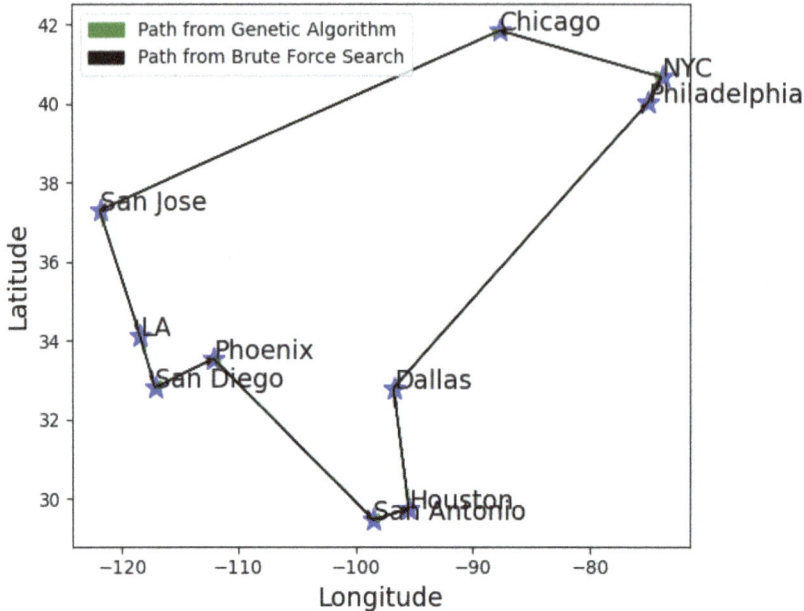

Figure 7-6. *The best route found by the Genetic Algorithm agrees with that from the brute force search*

A Traveling Consultant: Part 3

In previous two Sections, we have found a route to connect all ten cities in the shortest distance. Let us do something different. Let us travel from one start city to a destination city, for example, from New York to Los Angeles. Also, not all cities are directly connected. See the map in Figure 7-7 where numbers on the edge are the distances between two cities in miles, calculated using the Haversine formula.

CHAPTER 7 A TALE OF TEN CITIES

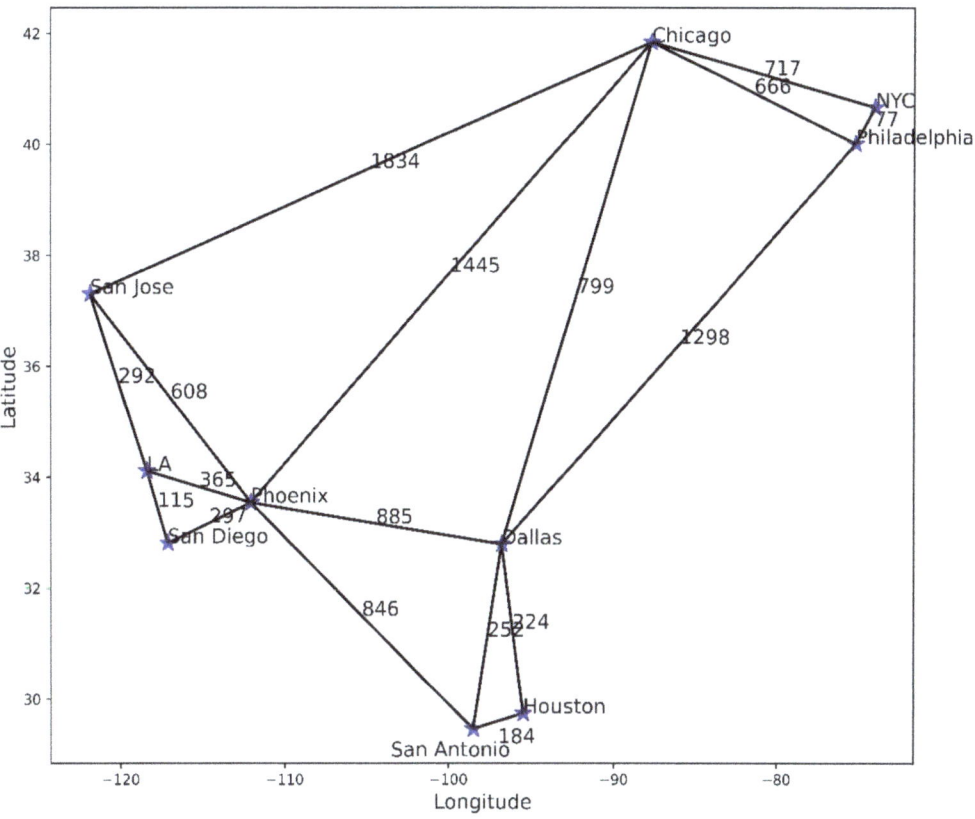

Figure 7-7. *A distance map between US cities. Numbers on edges are in miles*

Based on the map, there exist many routes from NYC to LA, such as NYC → Chicago → San Jose → LA or NYC → Philadelphia → Dallas → Phoenix → LA. But how to find the shortest one?

For finding the shortest path with positive weights, one typically uses Dijkstra's algorithm. Let us examine how it works with a simpler graph (Figure 7-8). The numbers on the graph are distances between places in miles, or you can think of them as the time to travel, in minutes. Either is fine. The goal is to find the shortest path from Home to Library. Below are the steps to follow.

CHAPTER 7   A TALE OF TEN CITIES

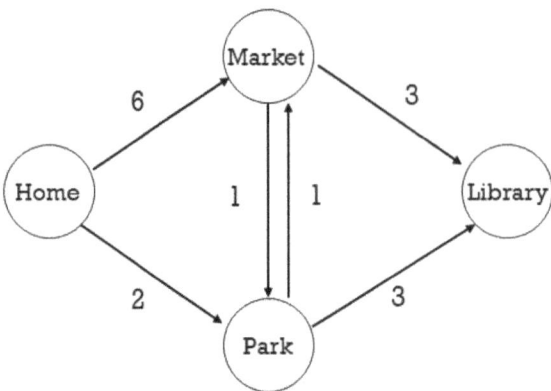

Figure 7-8. *A simple map for the local community*

Step 1: Tabulate the distances between the start node and other nodes; initial distances are infinity.

Start	End	Distance
Home	Market	∞
Home	Park	∞
Home	Library	∞

Step 2: Pick up the neighbors of Home, in this case, Market and Park, and update distances. There is a path to Market with a distance of 6 which is shorter than infinity, so replace infinity with 6. Same for Park, replace infinity with 2.

Start	End	Distance
Home	Market	6
Home	Park	2
Home	Library	∞

Step 3: Pick up Park to explore further, as it has the shortest distance among all. Park has two neighbors, Library and Market. The distance to Market will be 2 +1 = 3, which is smaller than the existing value, so replace 6 with 3. Same for Library, let us replace infinity with 2 + 3 = 5.

Start	End	Distance
Home	Market	3
Home	Park	2
Home	Library	5

Step 4: Although Park has the shortest distance in the table, we have already visited it. We will choose between **unvisited** nodes, i.e., Market and Library. Since Market has a shorter distance, pick up Market for further exploration. From Market, one can go to either Park or Library. If going to Park, the total distance will be 3 + 1 = 4 > 3; if going to Library, the total distance will be 3 + 3 = 6 > 5, so we reject both updates. The table stays the same.

Start	End	Distance
Home	Market	3
Home	Park	2
Home	Library	5

Step 5: Since Library has no outgoing paths, we do nothing about it and we have visited all nodes. The table tells the shortest distance from Home to all other places (Dijkstra's algorithm is a single-source shortest path algorithm). In particular, from Home to Library, the best route is Home → Park → Library with a total distance of 5 miles.

Dijkstra's algorithm shares similarity with Breadth-First Search (BFS, which we will discuss in detail in Chapter 8) in that it searches by looking at the neighbors, layer by layer. However, a BFS would recommend either Home → Park → Library or Home → Market → Library as the optimal path, as both only traverse two segments. If the distances between nodes are the same, then the shortest path problem can be solved by BFS.

A pure greedy search will yield a path of Home → Park → Market → Library as it picks up the node each time with the shortest distance locally. But the result of that path is 6, larger than the best value of 5. A Greedy Algorithm believes in the short-term incentive too much and often leads to a suboptimal result. In our Simulated Annealing example, we do not reject a swap with increasing total distance right away, but consider retaining it with a certain probability. By doing so, we make it possible to find a (near) optimal solution.

CHAPTER 7   A TALE OF TEN CITIES

Dijkstra's algorithm reminds us of Dynamic Programming in that it records the best route so far leading to the current node. For the next move, we will pick up the segment with the shortest distance – we are greedy here for this one move. In our example, we do not want to go to previous nodes during the search. Because, if removing this constraint, the search will bounce between Park and Market infinitely as there is a two-way path between them. By keeping track of the visited nodes, Dijkstra's algorithm is immune to cycles in the graph.

Dijkstra's algorithm does have a couple of limitations. First, it cannot handle the cases where the weights are negative, for which the Bellman–Ford algorithm can be used. Second, if the Library is to the east of Home, and the search map includes many nodes to the west of Home, as a human, we won't consider any places west of Home, but the algorithm will check all nodes, layer by layer. A better approach in this case would be using an A* algorithm that has heuristics incorporated.

The code for solving the current problem is displayed in Listing 7-4.

Listing 7-4. Apply Dijkstra's algorithm to find the shortest path between US cities

```
1.  import heapq
2.  from collections import defaultdict
3.  from utils import city_coordinates, cities, haversine_distance, drawArrow
4.  import matplotlib.pyplot as plt
5.
6.  N = 10
7.  cities_coord_dict = {city : coord for city, coord in zip(cities, city_coordinates)}
8.  edges = [["NYC", "Chicago"], ["NYC", "Philadelphia"], ["Chicago", "Philadelphia"],
9.           ["Chicago", "San Jose"], ["Chicago", "Phoenix"], ["Chicago", "Dallas"],
10.          ["Philadelphia", "Dallas"], ["Dallas", "Phoenix"], ["Dallas", "San Antonio"],
11.          ["Dallas", "Houston"], ["San Antonio", "Houston"], ["Phoenix", "San Antonio"],
12.          ["LA", "San Jose"], ["LA", "Phoenix"], ["LA", "San Diego"],
13.          ["San Jose", "Phoenix"], ["San Diego", "Phoenix"]]
14.
15. dists = [int(haversine_distance(*cities_coord_dict[city_1], *cities_coord_dict
    [city_2])) for city_1, city_2 in edges]
16.
17. graph = defaultdict(list)
18. for i in range(len(edges)):
19.     graph[edges[i][0]].append((edges[i][1], dists[i]))
20.     graph[edges[i][1]].append((edges[i][0], dists[i]))
21.
22. def shortest_path_between_cities(start_city, end_city):
23.     visited = {city: False for city in cities}
24.     distances = {city: float('inf') for city in cities}
25.     parent = {city: None for city in cities}
26.     parent[start_city] = start_city
27.     heap = [(0, start_city)]
28.     heapq.heapify(heap)
29.
30.     while heap:
```

```python
31.            dist, node = heapq.heappop(heap)
32.            if not visited[node]:
33.                distances[node] = dist
34.                visited[node] = True
35.                for k, d in graph[node]:
36.                    if not visited[k]:
37.                        new_dist = dist + d
38.                        if new_dist < distances[k]:
39.                            distances[k] = new_dist
40.                            parent[k] = node
41.                            heapq.heappush(heap, (new_dist, k))
42.
43.        # retrieve path
44.        if distances[end_city] == float('inf'):
45.            shortest_path = []
46.
47.        path = []
48.        node = end_city
49.        while node != start_city:
50.            path.append(node)
51.            node = parent[node]
52.        path.append(start_city)
53.        shortest_path = path[::-1]
54.
55.        print (distances)
56.        print (visited)
57.        print (parent)
58.        print (shortest_path)
59.        return shortest_path
```

Up to line 15 in Listing 7-4, we have prepared a list of inter-city distances using the Haversine formula, and then we move on to the graph part. Here we built a graph as an adjacency list (lines 17–20). Inside the `graph`, the key is the name of the city, whereas the value is its neighbors with a tuple value of (city, distance).

CHAPTER 7   A TALE OF TEN CITIES

In [3]: graph

Out[3]:

defaultdict(list,
            {'NYC': [('Chicago', 717), ('Philadelphia', 77)],
             'Chicago': [('NYC', 717),
              ('Philadelphia', 666),
              ('San Jose', 1834),
              ('Phoenix', 1445),
              ('Dallas', 799)],
             'Philadelphia': [('NYC', 77), ('Chicago', 666), ('Dallas', 1298)],
             'San Jose': [('Chicago', 1834), ('LA', 292), ('Phoenix', 608)],
             'Phoenix': [('Chicago', 1445),
              ('Dallas', 885),
              ('San Antonio', 846),
              ('LA', 365),
              ('San Jose', 608),
              ('San Diego', 297)],
             'Dallas': [('Chicago', 799),
              ('Philadelphia', 1298),
              ('Phoenix', 885),
              ('San Antonio', 252),
              ('Houston', 224)],
             'San Antonio': [('Dallas', 252),
              ('Houston', 184),
              ('Phoenix', 846)],
             'Houston': [('Dallas', 224), ('San Antonio', 184)],
             'LA': [('San Jose', 292), ('Phoenix', 365), ('San Diego', 115)],
             'San Diego': [('LA', 115), ('Phoenix', 297)]})

The meat of the algorithm is from lines 23–41. At line 23, we use a dictionary `visited` to keep track of visited nodes. Initially all nodes are not visited. At line 24, we keep track of optimal distances with initial values set as infinity in a dictionary `distances`. A parent dictionary is created at lines 25–26 to help retrieve the final optimal path. We use a min heap data structure because at each node, we will select the neighbor with the minimum total distance. From lines 30–41, if the heap is not empty, we pop a node from the heap (line 31), save its distance, and set the visited status to True. Then we loop over its neighbors. If the neighbor is not visited and the updated distance is smaller than the existing one (remember the default value is infinity), we update the distance, save the parent-child relation, and push the pair of updated distance and the neighboring city as a tuple to the heap.

From lines 43–53, we retrieve the path by leveraging the `parent` dictionary. Looking at the printed results below (the metadata printed out are from `distances`, `visited`, and `parent` dictionaries, respectively). The `distances` dictionary stores the shortest distances between NYC and other cities. The `visited` dictionary indicates that all nodes have been visited. After that comes the `parent` dictionary, which records the parent-child relationship. Finally, based on the `parent` dictionary, the shortest path between NYC and LA is retrieved.

```
In [4]: run Listing_7_4_dijkstra_shortest_path.py
{'NYC': 0, 'LA': 2527, 'Chicago': 717, 'Houston': 1599, 'Phoenix': 2162, 'Philadelphia': 77, 'San Antonio': 1627, 'San Diego': 2459, 'Dallas': 1375, 'San Jose': 2551}
{'NYC': True, 'LA': True, 'Chicago': True, 'Houston': True, 'Phoenix': True, 'Philadelphia': True, 'San Antonio': True, 'San Diego': True, 'Dallas': True, 'San Jose': True}
{'NYC': 'NYC', 'LA': 'Phoenix', 'Chicago': 'NYC', 'Houston': 'Dallas', 'Phoenix': 'Chicago', 'Philadelphia': 'NYC', 'San Antonio': 'Dallas', 'San Diego': 'Phoenix', 'Dallas': 'Philadelphia', 'San Jose': 'Chicago'}
['NYC', 'Chicago', 'Phoenix', 'LA']
```

As shown in red in Figure 7-9, the shortest path is NYC → Chicago → Phoenix → LA with a total distance of 2527 miles!

CHAPTER 7 A TALE OF TEN CITIES

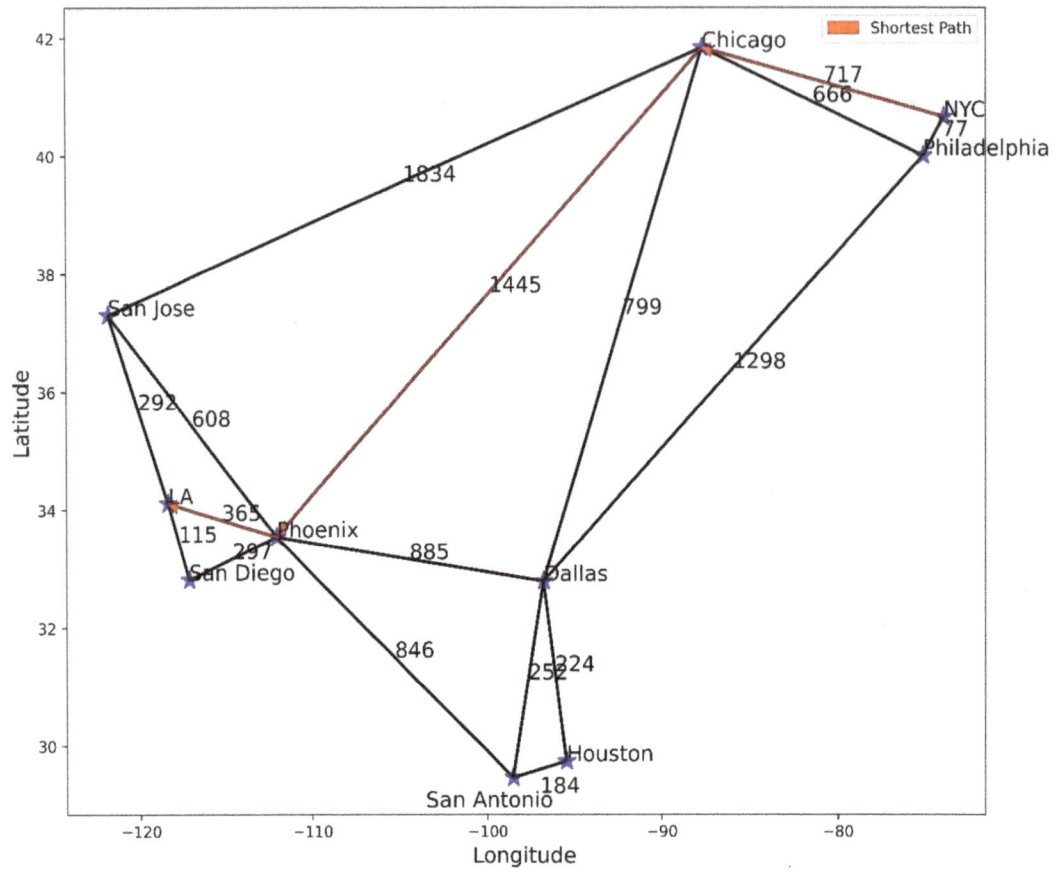

Figure 7-9. *The shortest path (red) from NYC to LA*

Build a Warehouse

The author's mind flies to many years later when his company has established excellent working relationships with all the clients in these ten major US cities. He asks himself: If we were to design a warehouse and want it to be closest to every city, where shall we build it? The distance between the warehouse location and the city can be readily calculated using the Haversine formula, given the latitude/longitude. The goal is to minimize this objective function: $\sum_{i=1}^{10} d(W, C_i)$ where W and C are coordinates of the warehouse and cities, respectively. The Haversine formula is great, but it involves trigonometric calculations.

Let us simplify things a bit, and assume we are on an x-y plane and the latitude/longitude of the cities are just x, y coordinates. Under these settings, the distance in this case will be the Euclidean distance.

Our target function then becomes $\sum_{i=1}^{10}\sqrt{(W_x - C_x^i)^2 + (W_y - C_y^i)^2}$. But how do we optimize this to get W?

There are certainly many ways of doing this, but let us try with an algorithm called Gradient Descent, which is widely used in machine learning optimization such as artificial neural networks.

The Gradient Descent consists of several steps.

(1) We calculate the partial derivative of the target function with respect to each variable.

(2) For each variable, we define a learning rate (nothing but a small number such as 0.001) and an initial guessed value.

(3) Since it is an iterative process, we will need a total number of rounds for iteration.

(4) For each round of iteration, we update the value for each variable, independently, by subtracting it from the step size value, which is the product of the learning rate and its evaluated partial derivative.

(5) The algorithm stops when either the predefined number of rounds is exhausted or any of the current step sizes is less than the predefined value.

(6) We trust the final variable values are optimized.

For the optimization, we can imagine a multidimensional parameter space. For the current problem, it will be a three-dimensional one with x, y being the coordinates of the warehouse and z being the total summed distances between cities and the warehouse. The partial derivative is nothing but the direction along which the search goes, and the step size tells how big a stride it should take downward, since we subtract it from the original value. The step size should be chosen carefully. If it is too large, it will overshoot the global minimum and bounce around in the parameter space. If it is too small, it will take a long time to converge.

CHAPTER 7 A TALE OF TEN CITIES

We can work out the partial derivatives for the target function using a bit of calculus; they are

$$\sum_{i=1}^{10} \frac{W_x - C_x^i}{\sqrt{\left(W_x - C_x^i\right)^2 + \left(W_y - C_y^i\right)^2}}$$

and

$$\sum_{i=1}^{10} \frac{W_y - C_y^i}{\sqrt{\left(W_x - C_x^i\right)^2 + \left(W_y - C_y^i\right)^2}}$$

As the initial guess for warehouse location, we can use the mean coordinates of ten cities. See code in Listing 7-5.

Listing 7-5. Find the location of a warehouse with Gradient Descent

```
1.  import math
2.  import matplotlib.pyplot as plt
3.  from utils import city_coordinates, cities, haversine_distance, drawArrow
4.
5.  X_COORD_MEAN = sum([x for x, _ in city_coordinates]) / len(city_coordinates)
6.  Y_COORD_MEAN = sum([y for _, y in city_coordinates]) / len(city_coordinates)
7.  ETA = 10**(-3) # learning rate
8.  MIN_STEP_SIZE = 10**(-8) # terminating condition for learning rate
9.  NUM_STEPS = 200000
10.
11. def euclidean_distance(x, y, coords):
12.     sum_distance = 0
13.     for coord_x, coord_y in coords:
14.         sum_distance += ((x - coord_x)**2 + (y - coord_y)**2)**0.5
15.     return sum_distance
16.
17. def partial_derivative_x_and_y(x, y, coords):
18.     partial_x = 0
19.     partial_y = 0
20.     for coord_x, coord_y in coords:
21.         partial_x += (x - coord_x) / ((x - coord_x)**2 + (y - coord_y)**2)**0.5
22.         partial_y += (y - coord_y) / ((x - coord_x)**2 + (y - coord_y)**2)**0.5
23.     return partial_x, partial_y
24.
25. def gradient_descent(x_guess = X_COORD_MEAN, y_guess = Y_COORD_MEAN):
26.     x = x_guess
27.     y = y_guess
28.     learning_rate_x = ETA
29.     learning_rate_y = ETA
30.     step_x = math.inf
31.     step_y = math.inf
32.
```

CHAPTER 7   A TALE OF TEN CITIES

```
33.     i = 0
34.     while i < NUM_STEPS and abs(step_x) > MIN_STEP_SIZE and abs(step_y) > MIN_STEP_SIZE:
35.         partial_x, partial_y = partial_derivative_x_and_y(x, y, city_coordinates)
36.         step_x = learning_rate_x * partial_x
37.         step_y = learning_rate_y * partial_y
38.         x -= step_x
39.         y -= step_y
40.         print (euclidean_distance(x, y, city_coordinates), "--->", step_x, step_y, i)
41.         i += 1
42.     return x, y
43.
44. def plot_result(x, y):
45.     # plot cities
46.     N = len(city_coordinates)
47.     for i in range(N):
48.         plt.scatter(city_coordinates[i][0], city_coordinates[i][1], s=150,
                marker='*', color = "b")
49.         plt.text(city_coordinates[i][0], city_coordinates[i][1], cities[i],
                fontsize = 14)
50.
51.     for i in range(N):
52.         drawArrow((x, y), city_coordinates[i], color = "gold", label = "")
53.
54.     plt.scatter(x, y, s=200, marker = "o", color = "gold")
55.     plt.xlabel("Longitude", fontsize = 14)
56.     plt.ylabel("Latitude", fontsize = 14)
57.     plt.tight_layout()
58.     plt.show()
59.
60. if __name__ == "__main__":
61.     x, y = gradient_descent()
62.     print (x, y)
63.     plot_result(x, y)
64.     total_distance = 0
65.     for lon, lat in city_coordinates:
66.         total_distance += haversine_distance(x, y, lon, lat)
67.     print (f"The shortest distance to ten biggest cities in US is {round(total_distance,
            2)} miles")
```

In [5]: run Listing_7_5_closest_to_ten_cities_location.py

...

149.51192560350339 ---> -7.335728941749375e-05 5.8535377291391026e-08 5988

149.51192022909186 ---> -7.331974340080793e-05 5.13951672452273e-08 5989

149.51191486018104 ---> -7.328221688855363e-05 4.426675941207603e-08 5990

149.51190949676516 ---> -7.32447098706358e-05 3.715013925573163e-08 5991

149.51190413883842 ---> -7.320722233696154e-05 3.004529226383057e-08 5992

149.51189878639508 ---> -7.316975427743488e-05 2.295220391734798e-08 5993

149.5118934394294 ---> -7.313230568198114e-05 1.587085972465374e-08 5994

149.5118880979356 ---> -7.309487654051183e-05 8.801245214490328e-09 5995

-97.82097427069056 32.6553725791288

The shortest distance to ten biggest cities in US is 8691.69 miles

CHAPTER 7   A TALE OF TEN CITIES

After running the program, the warehouse location has a longitude and latitude of (-97.82, 32.65); see Figure 7-10. And based on Google Maps, we can see it is located southwest of Dallas. The exact location is near a country road in Parker County, Texas (Figure 7-11).

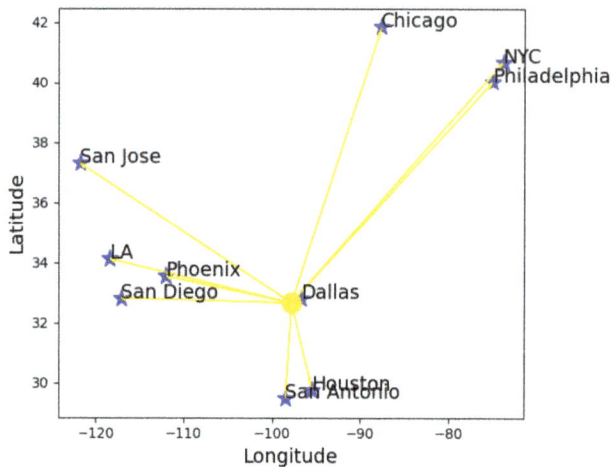

Figure 7-10. *The location of the warehouse is highlighted in a yellow dot*

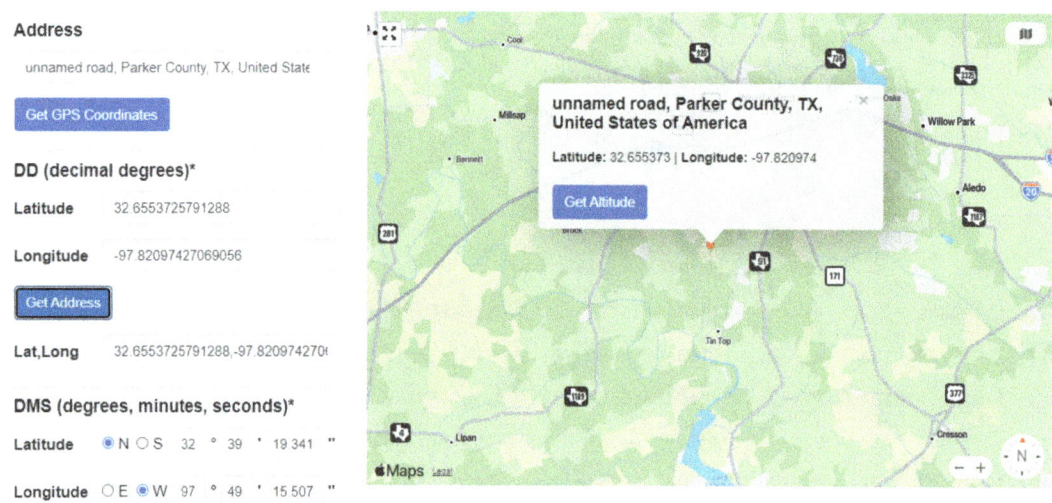

Figure 7-11. *The exact location of the warehouse based on Google Maps*

198

Group the Cities

Let us look at the cities one more time. This time, let us group them together based on the distances. If we group ten cities into three groups, which cities should be included in each group? Well, it seems NYC, Chicago, and Philadelphia could form a group. Dallas, Houston, and San Antonio can be grouped together. And the rest cities fall into the third group.

It becomes less clear how to group cities into two or four groups. Maybe we should let the computer draw boundary lines. We can use the popular unsupervised learning algorithm K-means Clustering here.

The way K-means works is summarized as below:

(1) It is an iterative algorithm; let us define the number of rounds as N.

(2) We need to know how many clusters we want to group the data into, e.g., K.

(3) We randomly pick up K points from all data points as an initial guess for the centroids.

(4) In each round of iteration, we

   a. Divide points into K groups based on distances to K centroids.

   b. Calculate the new centroids as the mean of K groups.

(5) We stop the algorithm when

   a. The predefined number of rounds N is reached.

   b. The total within-cluster sum of squared (WCSS) distances does not change much, say less than an epsilon value of 10^{-8}.

In Step 5, we mentioned the within-cluster sum of squares (WCSS) distances. For each cluster, we know the centroid and data points within the cluster. We can calculate the summed distances between the centroid and data points. We then sum up across the clusters to get one final value. The WCSS value will be used as a metric to evaluate the clustering. We can also use this parameter to decide K if it is not specified beforehand. In such a case, we create a plot of K as a function of WCSS where we should expect a steady decrease with K. In extreme cases, if we only have one cluster, this error term is the largest. On the other hand, if K equals the number of datapoints, we will have zero error. An optimal number of K resides between 1 and the total number of points. We can find the reflection point, a.k.a. "elbow," and choose that as our best-guessed K. This method is called "elbow method." See Listing 7-6 for code implementation of K-means Clustering.

CHAPTER 7   A TALE OF TEN CITIES

Listing 7-6. Cluster the cities using K-means Clustering

```python
1.  import matplotlib.pyplot as plt
2.  from collections import defaultdict
3.  from utils import city_coordinates, cities
4.  import random
5.  import math
6.  EPISILON = 10**(-8)
7.  N = len(city_coordinates)
8.
9.  def euclidean_distance(point_1, point_2):
10.     x1, y1 = point_1
11.     x2, y2 = point_2
12.     return math.sqrt((x1 - x2)**2 + (y1 - y2)**2)
13.
14. def find_average_coordinate(list_of_coordinates):
15.     x_sum, y_sum = 0, 0
16.     num_points = len(list_of_coordinates)
17.     for x, y in list_of_coordinates:
18.         x_sum += x
19.         y_sum += y
20.     return [x_sum / num_points, y_sum / num_points]
21.
22. def calculate_total_within_cluster_sum_of_squares(k_centroids, centroid_dict):
23.     total_sum_of_squares = 0
24.     for centroid_index in centroid_dict:
25.         for point_coord in centroid_dict[centroid_index]:
26.             total_sum_of_squares += euclidean_distance(k_centroids[centroid_index],
                    point_coord)
27.     return total_sum_of_squares
28.
29. def k_means_clustering(point_coords, num_clusters, num_iters):
30.     iter_count = 0
31.     # initial guess
32.     k_centroids = random.sample(point_coords, num_clusters)
33.     prev_total_within_cluster_sum_of_squares = math.inf
34.     while iter_count < num_iters:
35.         point_dict = {}
36.         # find new k centroids
37.         for point_coord in point_coords:
38.             distance_to_centroids = [(euclidean_distance(point_coord, k_centroid), i)
                    for i, k_centroid in enumerate (k_centroids)]
39.             closet_centroid_index = min(distance_to_centroids)[1]
40.             point_dict[tuple(point_coord)] = closet_centroid_index
41.
42.         centroid_dict = defaultdict(list)
43.         for point, centroid_index in point_dict.items():
44.             centroid_dict[centroid_index].append(list(point))
45.
46.         # udpate k centroids
47.         for i in range(num_clusters):
48.             if not centroid_dict[i]:
49.                 continue
50.             k_centroids[i] = find_average_coordinate(centroid_dict[i])
51.
52.         total_within_cluster_sum_of_squares                                          =
            calculate_total_within_cluster_sum_of_squares(k_centroids, centroid_dict)
```

200

```
53.         if abs(total_within_cluster_sum_of_squares - prev_total_within_cluster_
            sum_of_squares) <= EPSILON:
54.             break
55.         prev_total_within_cluster_sum_of_squares = total_within_cluster_sum_of_squares
56.         iter_count += 1
57.
58.     return k_centroids, centroid_dict, total_within_cluster_sum_of_squares
59.
60. def find_optimum_number_of_clusters(city_coordinates):
61.     num_clusters = range(1, N + 1)
62.     total_within_cluster_sum_of_squares_arr = []
63.     for num_cluster in num_clusters:
64.         cur_within_cluster_sum_of_squares_res = []
65.         for _ in range(10):
66.             _, _, total_within_cluster_sum_of_squares = k_means_clustering
                (city_coordinates, num_cluster, 1000)
67.             cur_within_cluster_sum_of_squares_res.append
                (total_within_cluster_sum_of_squares)
68.         total_within_cluster_sum_of_squares_arr.append(min
                (cur_within_cluster_sum_of_squares_res))
69.     plt.plot(num_clusters, total_within_cluster_sum_of_squares_arr, "ko-", lw=2)
70.     plt.xlabel("Number of Clusters", fontsize = 12)
71.     plt.ylabel("Total Within Cluster Sum of Squares", fontsize = 12)
72.     plt.title("Find Optimum Number of Clusters using Elbow Method", fontsize =12)
73.     plt.tight_layout()
74.     plt.show()
75.
76. def visualize_results(k_centroids, centroid_dict, colors = ["r", "b", "g", "m",
    "k", "c", "y", "tab:pink", "tab:brown", "tab:purple"]):
77.     for i, k_centroid in enumerate(k_centroids):
78.         for coord_x, coord_y in centroid_dict[i]:
79.             plt.scatter(coord_x, coord_y, c=colors[i], alpha = 0.6, s=50)
80.             plt.plot([coord_x, k_centroid[0]], [coord_y, k_centroid[1]], c = colors[i],
                alpha = 0.2)
81.         plt.scatter(k_centroid[0], k_centroid[1], marker='^', c=colors[i], s=70)
82.     # add city names
83.     for i in range(N):
84.         plt.text(city_coordinates[i][0], city_coordinates[i][1], cities[i],
            fontsize = 14)
85.     # title and labels
86.     plt.title(f'Clustering of Ten Major US Cities; n = {len(k_centroids)}',
        fontsize = 14)
87.     plt.xlabel('Longitude', fontsize = 12)
88.     plt.ylabel('Latitude', fontsize = 12)
89.     plt.tight_layout()
90.     plt.show()
91.
92. if __name__ == "__main__":
93.     k_centroids, centroid_dict, total_within_cluster_sum_of_squares =
    k_means_clustering(city_coordinates, 2, 1000)
94.     print (total_within_cluster_sum_of_squares)
95.     visualize_results(k_centroids, centroid_dict)
96.     find_optimum_number_of_clusters(city_coordinates)
```

CHAPTER 7   A TALE OF TEN CITIES

The final clustering results are sensitive to the initial choices of the centroids. In our program, we pick up city coordinates randomly as initial guesses. To find the optimal results, we can run the program several times and keep track of the WCSS – the clustering that yields the smallest WCSS will be the optimal clustering.

The best K-means Clustering for K=2 and 3 (Figure 7-12) has a WCSS of 79.12 and 36.95, respectively. The K=3 grouping aligns with our intuition.

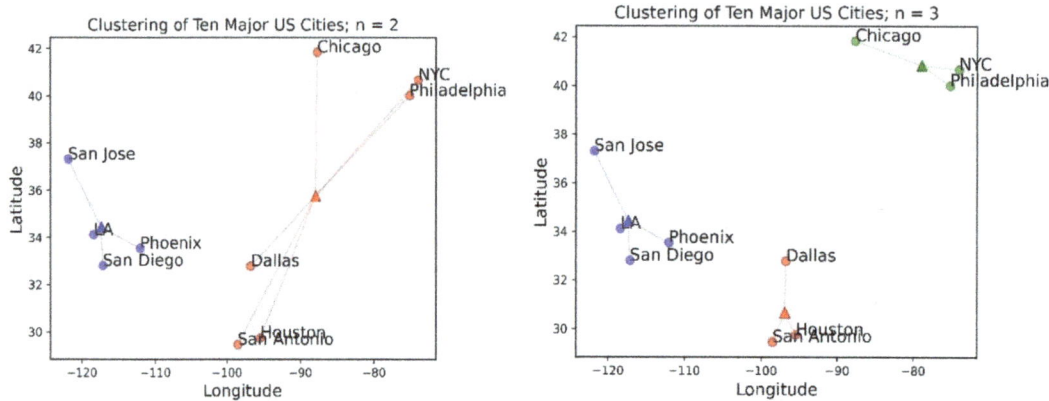

Figure 7-12. *Cluster the cities into two and three groups, respectively*

Let us see if we can find an optimal number of clusters. In Figure 7-13, WCSS is plotted as a function of the number of clusters K. The reduction in WCSS is dramatic for K up to 4 (from ~152.79 to ~20.73). There is a further reduction in WCSS beyond K=4, though the rate of the decrease is significantly reduced (from ~20.73 to 0). We can argue based on the "elbow method" that the optimum cluster is 4.

CHAPTER 7   A TALE OF TEN CITIES

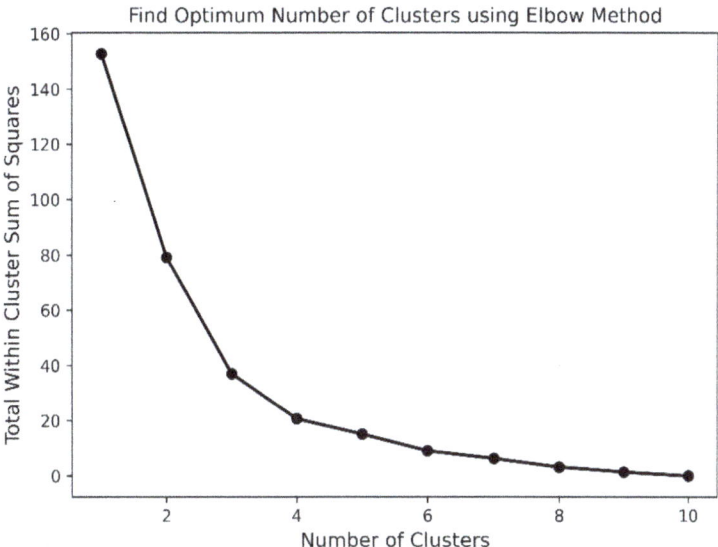

Figure 7-13. *The elbow method to find the optimal number of clusters*

The result in Figure 7-14 groups the cities into four distinct groups with a WCSS of ~20.64. Compared with the K=3 case in Figure 7-12, Chicago becomes the single point cluster, whereas the other three clusters remain the same.

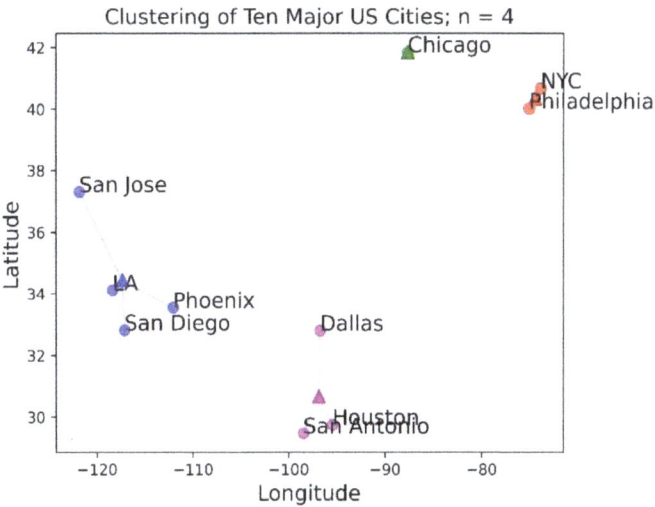

Figure 7-14. *Group cities into four groups*

After doing the previous exercises, we realize the limitations of K-means. First, the clustering results are heavily influenced by the initial choices of the centroids. In addition, K-means approximates the data points as spherical clusters – it fails at non-convex clusters,

203

for example, clusters of two concentric rings. Finally, the number of optimal clusters is a hyperparameter. The algorithm cannot determine it automatically (though in practice, the elbow method may help to a certain degree). Nonetheless, K-means is a simple and intuitive algorithm that is often the first tool to try for many clustering problems.

Application

The algorithms introduced in the Chapter are foundational to a variety of real-world applications. Both Simulated Annealing and Genetic Algorithm are optimization techniques that are widely used in many applications such as solving combinatorial optimization problems, hyperparameter tuning in machine learning, robotics and path planning, and financial portfolio optimization. Dijkstra's algorithm is the bedrock of routing and navigation systems, packet routing in computer networks, and logistics and supply chain management. Gradient Descent is one of the most important optimization techniques that is widely used in machine learning model training. For example, Stochastic Gradient Descent, its variant, is commonly used to update weights in deep neural networks by calculating gradients through backpropagation (a process of computing the derivative of the loss function with respect to each weight in the network). K-means Clustering finds applications in customer segmentation in marketing, anomaly detection, and object detection in computer vision.

As an example, let us see how we can apply Simulated Annealing to solve a Sudoku puzzle. The Sudoku we are going to solve is shown below where "x" represents a missing number from 1 to 9.

```
-------------------------
| 7 3 x | x x x | 8 4 x |
| 1 5 x | x x 7 | 2 x x |
| x x 8 | x 1 x | 3 x 5 |
-------------------------
| x 9 6 | x 5 x | x 8 3 |
| x x x | 6 x 3 | x x x |
| 5 4 x | x 2 x | 7 6 x |
-------------------------
| 3 x 2 | x 4 x | 6 x x |
| x x 7 | 2 x x | x 3 4 |
| x 1 5 | x x x | x 2 8 |
-------------------------
```

Sudoku contains nine 3×3 square blocks, and each of the blocks must contain all numbers 1 to 9 within its square. Additionally, each number can only appear *once* in a row or column of the 9×9 square.

The Sudoku can be solved using Backtracking which we will discuss in detail in Chapter 8. Here, we will try to solve it using Simulated Annealing. Our approach is this:

(1) For each 3×3 square block, we first figure out what missing numbers are and use them to replace "x" randomly. For example, for the first 3×3 block, only 2, 4, 6, 9 are missing, and we fill in "x" with them randomly.

(2) We record the cost by counting duplicated numbers in each row and column of the 9×9 square.

(3) We swap the allowed numbers in each 3×3 block randomly. If the swap reduces the cost, we accept it; if not, we accept it with a certain probability.

(4) A solution of Sudoku is found when the error is zero.

The complete code is listed in Listing 7-7. First, we use a seed of 1234 (line 4) to guarantee a reproducible result. Next, we store the board in a dictionary (lines 57-59) where the key is the (x, y) coordinate pair and the value is either the number in string format or "x", i.e., the missing number. A convenient print_board function is created to beautifully print the board to the console, see the puzzle above. The indexes and values of missing numbers are stored in a dictionary missing_numbers_dict which gets updated in the subsequent iterations. As a first attempt, Simulated Annealing would fill in the numbers from missing_numbers_dict to complete the puzzle (lines 29-45), which would certainly yield an incorrect solution. At lines 17-27, we quantify the cost as the summation of duplicated numbers at each row and each column of the 9×9 block; see calculate_total_cost(). In the steps that followed, we just keep randomly swapping two numbers in a 3×3 block (lines 47-54), until the total costs are reduced to 0. The main code for running the Simulated Annealing is from lines 64-89.

Listing 7-7. Solve a Sudoku puzzle with Simulated Annealing

```python
from copy import copy
from math import exp
import random
random.seed(1234)

def print_board(board):
    row_sep = '-'*25
    for i in range(9):
        if i % 3 == 0:
            print(row_sep)
        row = ""
        for c in range(9):
            row += board[(i, c)]
        print('| '+' '.join(row[0:3])+' | '+' '.join(row[3:6])+' | '+' '.join(row[6:])+' |')
    print(row_sep)

def calculate_total_cost():
    # total cost is the summation of duplicated numbers each row + each column
    total_counts = 0
    for i in range(9):
        row_count = 9 - len(set([board[(i,j)] for j in range(9)]))
        total_counts += row_count

    for j in range(9):
        col_count = 9 - len(set([board[(i,j)] for i in range(9)]))
        total_counts += col_count
    return total_counts

def fill_missing_numbers():
    for range_row in [range(0,3), range(3, 6), range(6,9)]:
        for range_col in [range(0,3), range(3, 6), range(6,9)]:
            block_numbers = ''
            unfilled_indexes = list()
            for i in range_row:
                for j in range_col:
                    if board[(i, j)] != 'x':
                        block_numbers += board[(i,j)]
                    else:
                        unfilled_indexes.append((i,j))
            remained_numbers = [str(num) for num in range(1, 10) if str(num) not in block_numbers]
            missing_numbers_dict[tuple(unfilled_indexes)] = remained_numbers
            random.shuffle(remained_numbers)
            # assign number
            for index, value in zip(unfilled_indexes, remained_numbers):
                board[index] = value

    def random_swap_numbers_in_a_block():
    indexes, numbers = random.choice(list(missing_numbers_dict.items()))
    if len(indexes) < 2:
        return
    i, j = random.sample(range(len(indexes)), 2)
    board[indexes[i]] = numbers[j]
    board[indexes[j]] = numbers[i]
    numbers[i], numbers[j] = numbers[j], numbers[i]
```

206

```python
55.
56.  if __name__ == "__main__":
57.      board = dict(
58.          zip(((i, j) for i in range(9) for j in range(9)),
59.          "73xxxx84x15xxx72xxxx8x1x3x5x96x5xx83xxx6x3xxx54xx2x76x3x2x4x6xxxx72xxx
             34x15xxxx28"))
60.      missing_numbers_dict = dict()
61.      # calculate the initial cost
62.      fill_missing_numbers()
63.      cur_cost = calculate_total_cost()
64.      # initial parameters for simulated annealing
65.      Tmax = 5000.0
66.      Tmin = 1e-3
67.      tau = 10000
68.      # start simulated annealing
69.      t = 0
70.      T = Tmax
71.      while T > Tmin:
72.          t += 1
73.          T = Tmax * exp(-t / tau)
74.          prev_cost = cur_cost
75.          prev_board = copy(board)
76.          random_swap_numbers_in_a_block()
77.          cur_cost = calculate_total_cost()
78.          diff_cost = cur_cost - prev_cost
79.          if diff_cost < 0:
80.              continue
81.          else:
82.              if exp(-diff_cost / T) > random.random():
83.                  continue
84.              else:
85.                  board = prev_board
86.                  cur_cost = prev_cost
87.          print (t, "--->", cur_cost)
88.          if cur_cost == 0:
89.              break
90.
91.      print_board(board)
```

Although it is not a "clever" approach that finds the solution by randomly swapping numbers, the Simulated Annealing does find the correct solution after ~100,000 iterations. It is worth mentioning that the current program can be further improved by, for example, defining a more sophisticated cost function.

CHAPTER 7   A TALE OF TEN CITIES

```
In [6]: run Listing_7_7_application_solving_sudoku.py
-------------------------
| 7 3 9 | 5 6 2 | 8 4 1 |
| 1 5 4 | 8 3 7 | 2 9 6 |
| 6 2 8 | 4 1 9 | 3 7 5 |
-------------------------
| 2 9 6 | 7 5 4 | 1 8 3 |
| 8 7 1 | 6 9 3 | 4 5 2 |
| 5 4 3 | 1 2 8 | 7 6 9 |
-------------------------
| 3 8 2 | 9 4 5 | 6 1 7 |
| 9 6 7 | 2 8 1 | 5 3 4 |
| 4 1 5 | 3 7 6 | 9 2 8 |
-------------------------
```

Summary

In the chapter, we learned five important algorithms based on the story of the ten most populous cities in the United States.

- The Simulated Annealing (SA) is a probabilistic optimization technique inspired by the process of annealing in metallurgy where controlled cooling of a metal leads to a state of low energy and optimal molecular arrangement. It balances the exploration and exploitation – it accepts a move that reduces the overall cost and conditionally accepts a move that increases the cost without rejecting it outright. It is this balance that makes SA escape local minima and freely explore the solution space and discover a better global solution.

- Genetic Algorithm (GA) borrows the idea of evolution and natural selection. It creates a population of chromosomes, picks up the best of them, and applies crossovers and mutations to them to produce the offsprings which replaces the worst chromosomes in the original population. It is through this iterative process (evolution) that we can find the best chromosome (the desired outcome). Both SA and GA seek better configuration/result through random perturbations to the current state iteratively.

- Dijkstra's algorithm finds the shortest path between two arbitrary nodes in a *non-negatively* weighted graph. For a graph with negative weights, we can instead use the Bellman–Ford algorithm to find the shortest path between nodes. Dijkstra's algorithm selects the node with the minimum distance from the source at each step and makes a local optimal choice by selecting the closest node and updating the distances to the neighboring nodes. It can be regarded as a Greedy Algorithm.

- The Gradient Descent algorithm is a powerful optimization technique that helps find the global (near) optimal solution in a convex function. The parameters get updated by a step size at each iteration, which is the product of the partial derivative and the learning rate. The iteration stops when either the step size is too small or the predefined number of iterations is reached.

- The K-means Clustering algorithm is a popular unsupervised learning algorithm. It works by iteratively updating the centroids of K groups. If the number of groups K is not predefined, we can use an "elbow" method to find the best value for K.

CHAPTER 8

Chess

Chess is a board game that has gained popularity around the globe. It is estimated that more than half a billion adults play it regularly. It has also become the trend that the highest title in professional chess, the Grand Master, is clinched by teenagers at an ever-decreasing age. The Indian wonderkid, Gukesh Dommaraju, stunned the world by beating defending champion Ding Liren in Singapore on December 12, 2024, with a score of $7^{1/2}$ vs. $6^{1/2}$, making him the youngest ever Chess World Champion at the age of 18!

In this chapter, we will review a few fun chess-inspired problems. We kick it off by introducing the binary tree and N-ary tree and their traversals, which serve as the foundation for solving the problems in the subsequent sections. We then review Knight's Tour, Knight's Jump, and N-queen problems where we will learn Depth-First Search, Breadth-First Search, and Backtracking algorithms. We move on to learn and implement the Monte Carlo Tree Search, which is the key component behind the AI agent, AlphaGo, that defeated the World Champion of Go. We wrap things up by discussing the real-life applications of the algorithms in this chapter.

Binary Tree and Its Traversals

In the "Application" section of Chapter 1, we have briefly introduced the binary tree and its pre-order, in-order, and post-order traversals using *recursion*. In this section, we will deep dive into more useful traversals using an *iterative* method with the help of a stack and queue data structure. Recall the tree discussed in Chapter 1 as shown in Figure 8-1. We can also view the tree from left to right; thus, we can see nodes are at different levels. For example, the root node is at level 1, nodes 2 and 3 are at level 2, and the rest are at level 3.

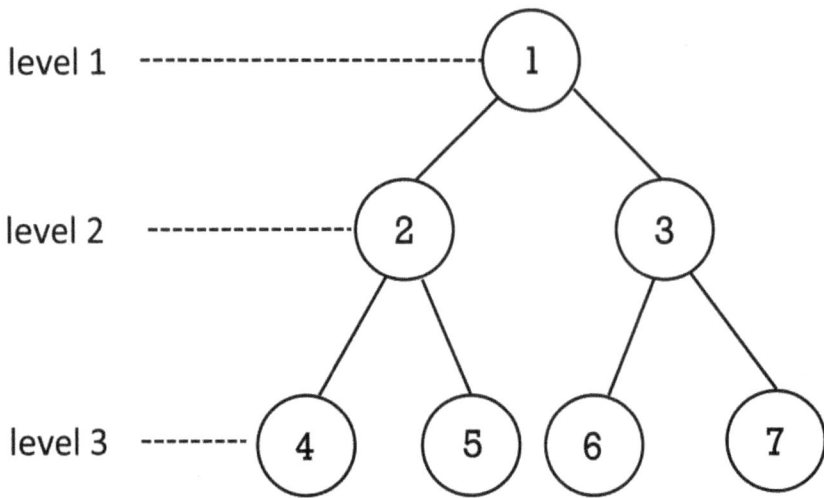

Figure 8-1. *An illustration of a binary tree with various levels*

There are various ways to traverse the tree. The two most common traversals leverage Depth-First Search (DFS) and Breadth-First Search (BFS). For DFS, as the name suggests, starting from the root node, it goes down its left branch repeatedly until it hits the bottom and then returns upward. In the example, the order of visits is 1 → 2 → 4 → 5 → 3 → 6 → 7. It explores in the order of root → left subtree → right subtree. In contrast, for BFS, it explores the nodes level by level. Thus, the order of visits is 1 → 2 → 3 → 4 → 5 → 6 → 7. BFS is often used to find the shortest path from one node to the other nodes, supposing that the segment between both nodes is of equal distance. In other words, BFS finds the minimum number of segments between two nodes.

To implement the traversals, we will use a stack for DFS and a queue for BFS. Recall that the stack is First In Last Out (FILO), whereas a queue is First In First Out (FIFO). In Python, we can use `list` to implement a stack and `deque` from the `collections` module for a queue. For both BFS and DFS, we first put the root node in the queue/stack. For the queue, we pop out the node from the front of it, whereas for a stack, we eject an element from the end. Another difference is that while in BFS, we push the left child and right child (if they exist) to the queue; in DFS, we will need to push the *right child first*, followed by the left child. In such way, the left child will be popped out first. The code implementation of DFS and BFS of a binary tree is in Listing 8-1.

Listing 8-1. DFS and BFS of a binary tree

```
1.  from collections import deque
2.  class TreeNode:
3.      def __init__(self, value):
4.          self.value = value
5.          self.left = None
6.          self.right = None
7.
8.  def breadth_first_search_traversal(root_node):
9.      BFS_values = []
10.     queue = deque([root_node])
11.     while queue:
12.         node = queue.popleft()
13.         BFS_values.append(node.value)
14.         if node.left:
15.             queue.append(node.left)
16.         if node.right:
17.             queue.append(node.right)
18.     return BFS_values
19.
20. def depth_first_search_traversal(root_node):
21.     DFS_values = []
22.     stack = [root_node]
23.     while stack:
24.         node = stack.pop()
25.         DFS_values.append(node.value)
26.         if node.right:
27.             stack.append(node.right)
28.         if node.left:
29.             stack.append(node.left)
30.     return DFS_values
```

For tree traversals using DFS and BFS, since we visit each node once, it is linear for both time and space complexity.

In the BFS case, we can also do a level-order traversal, i.e., by grouping the elements level by level. Instead of getting an array of [1, 2, 3, 4, 5, 6, 7], we shall expect [[1], [2, 3], [4, 5, 6, 7]]. The change to the previous code breadth_first_search_traversal in Listing 8-1 is minimal. At each level, we will need to empty out the entire queue to retrieve values; see Listing 8-2.

CHAPTER 8   CHESS

Listing 8-2. Level-order traversal of a binary tree

```
1.  def level_order_traversal(root_node):
2.      all_level_values = []
3.      queue = deque([root_node])
4.      while queue:
5.          cur_level_values = []
6.          for _ in range(len(queue)):
7.              node = queue.popleft()
8.              cur_level_values.append(node.value)
9.              if node.left:
10.                 queue.append(node.left)
11.             if node.right:
12.                 queue.append(node.right)
13.         all_level_values.append(cur_level_values)
14.     return all_level_values
```

Another task we often encounter is to find all paths from the root to the leaf. In Figure 8-2, we have four such paths, i.e., 1 → 2 → 4, 1 → 2 → 5, 1 → 3 → 6, and 1 → 3 → 7. We will store them in a list [[1, 2, 4], [1, 2, 5], [1, 3, 6], [1, 3, 7]]. For that, we can still use the stack data structure. But instead of storing only the integer value in a tree node, we store also an additional piece of information, i.e., the root-to-leaf path. See Figure 8-2 for the evolution of the stack until we get all four paths in correct order and implementation of code in Listing 8-3.

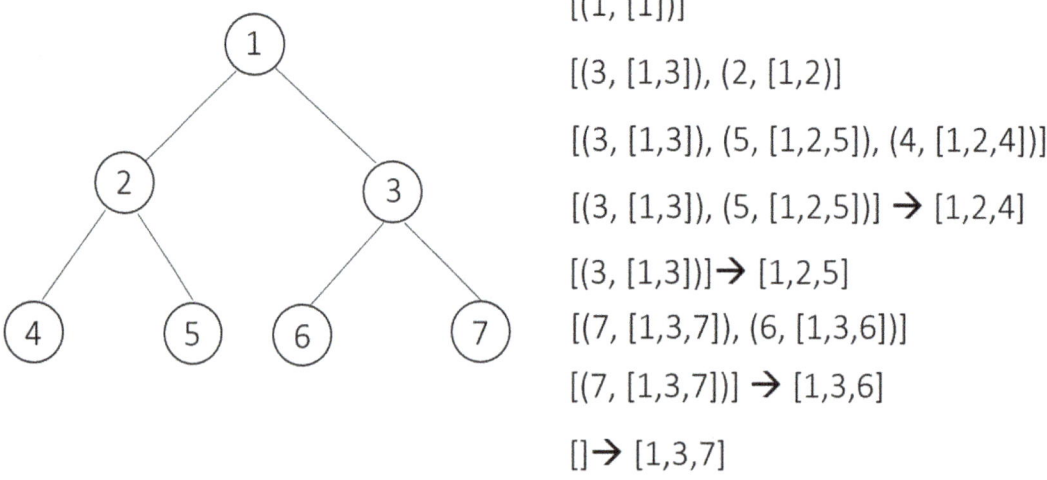

Figure 8-2. Find all root-to-leaf paths using a stack

Listing 8-3. Code to find all root-to-leaf paths in a binary tree

```python
1.  def root_to_leaf_paths(root_node):
2.      paths = []
3.      stack = [(root_node, [root_node.value])]
4.      while stack:
5.          node, path = stack.pop()
6.          if not node.left and not node.right:
7.              paths.append(path)
8.          if node.right:
9.              stack.append((node.right, path + [node.right.value]))
10.         if node.left:
11.             stack.append((node.left, path + [node.left.value]))
12.     return paths
```

N-ary Tree and Its Traversals

The N-ary tree is a more generic form of tree (Figure 8-3). In contrast to a binary tree that only allows up to two children for each node, an N-ary tree allows any number of child nodes. The concepts of root, leaf, and level from binary trees also apply here.

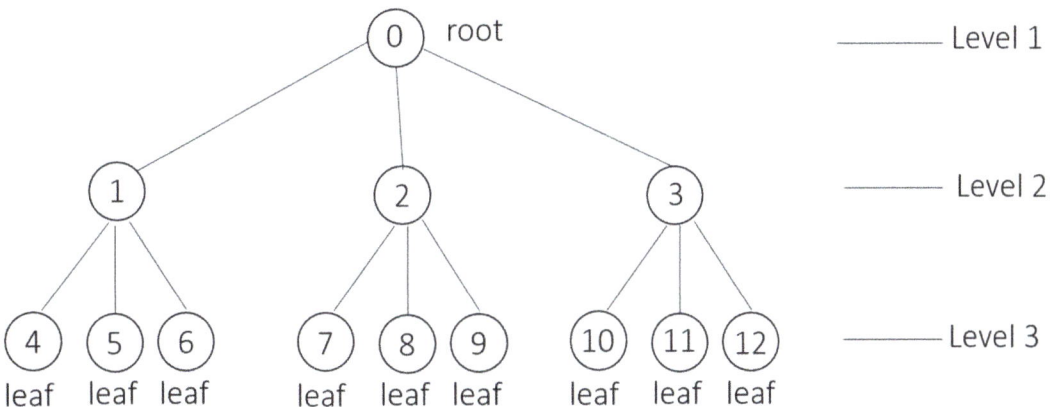

Figure 8-3. An illustration of an N-ary tree

In Listing 8-4, compared with the programmatic implementation of a binary tree, instead of the left and right child, we now initialize a `children` attribute in the `__init__` constructor. It uses a Python `list` to store any number of child nodes. Additionally, an `add_child` method is created to append any child node to the list. The tree we see above can be constructed using code from lines 10–34.

CHAPTER 8   CHESS

Listing 8-4. The class definition of a tree node for an N-ray tree

```
1.  class TreeNode:
2.      def __init__(self, value = None):
3.          self.value = value
4.          self.children = []
5.
6.      def add_child(self, child):
7.          self.children.append(child)
8.
9.  if __name__ == "__main__":
10.     root = TreeNode(0)
11.     child_1 = TreeNode(1)
12.     child_2 = TreeNode(2)
13.     child_3 = TreeNode(3)
14.     child_4 = TreeNode(4)
15.     child_5 = TreeNode(5)
16.     child_6 = TreeNode(6)
17.     child_7 = TreeNode(7)
18.     child_8 = TreeNode(8)
19.     child_9 = TreeNode(9)
20.     child_10 = TreeNode(10)
21.     child_11 = TreeNode(11)
22.     child_12 = TreeNode(12)
23.     root.add_child(child_1)
24.     root.add_child(child_2)
25.     root.add_child(child_3)
26.     child_1.add_child(child_4)
27.     child_1.add_child(child_5)
28.     child_1.add_child(child_6)
29.     child_2.add_child(child_7)
30.     child_2.add_child(child_8)
31.     child_2.add_child(child_9)
32.     child_3.add_child(child_10)
33.     child_3.add_child(child_11)
34.     child_3.add_child(child_12)
```

Let us do the traversals of an N-ary tree. The visiting order of nodes for Depth-First Search (DFS) is 0 → 1 → 4 → 5 → 6 → 2 → 7 → 8 → 9 → 3 → 10 → 11 →12. And for Breadth-First Search (BFS), the order of the sequence becomes 0 → 1 → 2 → 3 → 4 → 5 → 6 → 7 → 8 → 9 → 10 → 11 → 12. In Listing 8-5, the code implementation of DFS and BFS traversals of an N-ary tree only requires slight modifications to those of a binary tree (Listing 8-1). We still use stack and queue data structures, respectively, for DFS and BFS, but at lines 10 and 20, we loop through all children of a node.

Listing 8-5. DFS and BFS of an N-ary tree

```
1.  from collections import deque
2.
3.  def depth_first_search_traversal_n_ary_tree(root_node):
4.      DFS_values = []
5.      stack = [root_node]
6.      while stack:
7.          node = stack.pop()
8.          DFS_values.append(node.value)
9.          if node.children:
10.             stack.extend(node.children[::-1])
11.     return DFS_values
12.
13. def breadth_first_search_traversal_n_ary_tree(root_node):
14.     BFS_values = []
15.     queue = deque([root_node])
16.     while queue:
17.         node = queue.popleft()
18.         BFS_values.append(node.value)
19.         if node.children:
20.             queue.extend(node.children)
21.     return BFS_values
```

In terms of the level order traversal for an N-ray tree, we shall expect [[0], [1, 2, 3], [4, 5, 6, 7, 8, 9, 10, 11, 12]]. And the code implementation in Listing 8-6 is very similar to level-order traversal in the binary tree case (Listing 8-2). The only change is at lines 11–12. Instead of discussing the left and/or right child, here in the N-ary tree, we only have the `children` attribute.

Listing 8-6. Level-order traversal of an N-ary tree

```
1.  from collections import deque
2.
3.  def level_order_traversal_n_ary_tree(root_node):
4.      all_level_values = []
5.      queue = deque([root_node])
6.      while queue:
7.          cur_level_values = []
8.          for _ in range(len(queue)):
9.              node = queue.popleft()
10.             cur_level_values.append(node.value)
11.             if node.children:
12.                 queue.extend(node.children)
13.         all_level_values.append(cur_level_values)
14.     return all_level_values
```

Finally, let us implement the root-to-leaf path in Listing 8-7. We would expect [[0, 1, 4], [0, 1, 5], [0, 1, 6], [0, 2, 7], [0, 2, 8], [0, 2, 9], [0, 3, 10], [0, 3, 11], [0, 3, 12]] for current N-ary tree.

CHAPTER 8 CHESS

Listing 8-7. Find root-to-leaf paths in an N-ary tree

```
1.  def root_to_leaf_paths_n_ary_tree(root):
2.      paths = []
3.      stack = [(root, [root.value])]
4.      while stack:
5.          node, path = stack.pop()
6.          if not node.children:
7.              paths.append(path)
8.          else:
9.              for child in node.children[::-1]:
10.                 stack.append((child, path + [child.value]))
11.     return paths
```

Knight's Tour

The famous Knight's Tour problem asks that, starting from an arbitrary position of the chessboard, find the path of a knight such that it traverses every square of the board exactly only once. In chess, a knight moves in an "L" shape, that is, moves one square ahead, followed by a diagonal move. It is the only piece that can jump over other pieces. Before working on the standard 8×8 board, let us just try with a smaller board, say 3×3. For convenience, we can assign the Cartesian coordinates to each square where the bottom left square sits at (0, 0). In Figure 8-4, starting from (0, 0), we can either go to (1, 2) or (2, 1). Suppose at a first attempt, we pick up (1, 2), the next available square is (2, 0). When at (2, 0), since we cannot go back to (1, 2) as it has been visited, we go to (0, 1) instead. Moving on and the next sequential steps are (2, 2), (1, 0), (0, 2), and (2, 1). In sum, the full path is (0, 0) → (1, 2) → (2, 0) → (0, 1) → (2, 2) → (1, 0) → (0, 2) → (2, 1).

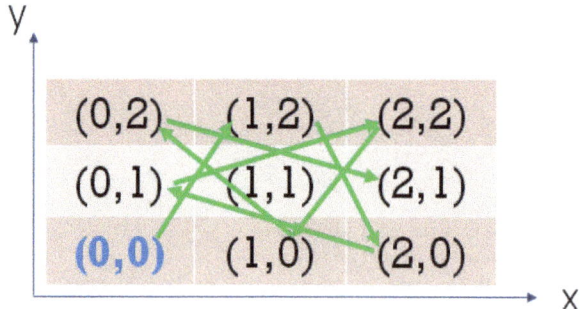

Figure 8-4. Jump the knight in a 3×3 board and start from position (0, 0) to (1, 2)

CHAPTER 8 CHESS

In this case, the knight does not jump to all squares on the board as the middle square is not reachable from (0, 0).

As discussed above, starting from (0, 0), we have two possible next moves, i.e., (1, 2) and (2, 1). We just demonstrated that picking up (1, 2) failed to complete the tour. Let us now try (2, 1); see Figure 8-5. The path is (0, 0) → (2, 1) → (0, 2) → (1, 0) → (2, 2) → (0, 1) → (2, 0) → (1, 2). Again, the center square (1, 1) is not reachable.

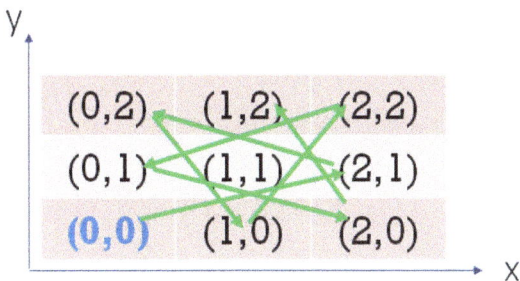

Figure 8-5. Jump the knight in a 3×3 board and start from position (0, 0) to (2, 1)

In such cases, a complete tour is not possible for a 3×3 board starting at (0, 0). In fact, it is not possible for a board of 3×3 or 4×4 size, regardless of the starting position. Also, exploring alternatively at (2, 1) demonstrates the idea of "*backtrack*," that is, if one path does not work, return to the previous checkpoint, build another path, and see if the new path works. This will become clearer if we construct a search tree for it as shown in Figure 8-6.

CHAPTER 8 CHESS

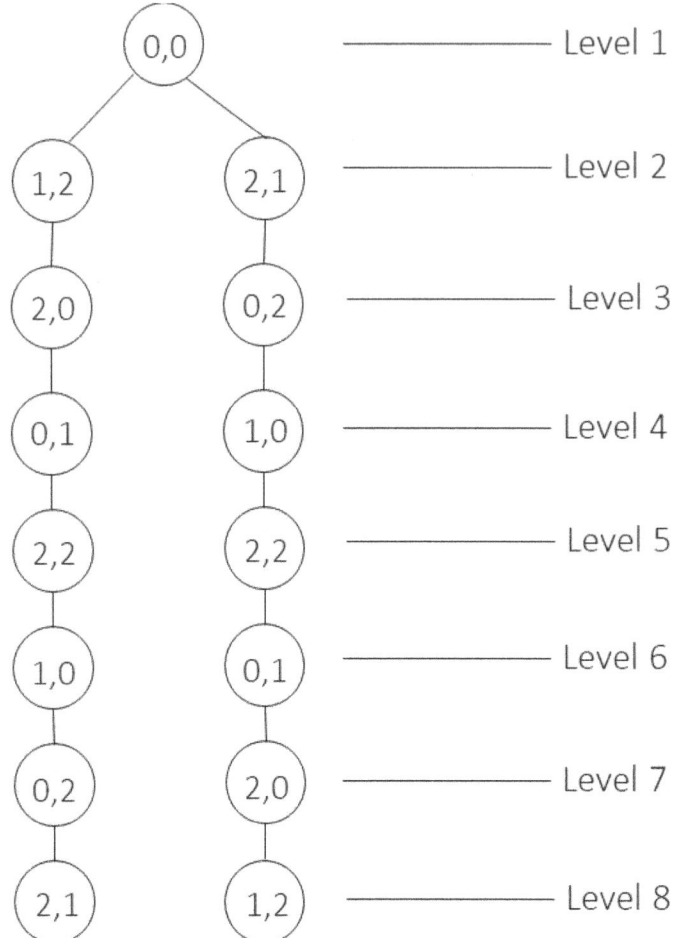

Figure 8-6. *A search tree for the knight jumping on a 3×3 board. Starting from (0, 0), the knight has two options: either go to (1, 2) or (2, 1)*

For a 3×3 board, the search tree starting from (0, 0) is a binary tree. However, for a bigger board and multiple starting points, this will turn into a huge N-ary tree. We can let each node store the positional information and mark every layer by the corresponding level number.

To solve the Knight's Tour problem, we can construct a search tree first. We can then traverse the tree using the Depth-First Search (DFS) algorithm until we find the target root-to-leaf path. We can stop it when the search hits the leaf node whose level number is equal to the number of the squares the knight needs to jump, including the initial square. In our case of a 3×3 board, the search shall stop at level 9.

As shown in Figure 8-6, during the initial search, we arrived at node (2, 1) at level 8, which is one level short of the target level. We then backtracked to the node (2, 1) at level 2 and continued the search. This time, the search explored the right subtree and stopped at (1, 2). Again, it could not reach level 9. Since we have traversed the entire tree, we failed to find a solution.

A couple of things to note. One is when constructing the tree, we do want to avoid nodes that have already been visited. For example, from (0, 0) → (1, 2) → (2, 0), at position (2, 0), it can jump to either (0, 1) or (1, 2). Since (1, 2) is already in the path, we skip it. In the code, we can designate a `visited` variable to keep track of the positions traversed and avoid repetition. Additionally, at the time of backtracking, we need to update the `visited` variable for the new path. In our example, after searching the left subtree, the `visited` variable stores the values of (0, 0), (1, 2), (2, 0), (0, 1), (2, 2), (1, 0), (0, 2), (2, 1). However, after backtracking to (2, 1) at level 2, the `visited` variable should be updated to store only values of (0, 0) and (2, 1). To make it easier to update `visited`, we can store one additional piece of information, i.e., the level information. After backtracking, the previous values in `visited` will be kept only when *their level numbers are less than the level of the current node*. By using the level information, we can decide when to backtrack. For example, when we hit the bottom of the left subtree, i.e., at node (2, 1, 8), and the next node in the stack is (2, 1, 2), we know it is time to backtrack, because the level 2 is less than level 8.

To implement a solution, we can use a *stack* data structure to keep track of the node that contains information of positions x, y, and level (Listing 8-8). At line 3, there are eight possible next moves for the knight, but they must be within the boundary of the board (line 19). Line 10 specifies the condition for the backtracking, and lines 11–12 update the visited positions. Finally, line 20 avoids the squares that have already been visited.

CHAPTER 8 CHESS

Listing 8-8. An initial implementation of Knight's Tour

```
1.  def knight_tour(initial_pos, R=8, C=8):
2.      target_level = R * C
3.      directions = [(-1,2), (1,2), (2,1), (2,-1), (1,-2), (-1,-2), (-2,-1), (-2,1)]
4.      stack = [(initial_pos[0], initial_pos[1], 1)] # level 1
5.      visited_positions = []
6.      while stack:
7.          prev_level = visited_positions[-1][-1] if visited_positions else 1
8.          x, y, cur_level = stack.pop()
9.          # backtrack --> update the visited
10.         if cur_level <= prev_level:
11.             while visited_positions and visited_positions[-1][-1] >= cur_level:
12.                 visited_positions.pop()
13.         # add to visited
14.         visited_positions.append((x, y, cur_level))
15.         # add children to stack
16.         for direction_x, direction_y in directions[::-1]:
17.             new_x = x + direction_x
18.             new_y = y + direction_y
19.             if 0 <= new_x < R and 0<= new_y < C:
20.                 if not any(new_x == pos_x and new_y == pos_y for pos_x, pos_y, _ in
                        visited_positions):
21.                     stack.append((new_x, new_y, cur_level + 1))
22.         if cur_level == target_level:
23.             return visited_positions
24.     return "Cannot tour the board"
25.
26. if __name__ == "__main__":
27.     print (knight_tour((2,2), R=5, C=5))
28.     print (knight_tour((2,3), R=8, C=8))
```

In [1]: run Listing_8_8_knights_tour_initial.py

[(2, 2, 1), (1, 4, 2), (3, 3, 3), (4, 1, 4), (2, 0, 5), (0, 1, 6), (1, 3, 7), (3, 4, 8), (4, 2, 9), (3, 0, 10), (1, 1, 11), (0, 3, 12), (2, 4, 13), (4, 3, 14), (3, 1, 15), (1, 0, 16), (0, 2, 17), (2, 3, 18), (4, 4, 19), (3, 2, 20), (4, 0, 21), (2, 1, 22), (0, 0, 23), (1, 2, 24), (0, 4, 25)]

Running the above code, we find the path for a 5×5 board in a fraction of a second, but it gets stuck for the standard 8×8 board. What is going on? The problem lies at line 3 of our code, where we specify the order of the equally likely moves. Our tiebreaker rule demands that the knight chooses to jump to the top left of the board first, and then top right, ..., in a clockwise fashion. In Figure 8-7, below, the knight at (2, 2) prioritizes (1, 4) over (3, 4), (4, 3), (4, 1), ..., (0, 3).

CHAPTER 8　CHESS

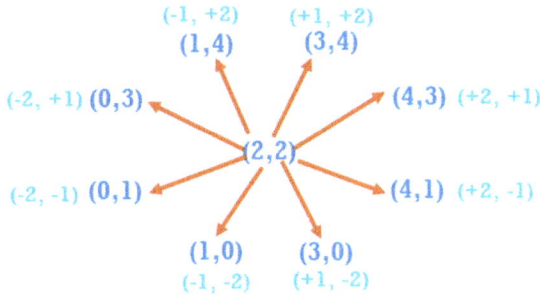

Figure 8-7. *Eight possible squares for a knight to jump to from an initial position of (2, 2)*

This does sound a bit arbitrary. After all, the DFS search considered here is an exponential algorithm. For an 8×8 board, the branching factor is ~5.25, which leads to a total of ~1.3×10^{46} possible nodes to explore. This is beyond the computing capability of our laptop.

To improve the efficiency of the program, we can inject some heuristics into it. Figure 8-8 shows the number of possible next moves for a knight landing at each square of an 8×8 board. As expected, the more central the knight is, the more possible moves there are. That is why the chess coaches often yell at the students, "Put your knight in the center!"

y									
7	2	3	4	4	4	4	3	2	
6	3	4	6	6	6	6	4	3	
5	4	6	8	8	8	8	6	4	
4	4	6	8	8	8	8	6	4	
3	4	6	8	8	8	8	6	4	
2	4	6	8	8	8	8	6	4	
1	3	4	6	6	6	6	4	3	
0	2	3	4	4	4	4	3	2	
	0	1	2	3	4	5	6	7	x

Figure 8-8. *Possible number of next squares to jump to for the knight on a chessboard*

CHAPTER 8   CHESS

The intuition here is that when picking up the next move from a series of equally allowed squares, prioritize the ones at the edge over those at the center. If the knight can finish exploring the edge positions first, it will be easy to complete the tour of the central area. From the central squares, it can jump to eight possible positions. On the contrary, if it starts in the middle, it would be hard for it to escape the central area to the edge and connect all the edge positions. The heuristic is called *Warnsdorff's algorithm*, named after H. C. von Warnsdorff, who conceived and published the idea in 1823.

With all these, the improved code is shown in Listing 8-9. The search for an 8×8 board indeed ends within a fraction of a second! The code from lines 1–13 generates the possible legal moves for all 64 positions on an 8×8 board and saves the result into a dictionary. This dictionary is used at line 39 to assist in finding the most plausible next move among equally allowed positions.

The complete Knight Tour starting from (0, 0) is (0, 0), (2, 1), (0, 2), (1, 0), (3, 1), (5, 0), (7, 1), (6, 3), (7, 5), (6, 7), (4, 6), (2, 7), (0, 6), (1, 4), (2, 6), (0, 7), (1, 5), (0, 3), (1, 1), (3, 0), (5, 1), (7, 0), (6, 2), (7, 4), (6, 6), (4, 7), (3, 5), (1, 6), (0, 4), (1, 2), (2, 0), (0, 1), (1, 3), (0, 5), (1, 7), (3, 6), (5, 7), (7, 6), (6, 4), (7, 2), (6, 0), (4, 1), (2, 2), (4, 3), (5, 5), (3, 4), (4, 2), (6, 1), (4, 0), (5, 2), (7, 3), (5, 4), (3, 3), (4, 5), (2, 4), (3, 2), (5, 3), (6, 5), (7, 7), (5, 6), (3, 7), (2, 5), (4, 4), (2, 3).

Listing 8-9. An improved version of Knight's Tour

```
1.  def num_possible_moves_for_each_position(R=8, C=8):
2.      directions = [(-1,2), (1,2), (2,1), (2,-1), (1,-2), (-1,-2), (-2,-1), (-2,1)]
3.      num_moves_for_positions = dict()
4.      for x in range(R):
5.          for y in range(C):
6.              counter = 0
7.              for direction_x, direction_y in directions:
8.                  new_x = x + direction_x
9.                  new_y = y + direction_y
10.                 if 0 <= new_x < R and 0<= new_y < C:
11.                     counter += 1
12.             num_moves_for_positions[(x, y)] = counter
13.     return num_moves_for_positions
14.
15. def knight_tour_warnsdorff_heuristics(initial_pos, R=8, C=8):
16.     target_level = R * C
17.     directions = [(-1,2), (1,2), (2,1), (2,-1), (1,-2), (-1,-2), (-2,-1), (-2,1)]
18.     stack = [(initial_pos[0], initial_pos[1], 1)] # level 1
19.     visited_positions = []
20.     num_moves_for_positions_dict = num_possible_moves_for_each_position(R, C)
21.     while stack:
22.         prev_level = visited_positions[-1][-1] if visited_positions else 1
23.         x, y, cur_level = stack.pop()
24.         # backtrack --> update the visited
25.         if cur_level <= prev_level:
```

```
26.            while visited_positions and visited_positions[-1][-1] >= cur_level:
27.                visited_positions.pop()
28.            # add to visited
29.            visited_positions.append((x, y, cur_level))
30.            # add children to stack
31.            possible_next_positions = []
32.            for direction_x, direction_y in directions:
33.                new_x = x + direction_x
34.                new_y = y + direction_y
35.                if 0 <= new_x < R and 0<= new_y < C:
36.                    if not any(new_x == pos_x and new_y == pos_y for pos_x, pos_y, _ in
                       visited_positions):
37.                        possible_next_positions.append((new_x, new_y))
38.            # sort next possible positions
39.        possible_next_positions.sort(key = lambda pos: num_moves_for_positions_dict[pos],
            reverse=True)
40.            for new_x, new_y in possible_next_positions:
41.                stack.append((new_x, new_y, cur_level + 1))
42.
43.            if cur_level == target_level:
44.                return visited_positions
45.        return "Cannot tour the board"
46.
47. if __name__ == "__main__":
48.     print (num_possible_moves_for_each_position())
49.     print (knight_tour_warnsdorff_heuristics((0,0), R=8, C=8))
```

In [2]: run Listing_8_9_knights_tour_warnsdorff.py

{(0, 0): 2, (0, 1): 3, (0, 2): 4, (0, 3): 4, (0, 4): 4, (0, 5): 4, (0, 6): 3, (0, 7): 2,
(1, 0): 3, (1, 1): 4, (1, 2): 6, (1, 3): 6, (1, 4): 6, (1, 5): 6, (1, 6): 4, (1, 7): 3,
(2, 0): 4, (2, 1): 6, (2, 2): 8, (2, 3): 8, (2, 4): 8, (2, 5): 8, (2, 6): 6, (2, 7): 4,
(3, 0): 4, (3, 1): 6, (3, 2): 8, (3, 3): 8, (3, 4): 8, (3, 5): 8, (3, 6): 6, (3, 7): 4,
(4, 0): 4, (4, 1): 6, (4, 2): 8, (4, 3): 8, (4, 4): 8, (4, 5): 8, (4, 6): 6, (4, 7): 4,
(5, 0): 4, (5, 1): 6, (5, 2): 8, (5, 3): 8, (5, 4): 8, (5, 5): 8, (5, 6): 6, (5, 7): 4,
(6, 0): 3, (6, 1): 4, (6, 2): 6, (6, 3): 6, (6, 4): 6, (6, 5): 6, (6, 6): 4, (6, 7): 3,
(7, 0): 2, (7, 1): 3, (7, 2): 4, (7, 3): 4, (7, 4): 4, (7, 5): 4, (7, 6): 3, (7, 7): 2}

[(0, 0, 1), (2, 1, 2), (0, 2, 3), (1, 0, 4), (3, 1, 5), (5, 0, 6), (7, 1, 7), (6, 3, 8),
(7, 5, 9), (6, 7, 10), (4, 6, 11), (2, 7, 12), (0, 6, 13), (1, 4, 14), (2, 6, 15), (0, 7,
16), (1, 5, 17), (0, 3, 18), (1, 1, 19), (3, 0, 20), (5, 1, 21), (7, 0, 22), (6, 2, 23),
(7, 4, 24), (6, 6, 25), (4, 7, 26), (3, 5, 27), (1, 6, 28), (0, 4, 29), (1, 2, 30), (2, 0,
31), (0, 1, 32), (1, 3, 33), (0, 5, 34), (1, 7, 35), (3, 6, 36), (5, 7, 37), (7, 6, 38),
(6, 4, 39), (7, 2, 40), (6, 0, 41), (4, 1, 42), (2, 2, 43), (4, 3, 44), (5, 5, 45), (3, 4,
46), (4, 2, 47), (6, 1, 48), (4, 0, 49), (5, 2, 50), (7, 3, 51), (5, 4, 52), (3, 3, 53),
(4, 5, 54), (2, 4, 55), (3, 2, 56), (5, 3, 57), (6, 5, 58), (7, 7, 59), (5, 6, 60), (3, 7,
61), (2, 5, 62), (4, 4, 63), (2, 3, 64)]

Minimum Jumps for a Knight

The next problem we are going to explore is the minimum number of jumps for a knight from one position to another on a chessboard. Recall the standard chessboard is 8×8, and thus, we can put the board in a Cartesian coordinate system and assign an (x, y) coordinate for each position; see Figure 8-9. We start from the bottom left (0, 0), all the way to the top right (7, 7). Also, the movement of a knight is a combination of two sub-moves: (1) move one step straight and (2) one step diagonally. For example, the knight at (0, 0) can jump to either (2, 1) or (1, 2) in one step.

Figure 8-9. *Put 64 squares of a chessboard in a Cartesian x-y system. The knight jumps in an "L"-shaped fashion*

Suppose a knight wants to jump from the bottom left (0, 0) to the top right position (7, 7). Theoretically, it can jump in eight directions. For example, as a first step, it can jump to any of (2, 1), (1, 2), (1, -2), (2, -1), (-1, 2), (-2, 1), (-1, -2), (-2, -1). But obviously, the negative coordinates are out of the board and thus need to be removed, leaving us with either (2, 1) or (1, 2) as the possible next move. Here, we can use BFS to find the shortest path. We use a queue to store (0, 0) and poll it, and push (2, 1) and (1, 2) to the queue, and repeat it until we reach the destination of (7, 7).

For a generic position (x, y), the knight can jump to any of these eight positions (x+2, y+1), (x+1, y+2), (x+1, y-2), (x+2, y-1), (x-1, y+2), (x-2, y+1), (x-1, y-2), (x-2, y-1) on the condition that new positions must within the chessboard. When coding a BFS solution, instead of just storing x and y coordinates of each move, we can store a third piece of information, i.e., the number of steps/BFS levels so far. The code for the minimum number of steps for a knight travelling on a chessboard is in Listing 8-10.

Listing 8-10. Minimum jumps for a knight between two squares

```
1.  from collections import deque
2.  DIRECTIONS = [(1,2), (2,1), (-1, 2), (-2,1), (1, -2), (2, -1), (-1, -2), (-2, -1)]
3.
4.  def min_moves_for_knight_bfs(start_pos, end_pos, size_of_board=8):
5.      start_pos_x, start_pos_y = start_pos
6.      end_pos_x, end_pos_y = end_pos
7.      num_moves = 0
8.      visited = set()
9.      queue = deque([(start_pos_x, start_pos_y, num_moves)])
10.     path_dict = dict()
11.
12.     while queue:
13.         cur_pos_x, cur_pos_y, num_moves_so_far = queue.popleft()
14.         if cur_pos_x == end_pos_x and cur_pos_y == end_pos_y:
15.             # retrieve the path
16.             paths = []
17.             while (end_pos_x, end_pos_y) != (start_pos_x, start_pos_y):
18.                 paths.append((end_pos_x, end_pos_y))
19.                 end_pos_x, end_pos_y = path_dict[(end_pos_x, end_pos_y)]
20.             paths.append((start_pos_x, start_pos_y))
21.             return num_moves_so_far, paths[::-1]
22.
23.         # 8 possible next moves for knight
24.         for direction_x, direction_y in DIRECTIONS:
25.             next_pos_x = cur_pos_x + direction_x
26.             next_pos_y = cur_pos_y + direction_y
27.             # make sure positions are valid
28.             if 0<=next_pos_x<= size_of_board-1 and 0<=next_pos_y<=size_of_board-1 and (next_pos_x, next_pos_y) not in visited:
29.                 queue.append((next_pos_x, next_pos_y, num_moves_so_far + 1))
30.                 visited.add((next_pos_x, next_pos_y))
31.                 path_dict[(next_pos_x, next_pos_y)] = (cur_pos_x, cur_pos_y)
32.
33. if __name__ == "__main__":
34.     print (min_moves_for_knight_bfs((0, 0), (7,7)))
```

In [3]: run Listing_8_10_min_moves_for_knight.py

(6, [(0, 0), (1, 2), (2, 4), (3, 6), (5, 7), (6, 5), (7, 7)])

In Listing 8-10, we define a DIRECTIONS variable at line 2 that specifies eight possible moves from the knight. The order of the moves does not affect the minimum number of steps, e.g., it needs six steps to go from (0, 0) to (7, 7). However, the shortest path depends on the order of directions. For example, if changing the order to [(1, -2), (2, -1), (-1, -2), (-2, -1), (1, 2), (2, 1), (-1, 2), (-2, 1)], we shall have a different path from (0, 0) to (7, 7). See the green and red paths in Figure 8-10.

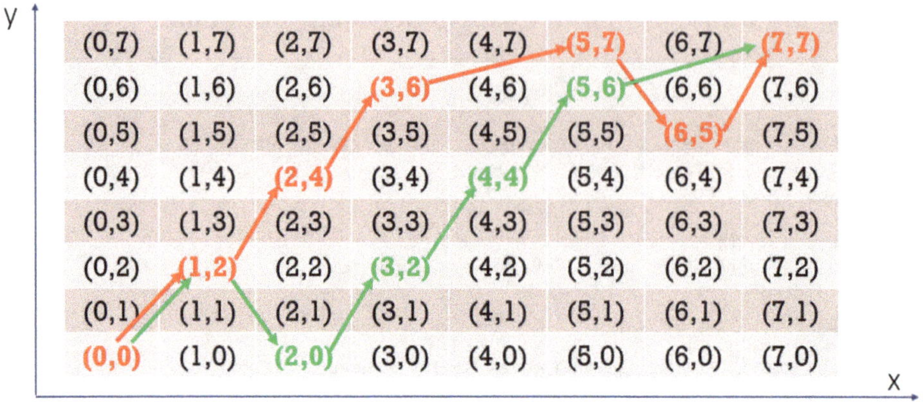

CHAPTER 8   CHESS

Figure 8-10. Two different ways to move from the bottom left to the top right

Eight Queens

Another famous chess-inspired problem is the Eight Queens problem. It asks for finding unique ways to place eight queens on a standard 8×8 board such that none of the queens attacks each other. We know the queen is the most powerful piece in chess: it can attack other pieces horizontally, vertically, and diagonally. The question was first proposed by Carl Friedrich Gauss in 1850, and he concluded there were 76 unique solutions. We will see whether he is correct or not by finding our own solutions.

Since there are a total of eight queens, we can plan to add queens to the board one by one. As illustrated in Figure 8-11, to place the first queen, we can freely pick up any of the 64 positions; for example, we place the queen at (0, 0). After the first queen, certain positions (a total of 22 positions) will be ruled out for the second queen; see the red arrows. In the second round, we randomly pick up (1, 2) which further excludes positions for placing other queens (green arrows). We can repeat it for the third round by placing a new queen at (2, 5) and the fourth round at (5, 1). We keep doing this until all positions are either chosen for placing queens or are eliminated. If we can find eight consecutive positions, then we have found a solution!

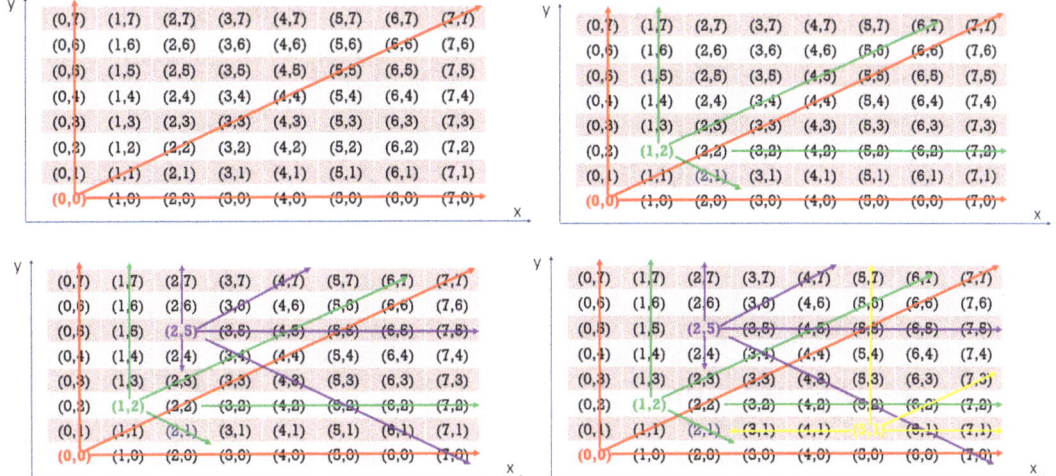

Figure 8-11. Put up to four queens on a chessboard. Arrows indicate the positions that get ruled out

Our strategy is essentially equivalent to constructing an N-ary tree as shown in Figure 8-12, where each node stores the position of a square on the chessboard.

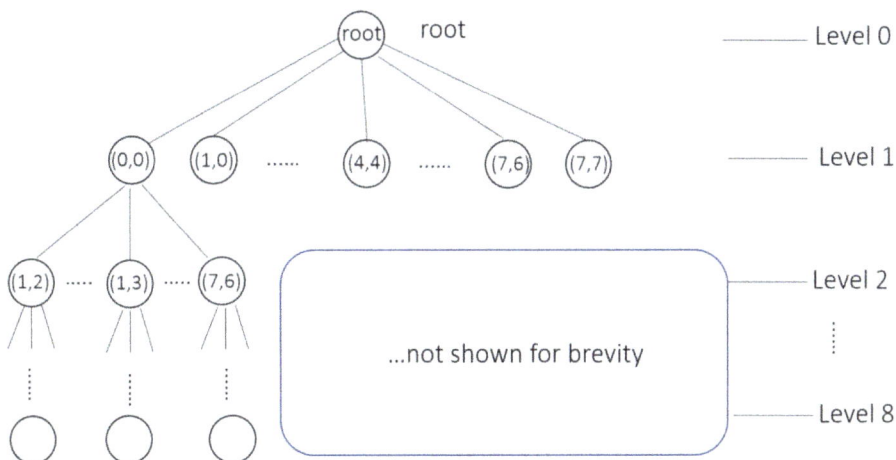

Figure 8-12. An N-ray tree for the Eight Queens problem

We create a dummy root node to get started. Level 1 has 64 nodes corresponding to each possible position on a chessboard. Each node at level 1 has its own child nodes: for example, node (0, 0) has 42 child nodes. The tree keeps on growing until it reaches the leaf

CHAPTER 8 CHESS

nodes. We can first construct such an N-ary tree and then find all root-to-leaf paths. If the length of the path is not equal to 8, we discard it; otherwise, it is one solution of placing eight queens legitimately, and we record it. The code is in Listing 8-11.

Listing 8-11. An initial attempt at the Eight Queens problem using an N-ary tree

```
1.  from copy import deepcopy
2.  import time
3.  class TreeNode:
4.      def __init__(self, value = None):
5.          self.value = value
6.          self.children = []
7.
8.      def add_child(self, child):
9.          self.children.append(child)
10.
11. class NQueens:
12.     def __init__(self, num_queens, board_size):
13.         self.num_queens = num_queens
14.         self.board_size = board_size
15.         self.coordinates = set((i,j) for i in range(self.board_size) for j in range(self.board_size))
16.         self.n_queens_solutions = set()
17.
18.     def root_to_leaf_paths_n_ary_tree(self, root):
19.         paths = []
20.         stack = [(root, [root.value])]
21.         while stack:
22.             node, path = stack.pop()
23.             if not node.children and len(path) == self.num_queens + 1: # check if the length of path equals num of queens
24.                 paths.append(path[1:]) # ignore the dummy root value
25.             else:
26.                 for child in node.children[::-1]:
27.                     stack.append((child, path + [child.value]))
28.         return paths
29.
30.     def allowed_positions_for_new_queens(self, existing_queen_positions):
31.         not_allowed_positions = set()
32.         for i in range(self.board_size):
33.             for j in range(self.board_size):
34.                 if any(r == i or j == c or abs(r - i) == abs(c - j) for r, c in existing_queen_positions):
35.                     not_allowed_positions.add((i, j))
36.         remaining_allowed_positions = deepcopy(self.coordinates) - not_allowed_positions
37.         return remaining_allowed_positions
38.
39.     def construct_n_ary_tree(self):
40.         root = TreeNode("root") # dummy root node
41.         stack = [(root, [])] # (node, exisiting queen positions)
42.         while stack:
43.             node, existing_queen_positions = stack.pop()
44.             if node.value == "root": # at root level
```

```
45.                  for i in range(self.board_size):
46.                      for j in range(self.board_size):
47.                          child = TreeNode((i, j))
48.                          node.add_child(child)
49.                          stack.append((child, existing_queen_positions + [(i, j)]))
50.              else:
51.                  allowed_positions = self.allowed_positions_for_new_queens
                                          (existing_queen_positions)
52.                  if not allowed_positions:
53.                      continue
54.                  for i, j in allowed_positions:
55.                      child = TreeNode((i,j))
56.                      node.add_child(child)
57.                      stack.append((child, existing_queen_positions + [(i, j)]))
58.          return root
59.
60.      def find_all_solutions(self):
61.          root = self.construct_n_ary_tree()
62.          paths = self.root_to_leaf_paths_n_ary_tree(root)
63.          for path in paths:
64.              path.sort()
65.              self.n_queens_solutions.add(tuple(path))
66.          return self.n_queens_solutions
67.
68. if __name__ == "__main__":
69.     t_start = time.time()
70.     eight_queens = NQueens(6, 6)
71.     print (eight_queens.find_all_solutions())
72.     t_end = time.time()
73.     print ("time consumed", t_end - t_start)
```

From lines 3–9, we define a TreeNode class with an add_child method. In the main class of NQueens, we first initialize the parameters for the number of queens, size of the board, (x, y) coordinates of all squares, and a placeholder for holding all solutions. At lines 18–28, we write a root_to_leaf_paths_n_ary_tree method to collect all root-to-leaf paths given a root node for an N-ary tree. Lines 30–37 are a helper function to find out the allowed squares given the positions of queens that have been placed. Lines 39–58 construct the N-ary tree, and lines 60–66 collect all correct solutions. At lines 69 and 72, we add two timestamps, one before running the code and one after. The difference tells the time cost to execute the program.

For six queens on a 6×6 board, the program returns four unique solutions in ~9 seconds.

$\{((0, 1), (1, 3), (2, 5), (3, 0), (4, 2), (5, 4)),$

$((0, 3), (1, 0), (2, 4), (3, 1), (4, 5), (5, 2)),$

$((0, 2), (1, 5), (2, 1), (3, 4), (4, 0), (5, 3)),$

$((0, 4), (1, 2), (2, 0), (3, 5), (4, 3), (5, 1))\}$

CHAPTER 8   CHESS

```
In [4]: run Listing_8_11_eight_queens_n_ary_tree.py
{((0, 1), (1, 3), (2, 5), (3, 0), (4, 2), (5, 4)), ((0, 3), (1, 0), (2, 4), (3, 1), (4,
5), (5, 2)), ((0, 2), (1, 5), (2, 1), (3, 4), (4, 0), (5, 3)), ((0, 4), (1, 2), (2, 0),
(3, 5), (4, 3), (5, 1))}
time consumed 8.823694944381714
```

The program gets stuck for seven queens, let alone eight queens. The N-ary tree constructed has too many branches to be realistically processed in a reasonable time. However, the fact that we obtain correct solutions for the six queens suggests that our code has no fundamental issue. But we need to optimize it to increase the speed.

In Listing 8-11, we represented the squares on the chessboard using (x, y) coordinates. In fact, we do not need **a pair of coordinates**; we only need **one**. We know beforehand that we can only place each queen in a separate row (if placing them in the same row, they would attack each other), so we only need to find the column index for each queen. Figure 8-13 shows one possible solution for eight queens with a solution represented as [0, 4, 7, 5, 2, 6, 1, 3]. These numbers represent the column index for each queen from bottom to top.

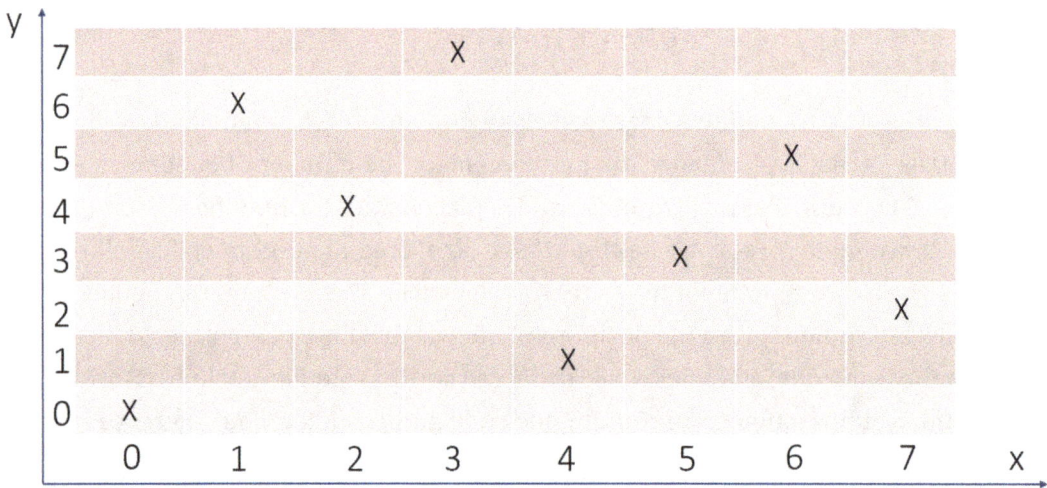

Figure 8-13. *One solution to the Eight Queens using only column indexes*

With this new insight, the N-ary tree is much simplified; see Figure 8-14. The tree node now only stores the column indexes of the queens. At level 0, we have a dummy root. At level 1 (we have decided to put a queen in row 0, i.e., the bottom of the board; see Figure 8-13), we can put the first queen in any of the eight columns. At this level, the nodes store indexes from 0 to 7, respectively. We continue to build a tree from node 0 in level 1. Node 0 in level 1 means we have a node with row index 0 and column index 0, i.e., place the first queen at the bottom left of the board. For its children, we can only put a second queen from columns 2 to 7 (the second queen will be placed at row 1). Putting a second queen in either column 0 or 1 will result in it being attacked by the first queen. We can continue the process to build the entire tree. Let us consider the size of the tree. For the first queen, we have eight possible positions. The second one, we have *at most* seven possible positions, and so on, so forth. The size of the tree is at most n! where n is the number of queens.

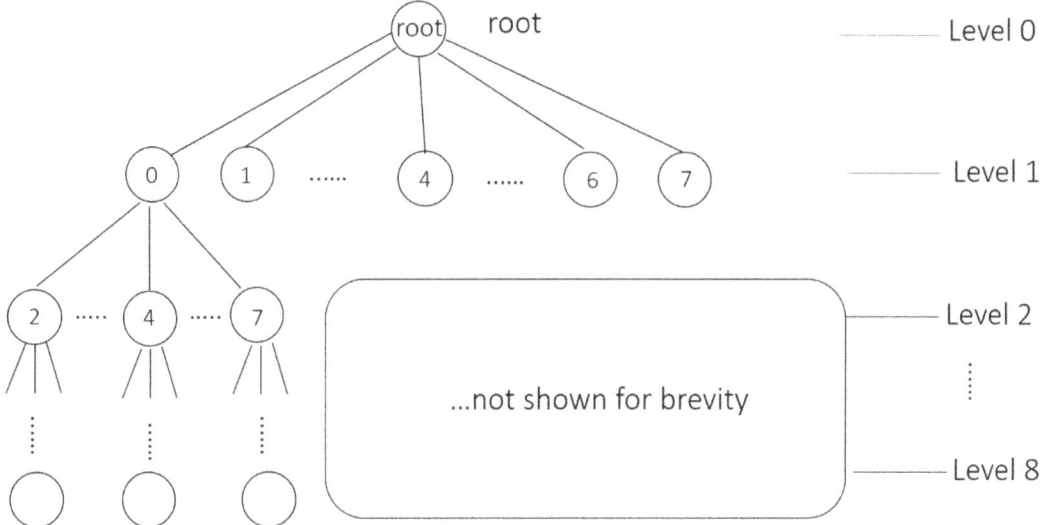

Figure 8-14. A simplified N-ary tree for the Eight Queens problem

The code implementation is in Listing 8-12. It resembles that of Listing 8-11 with a couple of improvements. First, we do not need a TreeNode class as defined at line 3 in Listing 8-11. Instead of using a value attribute of the tree node instance to access the coordinates (e.g., root.value in line 20 in Listing 8-11), we can directly collect them in a stack, for instance, col_idx in lines 39 and 45 in Listing 8-12. Second, instead of using two separate functions to construct a tree and traverse the tree as in Listing 8-11, in the current code, both steps are combined into one method, find_all_solutions, at line 30. The way it works is that we let each node carry another piece of information, i.e., the level number (see line 31). With this level of information, we can determine whether we have found a solution or not by comparing it with the desired number of queens self.num_queens (line 34).

Listing 8-12. Implementation of N-Queens using only column indexes

```python
1.  import time
2.  class NQueens:
3.      def __init__(self, num_queens, board_size):
4.          self.num_queens = num_queens
5.          self.board_size = board_size
6.          self.n_queens_solutions = []
7.
8.      def allowed_col_positions_for_new_queen(self, existing_queen_col_positions):
9.          # we put one queen in each row by default
10.         allowed_positions = []
11.         cur_row_idx = len(existing_queen_col_positions)
12.         forbidden_diagnoal_cols = []
13.         for existing_queen_row_pos, existing_queen_col_pos in enumerate(existing_queen_col_positions):
14.             pos_1 = existing_queen_col_pos + (cur_row_idx - existing_queen_row_pos) #col position to rule out due to diagonal attack
15.             pos_2 = existing_queen_col_pos - (cur_row_idx - existing_queen_row_pos) #col position to rule out due to diagonal attack
16.             if 0<=pos_1<self.board_size:
17.                 forbidden_diagnoal_cols.append(pos_1)
18.             if 0<=pos_2<self.board_size:
19.                 forbidden_diagnoal_cols.append(pos_2)
20.
21.         for col_idx in range(self.board_size):
22.             if col_idx in existing_queen_col_positions:
23.                 continue
24.
25.             if col_idx in forbidden_diagnoal_cols:
26.                 continue
27.             allowed_positions.append(col_idx)
28.         return allowed_positions
29.
30.     def find_all_solutions(self):
31.         stack = [("root", [], 0)] # (node, existing queen positions, level)
32.         while stack:
33.             cur_col_position, existing_queen_positions, level = stack.pop()
34.             if level == self.num_queens:
35.                 self.n_queens_solutions.append(existing_queen_positions)
36.
37.             if cur_col_position == "root": # at root level
38.                 for col_idx in range(self.board_size):
39.                     stack.append((col_idx, existing_queen_positions + [col_idx], 1))
40.             else:
41.                 allowed_positions = self.allowed_col_positions_for_new_queen(existing_queen_positions)
42.                 if not allowed_positions:
43.                     continue
44.                 for col_idx in allowed_positions:
45.                     stack.append((col_idx, existing_queen_positions + [col_idx], level + 1))
46.         return self.n_queens_solutions
47.
48. if __name__ == "__main__":
49.     t_start = time.time()
50.     eight_queens = NQueens(8,8)
51.     solutions = eight_queens.find_all_solutions()
52.     print (len(solutions))
53.     print (solutions)
54.     t_end = time.time()
55.     print ("time consumed", t_end - t_start)
```

The code performance has improved drastically. Now it takes 0.01 second for eight queens!

```
In [5]: run Listing_8_12_eight_queens_n_factorial.py
92
[[7, 3, 0, 2, 5, 1, 6, 4], [7, 2, 0, 5, 1, 4, 6, 3], [7, 1, 4, 2, 0, 6, 3, 5], [7, 1, 3,
0, 6, 4, 2, 5], [6, 4, 2, 0, 5, 7, 1, 3], [6, 3, 1, 7, 5, 0, 2, 4], [6, 3, 1, 4, 7, 0, 2,
5], [6, 2, 7, 1, 4, 0, 5, 3], [6, 2, 0, 5, 7, 4, 1, 3], [6, 1, 5, 2, 0, 3, 7, 4], [6, 1,
3, 0, 7, 4, 2, 5], [6, 0, 2, 7, 5, 3, 1, 4], [5, 7, 1, 3, 0, 6, 4, 2], [5, 3, 6, 0, 7, 1,
4, 2], [5, 3, 6, 0, 2, 4, 1, 7], [5, 3, 1, 7, 4, 6, 0, 2], [5, 3, 0, 4, 7, 1, 6, 2], [5,
2, 6, 3, 0, 7, 1, 4], [5, 2, 6, 1, 7, 4, 0, 3], [5, 2, 6, 1, 3, 7, 0, 4], [5, 2, 4, 7, 0,
3, 1, 6], [5, 2, 4, 6, 0, 3, 1, 7], [5, 2, 0, 7, 4, 1, 3, 6], [5, 2, 0, 7, 3, 1, 6, 4],
[5, 2, 0, 6, 4, 7, 1, 3], [5, 1, 6, 0, 3, 7, 4, 2], [5, 1, 6, 0, 2, 4, 7, 3], [5, 0, 4, 1,
7, 2, 6, 3], [4, 7, 3, 0, 6, 1, 5, 2], [4, 7, 3, 0, 2, 5, 1, 6], [4, 6, 3, 0, 2, 7, 5, 1],
[4, 6, 1, 5, 2, 0, 7, 3], [4, 6, 1, 5, 2, 0, 3, 7], [4, 6, 1, 3, 7, 0, 2, 5], [4, 6, 0, 3,
1, 7, 5, 2], [4, 6, 0, 2, 7, 5, 3, 1], [4, 2, 7, 3, 6, 0, 5, 1], [4, 2, 0, 6, 1, 7, 5, 3],
[4, 2, 0, 5, 7, 1, 3, 6], [4, 1, 7, 0, 3, 6, 2, 5], [4, 1, 5, 0, 6, 3, 7, 2], [4, 1, 3, 6,
2, 7, 5, 0], [4, 1, 3, 5, 7, 2, 0, 6], [4, 0, 7, 5, 2, 6, 1, 3], [4, 0, 7, 3, 1, 6, 2, 5],
[4, 0, 3, 5, 7, 1, 6, 2], [3, 7, 4, 2, 0, 6, 1, 5], [3, 7, 0, 4, 6, 1, 5, 2], [3, 7, 0, 2,
5, 1, 6, 4], [3, 6, 4, 2, 0, 5, 7, 1], [3, 6, 4, 1, 5, 0, 2, 7], [3, 6, 2, 7, 1, 4, 0, 5],
[3, 6, 0, 7, 4, 1, 5, 2], [3, 5, 7, 2, 0, 6, 4, 1], [3, 5, 7, 1, 6, 0, 2, 4], [3, 5, 0, 4,
1, 7, 2, 6], [3, 1, 7, 5, 0, 2, 4, 6], [3, 1, 7, 4, 6, 0, 2, 5], [3, 1, 6, 4, 0, 7, 5, 2],
[3, 1, 6, 2, 5, 7, 4, 0], [3, 1, 6, 2, 5, 7, 0, 4], [3, 1, 4, 7, 5, 0, 2, 6], [3, 0, 4, 7,
5, 2, 6, 1], [3, 0, 4, 7, 1, 6, 2, 5], [2, 7, 3, 6, 0, 5, 1, 4], [2, 6, 1, 7, 5, 3, 0, 4],
[2, 6, 1, 7, 4, 0, 3, 5], [2, 5, 7, 1, 3, 0, 6, 4], [2, 5, 7, 0, 4, 6, 1, 3], [2, 5, 7, 0,
3, 6, 4, 1], [2, 5, 3, 1, 7, 4, 6, 0], [2, 5, 3, 0, 7, 4, 6, 1], [2, 5, 1, 6, 4, 0, 7, 3],
[2, 5, 1, 6, 0, 3, 7, 4], [2, 5, 1, 4, 7, 0, 6, 3], [2, 4, 7, 3, 0, 6, 1, 5], [2, 4, 6, 0,
3, 1, 7, 5], [2, 4, 1, 7, 5, 3, 6, 0], [2, 4, 1, 7, 0, 6, 3, 5], [2, 0, 6, 4, 7, 1, 3, 5],
[1, 7, 5, 0, 2, 4, 6, 3], [1, 6, 4, 7, 0, 3, 5, 2], [1, 6, 2, 5, 7, 4, 0, 3], [1, 5, 7, 2,
0, 3, 6, 4], [1, 5, 0, 6, 3, 7, 2, 4], [1, 4, 6, 3, 0, 7, 5, 2], [1, 4, 6, 0, 2, 7, 5, 3],
[1, 3, 5, 7, 2, 0, 6, 4], [0, 6, 4, 7, 1, 3, 5, 2], [0, 6, 3, 5, 7, 1, 4, 2], [0, 5, 7, 2,
6, 3, 1, 4], [0, 4, 7, 5, 2, 6, 1, 3]]
time consumed 0.010978937149047852
```

Based on our program, there are 92 unique solutions for the Eight Queens problem. After all, the Great Gauss's answer was not off by a lot (his answer was 76).

Monte Carlo Tree Search

Humans have long dreamed of a supercomputer that is intelligent enough to surpass themselves, for example, in board games. The early computing systems were light-years away from this goal due to limitations of both computing power and algorithms. This changed when IBM's Deep Blue defeated the then Chess World Champion Garry Kasparov in 1997. Despite this breakthrough, some argue that the game of chess has such a small board that the computation is still manageable. In comparison, the board game of Go is many magnitudes more complex than chess. Its board is 19 by 19 with 361 possible positions, whereas chess has only 8 by 8 with 64 squares on the board. With a typical ~150 moves for Go, it has a total of ~250^{150}, or 10^{360} possible moves. To put it in scale, it is estimated that there may be 10^{78} to 10^{82} atoms in the known universe. However, in 2016, AlphaGo, the intelligent agent developed by DeepMind, defeated the Go World Champions Lee Sedol by 4 to 1. One of the key algorithms behind AlphaGo is Monte Carlo Tree Search (MCTS), which we will take a closer look at in this section.

The high-level idea behind MCTS is this. Since we have a vast search space, it is impossible to find the global solution, but instead, we find the solution as best as we can. When navigating through the search space, we will balance between *exploration* and *exploitation*. We may recall that the exploration and exploitation theme arises often in other algorithms such as Simulated Annealing where if a new step or new configuration improves the overall metric, we will accept it. But if it decreases the metric, we will not reject it right away but accept it with a certain probability. This is to say, even if an intermediate next step leads to a worse result, it is possible that in the long run, it can still lead to an overall better solution.

The mathematical parameter for balancing exploration and exploitation in MCTS is called UCB1 (UCB stands for Upper Confidence Bound). See the formula below:

$$UCB1_i = \overline{V_i} + C\sqrt{\frac{\ln(N)}{n_i}}$$

Here, N is the total visit counts of the parent node of the current node;, n is the total visit counts of the current node, and $\overline{V_i}$ is the average score of the current node, i.e., the ratio of total score and total number of visits. The first term promotes the average score (exploitation), and the second term emphasizes the visits (exploration). C is a factor, normally set as 2, to balance both [16].

Each tree node stores a total of five pieces of information: the score and the visit counts, its parent, its left child, and its right child. We can define a tree node class as in Listing 8-13. It stores these five pieces of information and has a `calculate_ucb1_score` method to calculate the score.

Listing 8-13. Define a tree node for MCTS

```
1.  import numpy as np
2.  import random
3.
4.  class Node:
5.      def __init__(self, total_score = 0, num_visits = 0):
6.          self.left = None
7.          self.right = None
8.          self.parent = None
9.          self.total_score = total_score
10.         self.num_visits = num_visits
11.
12.     def calculate_ucb1_score(self, c=2):
13.         if not self.num_visits:
14.             return np.inf
15.         # if at root node
16.         if not self.parent:
17.             return
18.         # at child node
19.         ubc1_score = (self.total_score / self.num_visits) + c * np.sqrt(np.log(self.parent.num_visits) / self.num_visits)
20.         return ubc1_score
```

Let us now see how MCTS works by giving a concrete example. Suppose we have an initial state with a tree stump of a root and two child nodes (Figure 8-15). All three nodes with zero total score (t_0) and zero visit counts (n_0).

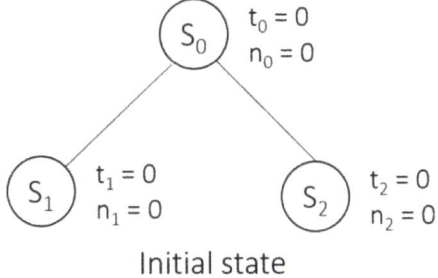

Figure 8-15. *Initial state of MCTS*

Next, as shown in Figure 8-16, starting from the root node S_0, we will need to select a child node. This is the **Selection** step. We select the node based on the UCB1 score. Since neither of the child node has been visited, the UCB1 scores are infinity for both. In such a case, we just pick up the first child node S_1.

Since S_1 has not been visited, we will perform a **Simulation** step, and by the end of the simulation, it will get a score V; in this case, it is 100. In terms of how the simulation is done, it depends on the application. For example, in the example of game of Go, given the first two moves, you can let the computer select the moves randomly until it completes the game. Then you will evaluate the final board and score it (e. g., if it is a win, give it a score of 1; a loss, 0; a draw, 0.5); that is V here.

CHAPTER 8   CHESS

After we obtain the score from the simulation, we do a **Backpropagation**, updating the total scores and visit counts upward till the root node. In this case, S_1 has an updated score of 100 and visit count of 1. Same for S_0. This completes the first iteration.

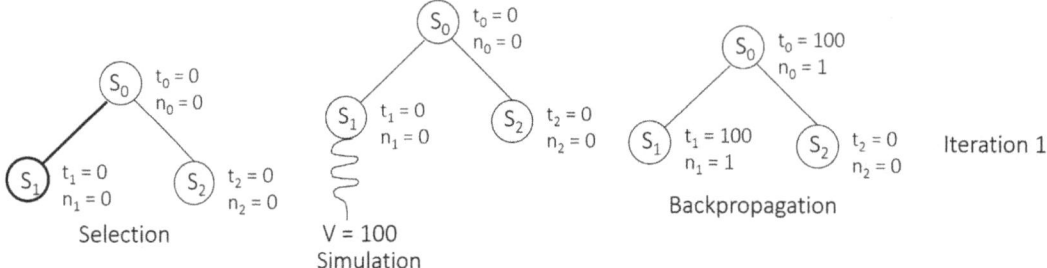

Figure 8-16. *First iteration of MCTS*

In the second iteration (Figure 8-17), we start from the root node S_0 and pick up its right child S_2 since its UCB1 score is infinity due to zero visits so far. Since S_2 has not been visited before, we do a Simulation and get a score of 30. Finally, we do a Backpropagation to update scores and visits of S_2 and S_0 and complete the iteration.

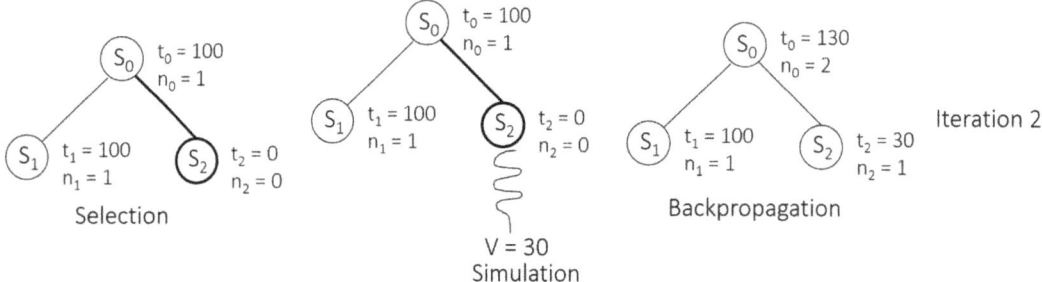

Figure 8-17. *Second iteration of MCTS*

The next iteration is a bit different (Figure 8-18). After we compare the UCB1 score of S_1 and S_2 and decide to go with S_1, instead of doing a simulation, we expand the nodes to have two new child nodes attaching to S_1. We do **Expansion** not Simulation because S_1 has been visited. The Simulation and Backpropagation steps are the same as the last two rounds.

238

CHAPTER 8 CHESS

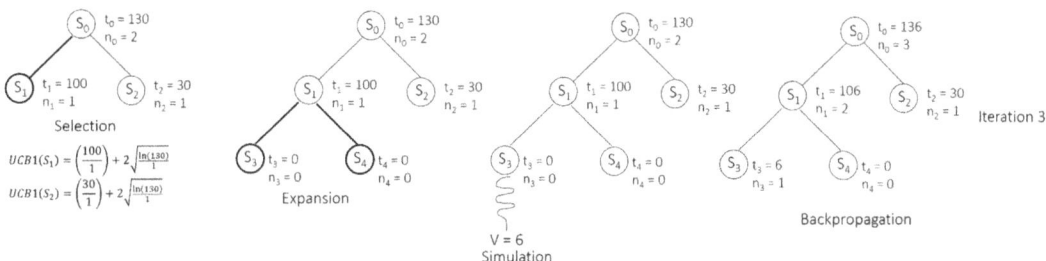

Figure 8-18. *Third iteration of MCTS*

In Figure 8-19, the fourth iteration should make sense now. We do not expand node S_4 since it has zero visit counts.

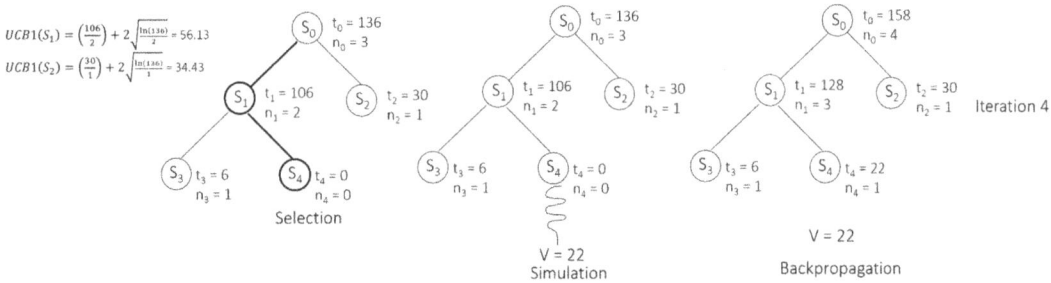

Figure 8-19. *Fourth iteration of MCTS*

The algorithm itself can be summarized in Figure 8-20. It has in general four steps: Selection, Expansion, Simulation, and Backpropagation. However, if the leaf node has not been visited, we do not do the Expansion step.

```
For 1, 2, ..., n iterations:
    (1) Start from the root node, go to the leaf node, select node based on UCB1 score
        (selection)
    (2) If the leaf node has 0 visits, do a simulation / rollout (simulation)
    (3) If the leaf node has >0 visits,
        (1) add two new child nodes (expansion)
        (2) move the current code to the left child node
        (3) do a simulation / rollout (simulation)
    (4) Backtrack from leaf node to root node, update visit counts and total scores up to
        the root node. (backpropagation)
```

Figure 8-20. *The pseudocode for MCTS*

CHAPTER 8 CHESS

To find the best path, one simply starts from the root and picks up a child based on its UCB1 score, until it hits the leaf node. A complete code of Monte Carlo Tree Search incorporating the four steps discussed above is implemented in Listing 8-14. Note that at lines 6 and 9, the roll-out results are hard-coded to compare against the result from the previous diagrams (Figure 8-15 to Figure 8-19), whereas in a real application, the random_roll_out_result method will be replaced by the actual code to do the simulation based on state values from nodes descending from the root.

Listing 8-14. A complete code of MCTS

```
1.  import numpy as np
2.
3.  class MonteCarloTreeSearch:
4.      def __init__(self, num_iters = 4):
5.          self.num_iters = num_iters
6.          self.ROLL_OUT_RESULTS = [22, 6, 30, 100]
7.
8.      def random_roll_out_result(self):
9.          return self.ROLL_OUT_RESULTS.pop()
10.
11.     def selection(self, node):
12.         if not node.left and not node.right:
13.             return node
14.
15.         if node.left and not node.right:
16.             return node.left
17.
18.         if not node.left and node.right:
19.             return node.right
20.
21.         if node.left and node.right:
22.             left_child_ucb1_score = node.left.calculate_ucb1_score()
23.             right_child_ucb1_score = node.right.calculate_ucb1_score()
24.             if left_child_ucb1_score > right_child_ucb1_score:
25.                 return node.left
26.             elif left_child_ucb1_score < right_child_ucb1_score:
27.                 return node.right
28.             else:
29.                 return node.left
30.
31.     def expansion(self, node):
32.         "add left and right children nodes"
33.         left_child_node = Node(0, 0)
34.         right_child_node = Node(0, 0)
35.         node.left = left_child_node
36.         node.right = right_child_node
37.         left_child_node.parent = node
38.         right_child_node.parent = node
39.
40.     def simulation(self):
41.         return self.random_roll_out_result()
42.
43.     def backpropagation(self, node, score):
44.         while node.parent:
```

```python
45.             node.num_visits += 1
46.             node.total_score += score
47.             node = node.parent
48.
49.         # root has no parent and update root separately
50.         node.num_visits += 1
51.         node.total_score += score
52.         return node
53.
54.     def perform_one_round_four_steps_simulation(self, node):
55.         # selection
56.         while node.left or node.right:
57.             node = self.selection(node)
58.
59.         # expansion
60.         if node.num_visits > 0:
61.             self.expansion(node)
62.             node = node.left
63.
64.         # simulation
65.         roll_out_val = self.simulation()
66.
67.         # backpropagation
68.         node = self.backpropagation(node, roll_out_val)
69.         return node
70.
71.     def perform_many_rounds_four_steps_simulation(self, node):
72.         if self.num_iters < 1:
73.             return
74.
75.         for _ in range(self.num_iters):
76.             node = self.perform_one_round_four_steps_simulation(node)
77.         return node
78.
79.     def return_best_path(self, root):
80.         path = [(root.total_score, root.num_visits)]
81.         while root:
82.             if root.left and not root.right:
83.                 path.append(((root.left.total_score, root.left.num_visits)))
84.                 root = root.left
85.             elif root.right and not root.left:
86.                 path.append(((root.right.total_score, root.right.num_visits)))
87.                 root = root.right
88.             elif root.left and root.right:
89.                 if root.left.num_visits:
90.                     average_score_left = root.left.total_score / root.left.num_visits
91.                 else:
92.                     average_score_left = np.inf
93.                 if root.right.num_visits:
94.                     average_score_right = root.right.total_score / root.right.num_visits
95.                 else:
96.                     average_score_right = np.inf
97.                 if average_score_left >= average_score_right:
98.                     path.append(((root.left.total_score, root.left.num_visits)))
99.                     root = root.left
100.                else:
101.                    path.append(((root.right.total_score, root.right.num_visits)))
102.                    root = root.right
103.            else:
104.                break
105.        return path
```

CHAPTER 8 CHESS

```
106.
107.        def print_tree(self, root, space=0, LEVEL_SPACE = 7):
108.            "Reference: https://stackoverflow.com/a/70318281"
109.            if not root:
110.                return
111.            space += LEVEL_SPACE
112.            self.print_tree(root.right, space)
113.            for i in range(LEVEL_SPACE, space):
114.                print(end = " ")
115.            print("|" + str(root.total_score) + ','+ str(root.num_visits) + "|<")
116.            self.print_tree(root.left, space)
117.
118.    if __name__ == "__main__":
119.        # construct a tree
120.        '''
121.            (0, 0)
122.            /    \
123.        (0,0)  (0,0)
124.
125.        '''
126.        # construct a shallow tree
127.        root_node = Node(0, 0)
128.        left_node = Node(0, 0)
129.        right_node = Node(0, 0)
130.        left_node.parent = root_node
131.        right_node.parent = root_node
132.        root_node.left = left_node
133.        root_node.right = right_node
134.
135.        mcts = MonteCarloTreeSearch(num_iters=4)
136.        new_root_node = mcts.perform_many_rounds_four_steps_simulation(root_node)
137.        print ("Visualize tree")
138.        mcts.print_tree(new_root_node)
139.        path = mcts.return_best_path(new_root_node)
140.        print ("Best path")
141.        print (path)
```

```
In [6]: run Listing_8_13_8_14_monte_carlo_tree_search.py
Visualize tree
        |30,1|<
|158,4|<
            |22,1|<
        |128,3|<
            |6,1|<
Best path
[(158, 4), (128, 3), (22, 1)]
```

After running the program, it is encouraging to see that the code returns the same result as that in Figure 8-19.

Application

Binary Trees and N-ary Trees

Both binary trees and N-ary trees are foundational to many aspects of computing and technology, helping efficiently structure and manage data in a way that enables fast searching, easy manipulation, and representation of complex relationships. In machine learning and AI, one uses decision trees for classification and regression tasks. In contrast to other black-box models such as deep neural networks, the white-box binary decision tree model is intuitive to understand. One just asks the question to repeatedly reduce the parameter space by half. On top of that, by combining many shallow trees (e.g., tree stumps), one can achieve superior prediction performance by ensemble methods such as Random Forest or Gradient Boosted Trees.

In programming languages, expressions are parsed using binary trees where operators are internal nodes and operands are leaves. For example, the following expression, $2 + 3 \times 5$ can be constructed by performing an in-order traversal of the binary tree shown in Figure 8-21 (recall in the "Application" section of Chapter 1, we learned the in-order traversal).

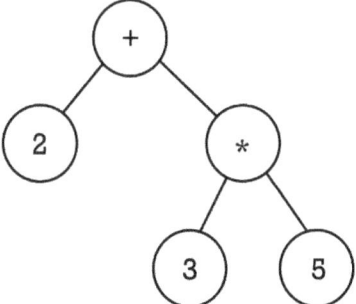

Figure 8-21. *An example of an expression tree*

A special type of binary tree, i.e., binary search tree (BST), stores information in an ordered fashion. If we run an in-order traversal on a BST such as the one in Figure 8-22, we shall get $1 \rightarrow 3 \rightarrow 4 \rightarrow 6 \rightarrow 7 \rightarrow 8 \rightarrow 10 \rightarrow 13 \rightarrow 14$, where the numbers are sorted in increasing order.

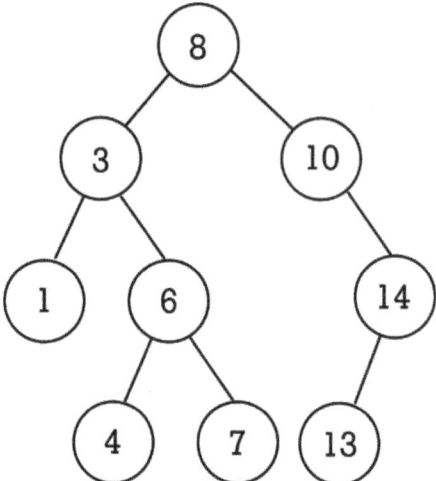

Figure 8-22. *An example of a binary search tree*

It is with this ordered nature, one can extract information using binary search with a logarithmic time (O(log n)) where *n* is the number of tree nodes. The BST is applied in index tables in a database and file system search where file names or directories are kept track of by the BST for quick searches and lookups.

We also learned the Huffman coding tree in the "Application" section of Chapter 3, which is often used to efficiently compress data. In file compression algorithms like ZIP or JPEG, Huffman coding is used to assign variable-length codes to characters based on their frequency of occurrence.

Similar to a binary tree, an N-ary tree finds applications in various areas. For example, companies use N-ary trees to represent employee hierarchies where each node represents an employee and the children represent direct reports. In addition, in operating systems (Windows, macOS, Linux), the file system is often represented as an N-ary tree where each directory (node) can contain many files and subdirectories (children). Finally, N-ary trees are used in network routers to store routing information. Each node might represent a different route, with branches representing different possible network paths or subnets.

DFS, BFS, and Backtracking

Depth-First Search explores as far as possible down a branch before backtracking. It is often used in scenarios where exploring all possible paths is important. Examples of DFS include file system traversal, topological sorting, and web crawlers. Breadth-

First Search explores neighbors' level by level, making it ideal for finding the shortest path in unweighted graphs or exploring all options in layers. BFS finds applications in the shortest path in unweighted graphs and social networks. Backtracking is a trial-and-error method for solving problems incrementally and undoing decisions when a problem's current path leads to an invalid state. Backtracking is useful in many areas such as puzzle solving and combinatorial problems.

Let us now leverage DFS and Backtracking to solve a puzzle of maze. Given a maze shown in Figure 8-23, where the black and blue colors denote blocks and paths, respectively. Each square in the maze has an (x, y) coordinate; for instance, the top left square is (0, 0), and the bottom right is (4, 4). Here the *x* axis is from top to bottom whereas the *y* axis is from left to right. Given a start position of (1, 1), find the path to reach the destination square of (4, 3).

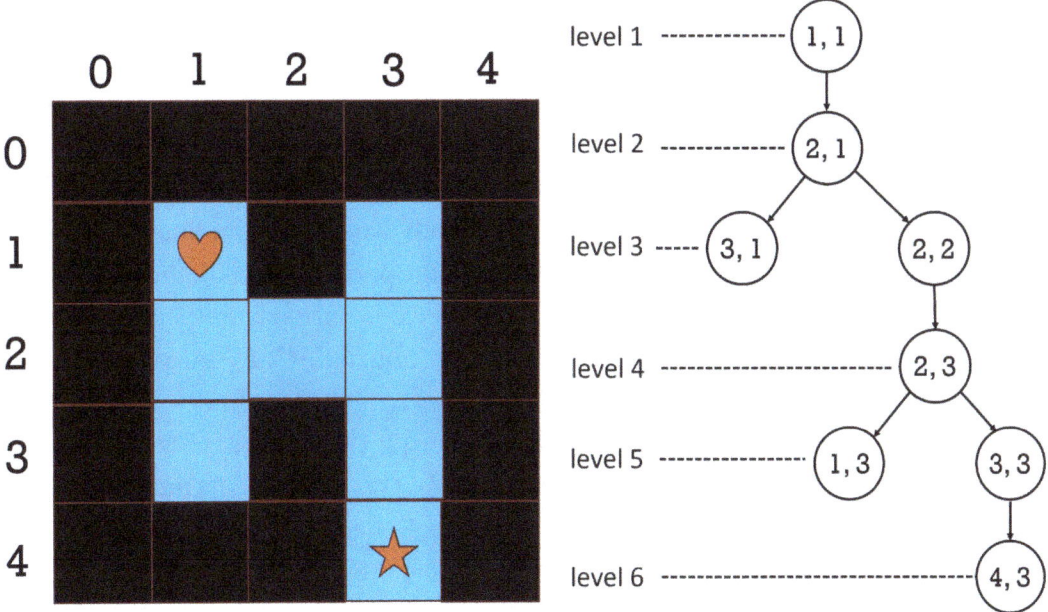

Figure 8-23. *A maze and its tree representation*

This problem resembles the Knight's Tour problem in Section "Knight's Tour". It involves Depth-First Search and Backtracking. Suppose we search for the next move in the order of upward, downward, leftward, and rightward. Starting from position (1, 1), we can construct a tree diagram as shown in Figure 8-23.

CHAPTER 8   CHESS

At (1, 1), we try moving upward, downward, leftward, and rightward. Only downward movement is allowed, and the new position becomes (2, 1). For the next positions, both (3, 1) and (2, 2) are possible, where (3, 1) has no next moves because (2, 1) is already visited. Thus, the tree continues from (2, 2) whose next move is (2, 3). At (2, 3), there are two new next moves, (1, 3) and (3, 3), where (1, 3) is a dead end. We continue from (3, 3) until we hit the target (4, 3).

From the discussion above, to implement a solution to solve this maze puzzle, we need:

(1) A stack data structure (in Python, we use a list) to perform a Depth-First Search of the tree where it stores three pieces of information, i.e., x coordinate, y coordinate, and level.

(2) A visited parameter to keep track of the positions that have been visited before.

(3) A path parameter to store the shortest path from start to finish.

In Listing 8-15, the maze is implemented as a two-dimensional matrix with binary values where 0 and 1 represent blocks and accessible squares, respectively (lines 41–45). At line 4, the stack holds the initial positions at level 1. At line 10, when the current positions equal the goal positions, we return the path. Note that from lines 17 to 22, we update the path by comparing the current level with the previous levels. If the current level is not larger than the previous ones, we pop out previous positions in the path until the condition is met. As an example, at level 3, after exploring node (3, 1), the path parameter is [(1, 1, 1), (2, 1, 2), (3, 1, 3)]. Then we explore node (2, 2, 3), since the current level is 3, which is the same as the last element in the path, i.e., (3, 1, 3), (3, 1, 3) must be removed. The path is now updated to [(1, 1, 1), (2, 1, 2), (2, 2, 3)]. This is essentially the *backtracking* in action: when one path reaches a dead end, we move on to explore the alternative ones. At line 27, we explore the neighboring positions in the order of up, down, left, and right. Note the directions at line 27, i.e., [(0, 1), (0, -1), (1, 0), (-1, 0)], correspond to, respectively, right, left, down, and up, in other words, the reversed order. This is due to the First In Last Out (FILO) nature of the stack. From lines 31–34, we check if the new position satisfies (1) the new position is within the boundary of the matrix, (2) the new position is accessible, and (3) the new position has not been visited. If it does, we push it (with an increased level) to the stack.

CHAPTER 8 CHESS

Listing 8-15. Solve a maze with backtracking

```
1.  def solve_maze(start_x, start_y, end_x, end_y, maze):
2.      R, C = len(maze), len(maze[0])
3.      level = 1
4.      stack = [(start_x, start_y, level)]
5.      visited = set()
6.      path = []
7.      while stack:
8.          print ('stack', stack)
9.          cur_x, cur_y, cur_level = stack.pop()
10.         if cur_x == end_x and cur_y == end_y:
11.             path.append((cur_x, cur_y, cur_level))
12.             return path
13.
14.         visited.add((cur_x, cur_y))
15.
16.         # update path
17.         while path:
18.             prev_level = path[-1][-1]
19.             if cur_level <= prev_level:
20.                 path.pop()
21.             else:
22.                 break
23.
24.         path.append((cur_x, cur_y, cur_level))
25.         print ('visited', visited)
26.
27.         for direction_x, direction_y in [(0, 1),(0, -1),(1, 0),(-1, 0)]: # right, left, down, up
28.             new_x = direction_x + cur_x
29.             new_y = direction_y + cur_y
30.             new_level = cur_level + 1
31.             if (0 <= new_x < R and
32.                 0 <= new_y < C and
33.                 maze[new_x][new_y] and
34.                 (new_x, new_y) not in visited):
35.                 stack.append((new_x, new_y, new_level))
36.
37.         print ("path", path)
38.
39. if __name__ == "__main__":
40.     # 0 is wall; 1 is path
41.     maze = [[0,0,0,0,0],
42.             [0,1,0,1,0],
43.             [0,1,1,1,0],
44.             [0,1,0,1,0],
45.             [0,0,0,1,0]]
46.
47.     print (solve_maze(1, 1, 4, 3, maze))
```

247

The intermediate results of the `stack`, `visited`, and `path` are printed out; see below.

```
In [7]: run Listing_8_15_application_solving_maze.py
stack [(1, 1, 1)]
visited {(1, 1)}
path [(1, 1, 1)]
stack [(2, 1, 2)]
visited {(1, 1), (2, 1)}
path [(1, 1, 1), (2, 1, 2)]
stack [(2, 2, 3), (3, 1, 3)]
visited {(3, 1), (1, 1), (2, 1)}
path [(1, 1, 1), (2, 1, 2), (3, 1, 3)]
stack [(2, 2, 3)]
visited {(3, 1), (1, 1), (2, 1), (2, 2)}
path [(1, 1, 1), (2, 1, 2), (2, 2, 3)]
stack [(2, 3, 4)]
visited {(2, 1), (3, 1), (1, 1), (2, 3), (2, 2)}
path [(1, 1, 1), (2, 1, 2), (2, 2, 3), (2, 3, 4)]
stack [(3, 3, 5), (1, 3, 5)]
visited {(2, 1), (3, 1), (1, 1), (2, 3), (2, 2), (1, 3)}
path [(1, 1, 1), (2, 1, 2), (2, 2, 3), (2, 3, 4), (1, 3, 5)]
stack [(3, 3, 5)]
visited {(2, 1), (3, 1), (1, 1), (2, 3), (3, 3), (2, 2), (1, 3)}
path [(1, 1, 1), (2, 1, 2), (2, 2, 3), (2, 3, 4), (3, 3, 5)]
stack [(4, 3, 6)]
[(1, 1, 1), (2, 1, 2), (2, 2, 3), (2, 3, 4), (3, 3, 5), (4, 3, 6)]
```

Monte Carlo Tree Search

The **Monte Carlo Tree Search** algorithm is tailor-made for solving decision problems. One of the recent novel applications of MCTS is in the field of drug discovery – designing drug molecules with desired properties, so-called *de novo* molecular design (Figure 8-24). The traditional small molecule discovery largely depends on the chemical knowledge of the pharmaceutical scientist who proposes candidate molecules that will be synthesized and characterized in the lab. The experiment results will be sent back to the scientist for the next round of improvement. The whole process is time-consuming and not efficient.

CHAPTER 8 CHESS

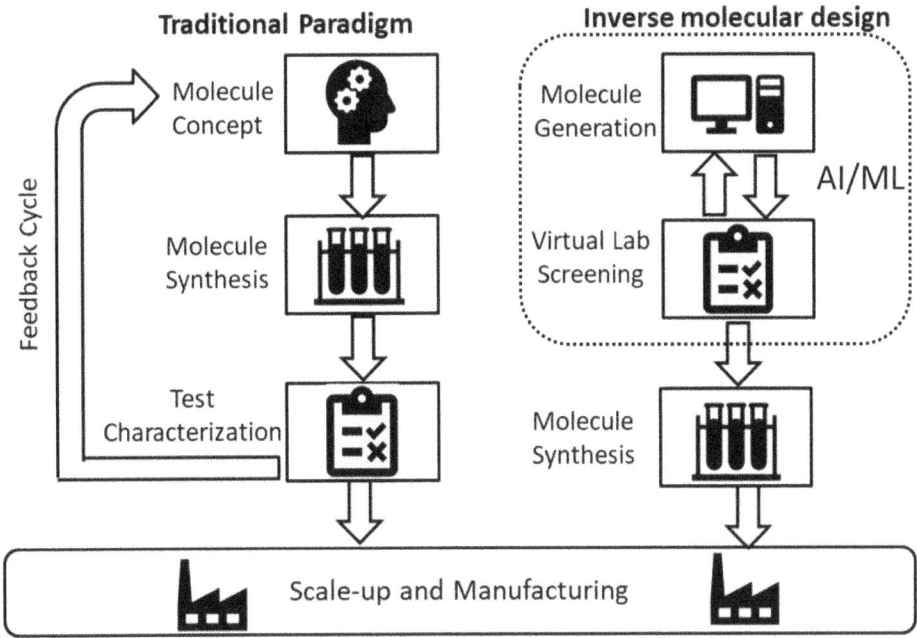

Figure 8-24. *Drug discovery: traditional paradigm vs. inverse molecular design*

A new paradigm that leverages the computer to screen molecule candidates is gaining traction in the pharmaceutical industry. The fast computer can generate a large number of candidates that will be evaluated by the same computer. At the end of the day, the most promising molecules will be proposed to the scientists and synthesized and evaluated in the lab.

Based on one recent research [17], one can use MCTS for inverse molecular design. The small molecule can be decomposed into basic building blocks, i.e., the chemical functional groups such as –OH (alcohol) and –COOH (acid). These groups can be pieced together to form a new molecule. As illustrated in Figure 8-25, the search process includes the same four steps, i.e., Selection, Expansion, Simulation, and Backpropagation. In the Simulation step, the tree continues to grow until the max depth of the tree is reached. If we concatenate all the functional groups along the best path, we will get a candidate molecule. We can then use a separate supervised machine learning model to predict the score of the molecule and backpropagate the score to the parent nodes sitting above.

CHAPTER 8　CHESS

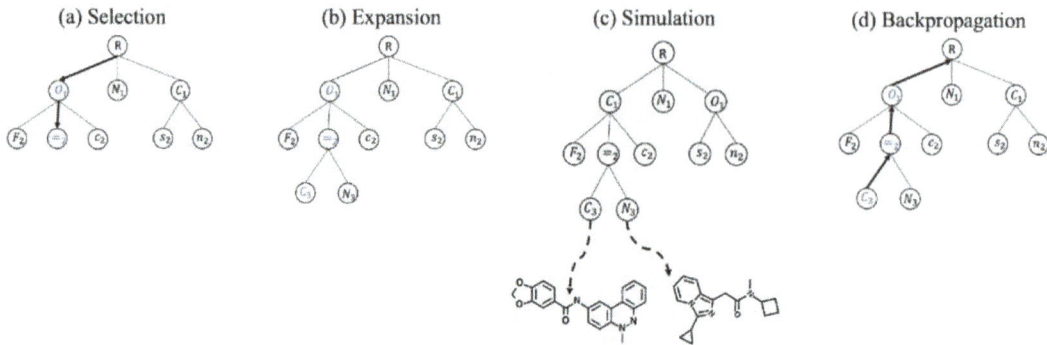

Figure 8-25. *Use MCTS to discover a new molecule*

For example, the following molecules in Figure 8-26 are novel molecules generated from MCTS [18].

Figure 8-26. *Novel molecules generated using MCTS*

Summary

In this chapter, we learned algorithms through solving a variety of chess-inspired problems. All these problems can be abstracted as the tree problems for which we learned the tree traversals extensively. The Depth-First Search algorithm essentially performs a pre-order traversal of the tree. Breadth-First Search explores the tree level by level. Backtracking finds the solution incrementally: if any of the intermediate explorations lead to a dead end, it will undo them, return to the previous decision point, and explore a different path. Finding a path in a maze, as discussed in the "Application" section of this chapter, is a great example of using backtracking. Finally, we learned the Monte Carlo Tree Search (MCTS) algorithm: it has four key steps: Selection, Expansion, Simulation, and Backpropagation. The MCTS balances exploration and exploitation and yields excellent results for searching a vast parameter space.

APPENDIX A

A Quick Review of Python

Basic Types and Data Types

Let us now review the basics of the Python programming language. Python is an interpreted language, which means it does not need to be compiled and can run code interactively. It is also dynamically typed – the type of the value is determined at runtime. For example, if we define x=5, then the data type for x will be inferred as integer. But if we change it to x="abc", then the type will be dynamically changed to string. In addition, Python supports programming several paradigms such as procedural, object-oriented, and functional programming. In procedural programming, the code is written with a sequential logic, and it will be executed orderly. Object-oriented programming is to encapsulate attributes and methods in a class. Functional programming is to treat a function as an input parameter to the existing function. For this matter, Python has decorators that serve the same purpose.

The basic built-in data types of Python are (1) int, to store integer values, such as x = 1; (2) float, to store float values, such as x = 1.0; (3) complex, to store complex numbers, such as x=3 + 5j; (4) bool, for Boolean values, either True or False; (5) str for string values such as x ="ABC"; and (6) None to indicate null values such as x=None.

The basic built-in data structures are list, tuple, dictionary, and set. The list is used to store an array of objects whose data types can differ. For example, l = ["a", 1, 1.0, None, True, [1,2,3]]. This list l contains six elements, all with a distinct data type. In other programming languages, the list is called an array instead.

A python list is mutable. For example, l[0]="b" will change the first element from "a" to "b". It supports index-based slicing. l[1:3] retrieves a subset of l, [1,1.0]. l[::-1] reverses the list. List also has a few built-in functions such as append and pop. The former adds one item to the end of the list, whereas the latter removes the last item from the list in O(1) time. Speaking of removing an item from the list, it is recommended to remove

© Chenyang Shi 2025
C. Shi, *Mastering Algorithms with Python*, https://doi.org/10.1007/979-8-8688-1799-1

APPENDIX A A QUICK REVIEW OF PYTHON

it from the end, which is done in constant time. If removing the item at the beginning of the list, it takes linear time O(N), where N is the size of the list. In such a case, one can use another data structure double-ended queue, deque, from Python, which is internally implemented as a doubly linked list. It can be imported as follows: `from collections import deque`, and it supports append, pop, and appendleft, popleft in an amortized O(1) time. In general, inserting and removing elements in the middle of a list or deque is slow and takes O(N) time.

Tuple stores the elements inside a round bracket. For example, t=("a", 1, 1.0, None, True, [1,2,3]). A tuple has similar features to a list – it retrieves elements based on the index or a slice of indexes. But unlike a list, it is immutable – you cannot change the value of its element. An assignment of t[0]="b" will raise a TypeError.

A dictionary stores data of key/value pairs in a syntax of curly brackets, e.g., d={"a": 1, "b": None, "c": True, "d": [1,2,3]}. You can retrieve the value by using a square bracket d["a"], which returns 1, and add a new key/value pair to the dictionary, such as d["e"]=1.0. When adding data to a dictionary, if the key already exists, it replaces its old value with the new one. When retrieving the value from the dictionary, if the key is nonexistent, it raises an error. In such a case, one can use d.get(key, default_value) where key is to be searched inside a dictionary, and if key is not found, then default_value will be returned. For example, d.get("z", 100) will return 100 as "z" is not in d. Not all data types can be used as the key in a dictionary. List cannot. It will raise a TypeError, mentioning unhashable type: "list". In such a case, instead of a list, convert it to a tuple. For example, d[["a", "b", "c"]] causes an error, but d[("a","b","c")] does not.

A Python set stores the data in curly brackets. Like the dictionary case, it does not allow an unhashable data type such as a list. Also, it only keeps one copy of the duplicated elements. For example, if defining a set as s={"a", 1, 1.0, None, True, (1,2,3)}, it will be saved as {(1, 2, 3), 1, None, 'a'}. Two things to notice here: (1) 1, 1.0, and True become a single element of 1. (2) The original order of the elements is not preserved. You can use built-in functions for set to add element such as s.add("b") → {(1, 2, 3), 1, None, 'a', 'b'} or combine sets such as s.union({1,2,3,"a",b,"c"}) → {(1, 2, 3), 1, 2, 3, None, 'a', 'b', 'c'} or find common elements of two sets such as s.intersection({1,2,3})→-{1}.

Boolean Logic and Flow Control

Python evaluates a logic expression and returns either True or False. Suppose x =100, then x>0 returns True. x in [100, "a", "b"] also returns True. Additionally, one can use the reserved keywords and, or, not to evaluate the combination of logic expressions. For example, (x % 2 ==0) and (x >0) → True, (x % 2 ==0) or (x > 200) → True and not (x > 0) → False.

One can use if, elif, and else to control the flow of a program. For example, here is a piece of program for Fizz buzz in Listing A-1. The rule to play Fizz buzz is that starting from 1 and counting incrementally, one shouts "Fizz" if the number is divisible by 3, "Buzz" by 5, and "Fizzbuzz" by both 3 and 5; otherwise, one says the number itself.

Listing A-1. Code for Fizz buzz using a for loop

```python
for num in range(1, 101):
    if num % 3 == 0 and num % 5 == 0:
        print ("Fizzbuzz")
    elif num % 3 == 0:
        print ("Fizz")
    elif num % 5 == 0:
        print ("Buzz")
    else:
        print (num)
```

The range(start, end, step) function is a sequence object that only stores start, end, and step information. It is not a Python list, though you can convert it to one by using list(range(1, 100, 2)) syntax. It is this laziness that makes range(1000000000) possible because not all these vast numbers of integers are assigned at once in the memory.

One can use a for loop to loop through a Python iterable such as a list, a tuple, or a range object. Some examples are shown below in Listing A-2. In the third example, we use the d.items() to get key and value pairs.

Listing A-2. Loop through a Python iterable

```python
for i in range(10):
    print (i)

for num in [100, 200, 300]:
    print (num)

for key, value in {'a': 1, 'b': None, 'c': True, 'd': [1,2,3]}.items():
    print (f"Key --> {key} : value -->{value}")
```

APPENDIX A   A QUICK REVIEW OF PYTHON

To retrieve both index and value of an iterable, one can use the enumerate function (Listing A-3).

Listing A-3. Use of enumerate

```
1.  for i, num in enumerate([100, 200, 300]):
2.      print (i, num)
```

In addition to a for loop, one can use a while loop to enumerate the iterable. Here is the code for the Fizzbuzz using a while loop (Listing A-4). Do not forget to increment the number by one each iteration at line 11. Otherwise, it will loop infinitely.

Listing A-4. Code for Fizz buzz using a while loop

```
1.   num = 1
2.   while num < 101:
3.       if num % 3 == 0 and num % 5 == 0:
4.           print ("Fizzbuzz")
5.       elif num % 3 == 0:
6.           print ("Fizz")
7.       elif num % 5 == 0:
8.           print ("Buzz")
9.       else:
10.          print (num)
11.      num += 1
```

You can use continue to skip an iteration, and use break to exit the loop (Listing A-5). For example, if you do not want to see Fizzbuzz, you can simply add a continue statement at line 3 to skip it.

Listing A-5. Use of continue to skip logic

```
1.   for num in range(1, 101):
2.       if num % 3 == 0 and num % 5 == 0:
3.           continue
4.       elif num % 3 == 0:
5.           print ("Fizz")
6.       elif num % 5 == 0:
7.           print ("Buzz")
8.       else:
9.           print (num)
```

If you want to stop the loop once you find the Fizzbuzz for the first time, you can exit the loop (Listing A-6). Note the break at line 5. The program stops at its 15th iteration.

Listing A-6. Use of a break to break logic

```
1.  num = 1
2.  while num < 101:
3.      if num % 3 == 0 and num % 5 == 0:
4.          print ("Fizzbuzz")
5.          break
6.      elif num % 3 == 0:
7.          print ("Fizz")
8.      elif num % 5 == 0:
9.          print ("Buzz")
10.     else:
11.         print (num)
12.     num += 1
```

To write loops in Python, for simplicity's sake, one often uses list comprehension. For example, to find all the even numbers between 1 and 100. One can simply write the following one-line expression (Listing A-7).

Listing A-7. Find even numbers using list comprehension

```
1.  even_numbers = [num for num in range(1, 101) if num % 2 == 0]
```

The same technique can be used to quickly create a dictionary with pairs of numbers and corresponding letters (Listing A-8).

Listing A-8. Create a dictionary using list comprehension

```
1.  import string
2.  alphabet_dict = {number: alphabet for number, alphabet in zip(range(26),
    string.ascii_lowercase)}
```

Functions

To reuse the code, one can write Python functions. It starts with a keyword def. A function name is usually in snake case, and arguments of the function are in parentheses. Here is a simple example to calculate the sum of two numbers (Listing A-9). Note that in Python a four-space indentation is often adopted.

Listing A-9. A simple function to add two numbers

```
1.  def my_function(a, b):
2.      return a + b
```

APPENDIX A   A QUICK REVIEW OF PYTHON

One can also specify the default values for a and b (Listing A-10).

Listing A-10. A simple function to add two numbers with default values specified

```
1.  def my_function(a=1, b=2):
2.      return a + b
```

For a simple function in Listing A-10, one can write a one-liner using the anonymous lambda function, i.e., my_function = lambda a, b: a + b. Here, we do not need a name for the function. The lambda function is convenient. For example, if we want to sort a list of paired elements, e.g., l = [("b", 0), ("a", 3), ("c", -1)], we can leverage the built-in sort function, which takes a key as an argument. If we want to sort the tuples based on the alphabet, one can write l.sort(key=lambda x: x[0]). Alternatively, if sorting the tuples based on the numeric values, one can write l.sort(key=lambda x: x[1]) instead.

For a normal Python function, you can also use args and kwargs to dynamically assign arguments (Listing A-11). Here, args takes a tuple of values, and kwargs takes a dictionary as input.

Listing A-11. Use of args and kwargs in a function

```
1.  def my_function(*args, **kwargs):
2.      print (f"args --> {args}")
3.      print (f"kwargs --> {kwargs}")
4.
5.  print (my_function(100, 200, a=300, b=400))
```

While you can import Python built-in packages, such as datetime or math, or a community package such as numpy or pandas, you can also create your package. You typically create a folder structure as in Figure A-1. It is recommended to include an empty __init__.py at the root level of package/subpackage to make it recognizable. With a tree structure such as the one shown below, you can import your module by import my_packge.sub_package.my_module.

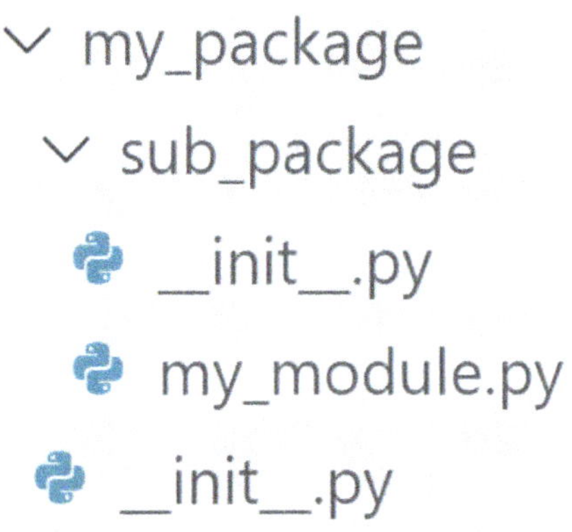

APPENDIX A   A QUICK REVIEW OF PYTHON

```
∨ my_package
   ∨ sub_package
       🐍 __init__.py
       🐍 my_module.py
   🐍 __init__.py
```

Figure A-1. *Recommended directory structure for a custom Python package*

Generators

A generator is another way to store a sequence of data. It can be created using list comprehension but with a round bracket. In Listing A-12, the first line of code creates a generator holding values from 1 to 100. The pronounced difference to other types of sequence data structures such as a list or a tuple is that in a generator, the objects are not explicitly saved in memory until they are called. You can either use my_generator.__next__() or next(my_generator) to iteratively get the element from the generator or exhaust the generator in one shot using a list function.

Listing A-12. *A simple example of a generator*

```python
1. my_generator_1 = (num for num in range(1, 101))
2. my_generator_1.__next__()
3. my_generator_1_list = list(my_generator_1)
```

Alternatively, one can use a function for generators (Listing A-13). At the end of the function, instead of a return, use yield.

APPENDIX A A QUICK REVIEW OF PYTHON

Listing A-13. Create a generator using a function

```
1.  def my_generator_function(lower_bound, upperbound):
2.      for num in range(lower_bound, upperbound):
3.          yield num
4.
5.  my_generator_2 = my_generator_function(1, 101)
6.  my_generator_2.__next__()
7.  my_generator_2_list = list(my_generator_2)
```

Similar to generators, in Python, several other functions are also evaluated lazily. We already know the `range` function is one of them. Others include `map` and `filter`.

For example, we can square a list of numbers, we can use the `map` function where it takes a function as the first argument and the sequence of data as the second (Listing A-14). The result is a generator for which you can retrieve values one-by-one using `__next__()` or get all using a `list` function.

Listing A-14. The use of a `map` to create a generator

```
1.  nums = [num for num in range(1, 101)]
2.  nums_squared = map(lambda x: x**2, nums)
3.  nums_squared.__next__()
4.  nums_squared_list = list(nums_squared)
```

We can use a `filter` to filter a sequence given a condition. Say, we want to find the odd numbers in a sequence (Listing A-15).

Listing A-15. The use of a `filter` to create a generator

```
1.  nums = [num for num in range(1, 101)]
2.  nums_filtered = filter(lambda x: x%2 == 1, nums)
3.  nums_filtered.__next__()
4.  nums_filtered_list = list(nums_filtered)
```

We can combine `map` and `reduce` functions. In the example below, we first square the numbers using the `map` function and sum them up using the `reduce` function (Listing A-16). Note `reduce` function needs to be imported from `functools`.

Listing A-16. An example use of `map` and `reduce`

```
1.  # an example of map-reduce
2.  from functools import reduce
3.  nums = [num for num in range(1, 101)]
4.  nums_squared = map(lambda x: x**2, nums)
5.  nums_summation = reduce(lambda acc, nxt : acc + nxt, nums_squared)
```

APPENDIX A   A QUICK REVIEW OF PYTHON

The map and reduce functions are the bedrocks of the big data analytics tools such as Apache Hadoop.

Classes

As mentioned at the beginning of this chapter, Python supports object-oriented programming. To do so, one can define a class. Listing A-17 is an example of a TreeNode class where in the __init__ constructor, we specify that each tree node has a left child and a right child and holds a value. The name of the class follows the camel case.

Listing A-17. A Python class for defining a binary tree node

```python
class TreeNode:
    def __init__(self, val):
        self.left = None
        self.right = None
        self.val = val

if __name__ == "__main__":
    root = TreeNode(10)
    root.left = TreeNode(5)
    root.right = TreeNode(20)
    print (root.val)
    print (root.left.val)
    print (root.right.val)
```

One can include a series of magic functions into the class (Listing A-18). __repr__ function gives a nice string representation for an object. __eq__, __lt__, and __gt__ specify how to compare two TreeNode objects, whereas __add__, __sub__, and __mul__ define how to do basic arithmetic operations given two TreeNode objects. Finally, __call__ enables you to call your object instance like a regular function. In Listing A-18, we just increase the value of a node by 1. At line 43, the value for node 1 has been increased from 100 to 101.

APPENDIX A   A QUICK REVIEW OF PYTHON

Listing A-18. TreeNode class with magic functions

```python
class TreeNode:
    def __init__(self, val):
        self.left = None
        self.right = None
        self.val = val

    def __repr__(self):
        return f"Current Tree Node has a value of {self.val}"

    def __eq__(self, other):
        return self.val == other.val

    def __lt__(self, other):
        return self.val < other.val

    def __gt__(self, other):
        return self.val > other.val

    def __add__(self, other):
        return self.val + other.val

    def __sub__(self, other):
        return self.val - other.val

    def __mul__(self, other):
        return self.val * other.val

    def __call__(self):
        self.val += 1

if __name__ == "__main__":
    node_1 = TreeNode(100)
    node_2 = TreeNode(50)
    print (node_1)
    print (node_2)
    print (node_1 > node_2)
    print (node_1 == node_2)
    print (node_1 < node_2)
    print (node_1 + node_2)
    print (node_1 - node_2)
    print (node_1 * node_2)
    # call
    node_1()
    print (node_1)
```

```
In [1]: run Listing_A_18_class_magic_functions.py
Current Tree Node has a value of 100
Current Tree Node has a value of 50
True
False
False
150
50
5000
Current Tree Node has a value of 101
```

One can reuse class code and avoid repetition via **class inheritance**. See the example in Listing A-19.

Listing A-19. The example of class inheritance

```python
1.  import numpy as np
2.  class TreeNode:
3.      def __init__(self, val):
4.          self.left = None
5.          self.right = None
6.          self.parent = None
7.          self.val = val
8.
9.      def __repr__(self):
10.         return f"Current Tree Node has a value of {self.val}"
11.
12. class MonteCarloTreeNode(TreeNode):
13.     def __init__(self, total_score, num_visits):
14.         self.num_visits = num_visits
15.         super().__init__(val=total_score)
16.
17.     def __repr__(self):
18.         return f"Current Tree Node has a value of {self.val} and a total visit of {self.num_visits}"
19.
20.     def calculate_ucb1_score(self, c=2):
21.         if not self.num_visits:
22.             return np.inf
23.         # if at root node
24.         if not self.parent:
25.             return
26.         # at child node
27.         ubc1_score = (self.val / self.num_visits) + c *
            np.sqrt(np.log(self.parent.num_visits) / self.num_visits)
```

APPENDIX A   A QUICK REVIEW OF PYTHON

```python
28.            return ubc1_score
29.
30.     def print_tree(self, root, space=0, LEVEL_SPACE = 7):
31.         "Reference: https://stackoverflow.com/a/70318281"
32.         if not root:
33.             return
34.         space += LEVEL_SPACE
35.         self.print_tree(root.right, space)
36.         for i in range(LEVEL_SPACE, space):
37.             print(end = " ")
38.         print("|" + str(root.val) + ','+ str(root.num_visits) + "|<")
39.         self.print_tree(root.left, space)
40.
41. if __name__ == "__main__":
42.     root_node = MonteCarloTreeNode(100, 10)
43.     left_node = MonteCarloTreeNode(20, 50)
44.     right_node = MonteCarloTreeNode(40, 60)
45.     left_node.parent = root_node
46.     right_node.parent = root_node
47.     root_node.left = left_node
48.     root_node.right = right_node
49.
50.     print (root_node)
51.     print (left_node.calculate_ucb1_score())
52.     print (right_node.calculate_ucb1_score())
53.     root_node.print_tree(root_node)
```

From lines 2 to 10, we define a parent class TreeNode that accepts a value in the constructor and has a __repr__ magic method for printing the class object in a neat format.

Next, we have a child class MonteCarloTreeNode that inherits the parent class TreeNode. For a node in the Monte Carlo tree, it records two pieces of information, the total score and the number of visits to the node. At line 14, we initialize the number of visits, whereas at line 15, we use a super().__init__() to inherit all the initial values from the parent class. Here, since the parent class also has a val attribute, we assign total_score to val.

In the MonteCarloTreeNode class, in addition to the __init__ constructor, we also define several methods. Since each node now has one extra value, i.e., the number of visits, the __repr__ is modified to include it. Two more methods are also included: calculate_ucb1_score is used to calculate the UCB1 score of each child node, and print_tree is used to print the tree to a terminal.

```
In [2]: run Listing_A_19_class_inheritance.py
Current Tree Node has a value of 100 and a total visit of 10
0.8291932052578694
1.0584646667461333
        |40,60|<
|100,10|<
        |20,50|<
```

Multiple inheritance, that is, a child class derives information from multiple parent classes, is also possible. If there is a conflict of methods from the parent classes, Python will consider the first matching method following the order of the parent classes. For more complex classes, Python relies on **Method Resolution Order** to resolve the conflict.

Decorators

In Python, a function is considered an object, just like other primitive data types. You can use a function as an input to another function. In the first example in Listing A-20, from lines 2–6, it calculates the nth number of a Fibonacci sequence. The recursive function performs tons of repetitive calculations and thus is very slow for a large n number, e.g., n = 100. However, if adding a built-in decorator @lru_cache at line 2, leveraging the cached value of the previous Fibonacci number, the code execution will be much faster. For example, the code returns fibonacci(100) in a fraction of a second.

From lines 8–17, the staticmethod decorator is used inside a class, which makes the method a stand-alone function and can be called independently. You can use MyClass.calculate_squares to call the function within the class.

We can also define our own decorator as shown from lines 19–25. An introduction decorator is nothing but a Python function that takes in another function as input. Within the body of the introduction function, a nested wrapper function is defined where actions that will be applied to target functions are detailed. Note the *args and **kwargs in the wrapper function will pick up any arguments in the target function. In the end, the wrapper function is returned. To use the decorator, just add @introduction to the target function greet. Three sentences are printed to the console. Note the wraps decorator from functools is used. By calling it, it will give the correct identity for the greet function, e.g., greet.__name__ returns greet. If not including the wraps decorator, greet.__name__ returns wrapper.

APPENDIX A   A QUICK REVIEW OF PYTHON

This just scratches the surface of Python decorators. Feel free to refer to document [19] for more information.

Listing A-20. The examples of decorators

```python
from functools import lru_cache, wraps
@lru_cache
def fibonacci(n):
    if n <=1:
        return n
    return fibonacci(n-1) + fibonacci(n-2)

class MyClass:
    def __init__(self, nums):
        self.nums = nums

    @staticmethod
    def calculate_squares(x):
        return x**2

    def squaring_arr(self):
        return [MyClass.calculate_squares(num) for num in self.nums]

def introduction(func):
    @wraps(func)
    def wrapper(*args, **kwargs):
        print ("Before introducing myself...")
        func(*args, **kwargs)
        print ("After introducing myself...")
    return wrapper

@introduction
def greet(name):
    print (f"Hello my name is {name}")

if __name__ == "__main__":
    print (fibonacci(100))
    my_class = MyClass(nums = [1,2,3,4,5])
    print(my_class.calculate_squares(10))
    print(my_class.squaring_arr())
    greet("Thomas")
```

```
In [3]: run Listing_A_20_decorators.py
3542248481792619150750
100
[1, 4, 9, 16, 25]
Before introducing myself...
Hello my name is Thomas
After introducing myself...
In [4]: greet
Out[4]: <function __main__.greet(name)>
In [5]: greet.__name__
Out[5]: 'greet'
In [6]: help(greet)
Help on function greet in module __main__:
greet(name)
```

Miscellaneous

Python offers type hints capability to quickly verify the type of data structures used as inputs/outputs in a function. It also provides `multiprocessing` and `asyncio` modules for writing parallel processing and asynchronous code, respectively. A wide variety of mature packages from the vibrant Python community are available for various real-world applications, such as `numpy`, `pandas` for data analytics, `sklearn`, `tensorflow`, and `pytorch` for machine learning and deep learning. One can easily install these packages by using `pip` or `conda`.

In real-life code development, developers use code repositories such as GitHub or Bitbucket to share and review each other's code. The well-tested code stays in the main/master branch. If a developer wants to make a change to the main branch, they create a feature branch based on the main branch, make modifications, and submit a pull request (PR). If it passes the peer review, the PR is merged into the main branch. It is often the case that any change to the main branch triggers the continuous integration/continuous development (CI/CD) process that leverages tools such as Jenkins, GitHub Actions, and AWS CodePipeline.

For complex code development, the developers leverage the logging and debugging features of code editors to catch bugs/errors. Popular editors for Python projects include PyCharm, Visual Studio Code, Sublime Text, Vim, and Spyder.

The life cycle of code development is divided into different phases: the team first starts with Development (DEV), System Integration Testing (SIT), then User Acceptance Testing (UAT), and finally Production (PROD) phase. Throughout the code development life cycle, the team can leverage tools such as `pytest` to test code and catch errors.

APPENDIX B

Environment Setup and Package Installation

While the majority of the code snippets are written from scratch using the built-in functions from Python, several other community packages are also used such as `numpy` and `OpenCV`. To install these packages, one possible way is to create a virtual environment, activate it, and install them using `pip`. Below are the detailed steps.

1. Download and install the latest version of Python available at https://www.python.org/downloads/.

2. Open a terminal, create a virtual environment named `algo-env` by entering `python -m venv algo-env`.

3. Activate `algo-env` by entering `algo-env\Scripts\activate` on Windows or `source algo-env/bin/activate` on Unix or MacOS.

4. Create a `requirements.txt` using tools such as Notepad which records the names and the versions of the packages that will be installed. Shown in Figure B-1 are the packages used in the book. Note that these packages are not the latest versions. To install the latest versions, just remove the version numbers (and the double equal signs), leaving only the package names.

APPENDIX B   ENVIRONMENT SETUP AND PACKAGE INSTALLATION

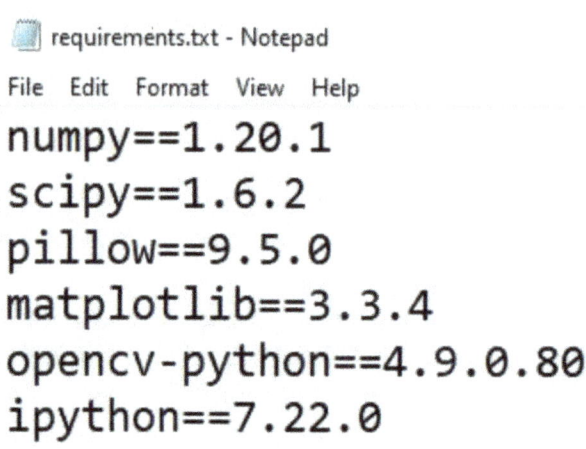

Figure B-1. *Additional community packages and versions used in the book*

5. To install the packages, type `pip install -r requirements.txt`.
6. To deactivate the virtual environment, type `deactivate` into the terminal.

APPENDIX C

References

[1] Bentley, Jon Louis; Haken, Dorothea; Saxe, James B. (September 1980), "A general method for solving divide-and-conquer recurrences," ACM SIGACT News, 12 (3): 36–44.

[2] CS 6515: Intro to Graduate Algorithms at Georgia Tech by Prof. Eric Vigoda, https://omscs.gatech.edu/cs-6515-intro-graduate-algorithms

[3] J. Dongarra and F. Sullivan, Guest Editors Introduction to the top 10 algorithms. https://www.computer.org/csdl/magazine/cs/2000/01/c1022/13rRUxBJhBm

[4] PhD thesis by Chenyang Shi, Local structure and lattice dynamics study of low dimensional materials using atomic pair distribution function and high energy resolution inelastic x-ray scattering (https://academiccommons.columbia.edu/doi/10.7916/D8KO7BX6/download).

[5] Kruskal, J. B. (1956). On the shortest spanning subtree of a graph and the traveling salesman problem. Proceedings of the American Mathematical Society. 7 (1): 48–50.

[6] Prim, R. C. (November 1957), Shortest connection networks and some generalizations, Bell System Technical Journal, 36 (6): 1389–1401.

[7] Avidan S, Shamir A (2007) Seam carving for content-aware image resizing. In: ACM SIGGRAPH 2007 Papers, p. 10.

[8] Broadway_tower.jpg: Newton2, CC BY 2.5 <https://creativecommons.org/licenses/by/2.5>, via Wikimedia Commons https://en.wikipedia.org/wiki/Seam_carving

APPENDIX C REFERENCES

[9] https://www.youtube.com/watch?v=1cUUfMeOijg

[10] Matsumoto, M.; Nishimura, T. (1998). "Mersenne twister: a 623-dimensionally equidistributed uniform pseudo-random number generator." ACM Transactions on Modeling and Computer Simulation. 8 (1): 3–30.

[11] https://en.wikipedia.org/wiki/PERT_distribution

[12] The integral is taken from Chapter 10.2 from the Computational Physics by Dr. Mark Newman.

[13] https://www.computer.org/csdl/magazine/cs/2000/01/c1022/13rRUxBJhBm

[14] United States Administrative Divisions Cities.svg: Nandhp, CC by 3.0 <https://creativecommons.org/licenses/by-sa/3.0/deed.en>, via Wikimedia Commons https://en.wikipedia.org/wiki/List_of_United_States_cities_by_population

[15] Inman, James (1835) [1821]. Navigation and Nautical Astronomy: For the Use of British Seamen (3 ed.). London, UK: W. Woodward, C. & J. Rivington.

[16] https://www.youtube.com/watch?v=UXW2yZnd17U

[17] Yang et al., Sci. Technol. Adv. Mater. (2017), 18, 973.

[18] The figure is adapted from the author's own research.

[19] PEP 318 – Decorators for Functions and Methods. https://peps.python.org/pep-0318/.

Index

A

Above and below the
 mean test, 140
add_child method, 215, 231
Autocorrelation test, 141

B

Back-end logic development, 19
Backtracking, 244–246
BFS, *see* Breadth-First Search (BFS)
Binary search, 20, 21
Binary search tree (BST), 243, 244
Binary tree, 12–16, 211
 aspects, 243
 BFS, 212, 213
 BST, 243, 244
 DFS, 212
 expressions, 243
 level-order traversal, 213
 levels, 211, 212
 logarithmic time, 244
 root-to-leaf paths, 214
Black-box models, 243
Breadth-First Search (BFS), 212, 216, 245, 250
Brute force method, 62
BST, *see* Binary search tree (BST)
Bubble Sort algorithm, 22, 26
Business trip, 173

C

Caesar cipher, 117, 119
 implementation, 118
Cartesian system, 144
Chess, 211
 board, 236
 Eight Queens problem (*see* Eight Queens problem)
 Knight's Tour problem (*see* Knight's Tour problem)
 minimum jumps for a Knight, 225, 227, 228
 problems, 211
Chromosome, 181
CI/CD process, *see* Continuous integration/continuous development (CI/CD) process
Commercial Forecasting, 149
construct_huffman_tree, 85
Continuous integration/continuous development (CI/CD) process, 265
Cryptosystem, 125
Cumulative energy, 112
Cumulative energy matrix, 113

D

Depth-First Search (DFS), 212, 216, 220, 244, 250
Desert Island Generator, 137, 138

INDEX

DFS, *see* Depth-First Search (DFS)
DFT matrix, *see* Discrete Fourier Transform (DFT) matrix
Dijkstra's algorithm, 204, 209
Dirichlet distribution, 147
Discrete Fourier Transform (DFT) matrix, 44
Divide-and-conquer algorithm, 19, 40
    binary search, 20, 21
    Bubble Sort, 22, 26
    FFT algorithm, 42–50
    guess number, 19, 20
    Insertion Sort, 22, 26
    Merge Sort, 24–26
    multiplication, two positive integers, 30–36
    Quick Sort, 26–29
    Selection Sort, 22, 26
Dynamic programming (DP), 89, 102, 103, 115
    and backtracking, 109
    character of string, 100
    characters, 98
    code implementation, 101
    common subsequence, 99
    knapsack problem, 104, 105
    one-dimensional table, 107
    subsequence and substring, 97
    table, maximum common substring, 100
    two-dimensional, 106

E

Eight Queens problem
    add queens/positions, 228, 229
    find_all_solutions method, 233
    implementation, column indexes, 233
    improved code, 235
    initial attempt, 230
    N-ary tree, 229, 232, 233
    nodes, 229
    power, 228
    root_to_leaf_paths_n_ary_tree method, 231
    6×6 board, 231
    solution, 232
    TreeNode class, 231, 233
Euclid's algorithm, 128, 129

F

Fast Fourier Transform (FFT) algorithm, 42, 44–47, 49
fast_modular_arithmetic method, 132
Fermat's Little Theorem, 117, 127
FFT algorithm, *see* Fast Fourier Transform (FFT) algorithm
Fibonacci number, 89, 92
    calculation tree, 91
    design a solution, 93
    dynamic programming, an array, 92
    generic procedures, 94
    golden ratio, 93
    mathematical expression, 93
    mathematical formula, 92
    naïve approach, 95
    optimization, 93
    parameters, 92
    prefix sum, 95
    recursion, 90
    space, 92
    time and space, 95

Fibonacci problem, 97
Fibonacci sequence, 90, 94
FIFO, *see* First In First Out (FIFO)
FILO, *see* First In Last Out (FILO)
First In First Out (FIFO), 212
First In Last Out (FILO), 212, 246
Fourier coefficients, 41, 42
Fourier transform technique, 46
Fractal, 6

G

Gaussian distribution, 160
Genetic algorithm (GA), 180, 204, 208
Gradient Descent, 195, 204, 209
Greatest Common Divisor, 121
    integers, 122
Greedy Algorithm, 53, 81, 103
    to build TV towers, 61–63
    on class scheduling problem, 55–57
    on coin change problem, 53–55
    Huffman coding, 81, 84–86
    on jumping frog example, 57–61
    MST (*see* Minimum spanning tree (MST))

H

Haversine formula, 173, 186, 191, 194
H-trees, 6–8
Huffman coding, 81, 84–86, 244
Huffman Tree, 82–86

I, J

IFFT algorithm, 44–46, 48
Insertion Sort algorithm, 22, 26
Inverse Fourier transform, 46

K

K-means clustering, 204, 209
    group the cities
        clusters, 202
        datapoints, 199
        elbow method, 199, 202, 203
        groups, 203
        implementation, 199
        limitations, 203
        optimal number, 202
        steps, 199
        WCSS distances, 199
Knapsack problem, 106
Knight's Tour problem
    backtracking, 221
    3×3 board, 218-220
    5×5 board, 222
    8×8 board, 223
    Cartesian coordinates, 218
    DFS algorithm, 220
    implementation, 221
    improved code, 224
    knight jumping
        possible moves, 223
        possible square, 222, 223
        search tree, 219, 220
    moves, 219
    path of knight, 218
    stack data structure, 221
    visited variable, 221
    Warnsdorff's algorithm, 224
Kruskal's algorithm, 66, 67, 74, 75, 77

L

Lambda function, 256

INDEX

LCG, *see* Linear Congruential Generator (LCG)
Linear Congruential Generator (LCG), 137

M

Manhattan Project, 135
Markov Chain Monte Carlo (MCMC), 156–158, 171
matplotlib package, 7
Matrix operation, 159
Maximum reachable index, 59–61
Maze puzzle
    backtracking, 246
    moves, 246
    positions/levels, 246
    representation, 245
    requirements to solve, 246
    results, 248
    solving, 247
MCMC, *see* Markov Chain Monte Carlo (MCMC)
MCTS, *see* Monte Carlo Tree Search (MCTS)
Merge Sort algorithm, 24–26
Metropolis algorithm, 163
Metropolis–Hastings (M-H) algorithm, 135, 162-163, 171
Mid-square method, 136, 137
Minimum spanning tree (MST), 65, 66, 76, 77
    Kruskal's algorithm, 66–78
    Prim's algorithm, 76–81
Modulo operation, 118
Monte Carlo integration, 150, 151, 153
MonteCarloIntegration class, 154
Monte Carlo methods, 135, 146, 152, 154, 165, 171
Monte Carlo simulation, 138, 144, 149, 167, 169
MonteCarloTreeNode class, 262
Monte Carlo Tree Search (MCTS), 236, 250
    algorithm, 239, 248
    code, 240
    exploration/exploitation, 236
    idea, 236
    initial state, 237
    iterations, 237–239
    new molecule, 249, 250
    novel molecules, 250
    random_roll_out_result method, 240
    traditional paradigm *vs.* inverse molecular design, 248, 249
    tree nodes, 236
    UCB1, 236
MST, *see* Minimum spanning tree (MST)

N

Naïve approach, 31, 36, 38, 96
N-ary tree
    applications, 244
    aspects, 243
    BFS, 216
    DFS, 216
    Eight Queens problem, 229, 232, 233
    generic form, 215
    level order traversal, 217
    root-to-leaf paths, 217
    tree node, 215
Nonnegative integer, 3
Numpy, 111
numpy.random module, 148
Nyquist frequency, 47

O

Object-oriented programming, 251
Optimization techniques, 204
Ordinary differential
    equations (ODEs), 166

P

Pair distribution function (PDF)
    technique, 46
PDF technique, *see* Pair distribution
    function (PDF) technique
PGP, *see* Pretty Good Privacy (PGP)
Polynomial multiplication, 36
Pretty Good Privacy (PGP), 134
Primality test, 127
Prime numbers, 123–126, 130
    integer, 124
    N-digit number, 123
Prim's algorithm, 76, 78, 80, 81
Pseudorandom numbers (PRNs), 137, 138
Python, 138, 141, 251
    classes
        binary tree node, 259
        class inheritance, 261
        MonteCarloTreeNode class, 262
        multiple inheritance, 263
        TreeNode class, 259, 260
    code development, 265, 266
    create dictionary, 255
    data structures, 251
    data types, 251
    decorators, 263
    dictionary, 252
    enumerate function, 254
    environment setup, 267, 268
    even numbers, 255
    Fizzbuzz
        break statement, 254
        continue statement, 254
        for loop, 253
        while loop, 254
    functions, 255–257
    generators, 257, 258
    iterable, 253
    list, 251, 252
    logic expressions, 253
    magic functions, 259
    packages, 256, 265
    packages installation, 267, 268
    paradigms, 251
    set, 252
    tuple, 252
    type hints capability, 265

Q

Quick Sort algorithm, 26–29

R

Random numbers, 127, 135–137
    independence, 140
    LCG, 137
    mid-square method, 136
    Monte Carlo method, 135
    null hypothesis, 139
Recursion, 1
    algorithm, 2
    binary tree, 12–16
    call stack, factorial function, 3
    functions for sum of integers, 4
    to H-trees, 6–8
    implementation, factorial function, 2
    number of paths in grid, 4–6
    recursive code to solve the Tower of
        Hanoi, 9–11

RecursionError, 3
Repeated squaring method, 128
RSA algorithm, 132, 134
RSA Cryptosystem, 117, 134
rsa_decrypt method, 132
RSA public key Cryptosystem, 120

S

SA, *see* Simulated annealing (SA)
Seam Carving, 110, 111
SciPy's quad method, 152
seam_carving function, 113
Secure Sockets Layer (SSL), 134
Selection Sort algorithm, 22, 26
Sieve of Eratosthenes, 125
Simulated annealing (SA), 180, 204, 208
SIT, *see* System Integration Testing (SIT)
SSL, *see* Secure Sockets Layer (SSL)
Statistical tests, 142
Stochastic Gradient Descent, 204
Sudoku
    backtracking, 205
    blocks, 205
    missing number, 204
    print_board function, 205
    SA, 205
    solving, SA, 206
    sophisticated cost function, 207
sum_n_integers(n), 3
System Integration Testing (SIT), 266

T

Tower of Hanoi, 9, 11
Trapezoid Rule, 150
Traveling Salesman problem (TSP)
    Dijkstra's algorithm, 187
        best route, 189
        BFS, 189
        distances dictionary, 193
        dynamic programming, 190
        graph, 191
        heap, 192
        limitations, 190
        local community, 187, 188
        Market/Park/Library, 188–190
        nodes, 188
        parent dictionary, 192, 193
        short-term incentive, 189
        US cities, shortest path, 190, 193, 194
        visited dictionary, 192, 193
    GA
        best route, 186
        brute force solution, 183
        chromosomes/parents, 181
        code, 183
        crossover, 181, 182
        mutation, 182, 183
        vs. SA, 183
        swapping, 182
    US cities, 173, 174
        accept it with a certain probability, 177
        best route, 173, 175
        brute force approach, 175, 176
        calculate_total_distance function, 176
        cooling process, 180
        distance map, 187
        distance, two cities, 173
        longitude and latitude, 174
        routes, 187
        shortest route, 176
        Simulated annealing (SA), 177, 180

solution, 176, 177
total distance, 176
TSP, *see* Traveling Salesman problem (TSP)
TreeNode class, 259

U, V

UAT, *see* User Acceptance Testing (UAT)
UCB, *see* Upper Confidence Bound (UCB)
UI design, *see* User Interface (UI) design
Union Find, 69, 73–75
Up and down test, 140
Upper Confidence Bound (UCB), 236
User Acceptance Testing (UAT), 266
User Interface (UI) design, 19

W, X, Y, Z

Warehouse, 194
    Gradient Descent
        location, 196, 198
        optimization, 195
        steps, 195
        target function, 196
    target function, 195
Warnsdorff's algorithm, 224
Wikipedia, 173

GPSR Compliance

The European Union's (EU) General Product Safety Regulation (GPSR) is a set of rules that requires consumer products to be safe and our obligations to ensure this.

If you have any concerns about our products, you can contact us on

ProductSafety@springernature.com

In case Publisher is established outside the EU, the EU authorized representative is:

Springer Nature Customer Service Center GmbH
Europaplatz 3
69115 Heidelberg, Germany